# Punishing Poverty

# Punishing Poverty

*How Bail and Pretrial Detention*
*Fuel Inequalities in the*
*Criminal Justice System*

Christine S. Scott-Hayward
and Henry F. Fradella

UNIVERSITY OF CALIFORNIA PRESS

University of California Press, one of the most
distinguished university presses in the United States,
enriches lives around the world by advancing scholarship
in the humanities, social sciences, and natural sciences. Its
activities are supported by the UC Press Foundation and
by philanthropic contributions from individuals and institutions. For more information, visit www.ucpress.edu.

University of California Press
Oakland, California

Library of Congress Cataloging-in-Publication Data

Names: Scott-Hayward, Christine S., author. | Fradella,
Henry F., author.
Title: Punishing poverty : how bail and pretrial
detention fuel inequalities in the criminal justice
system / Christine S. Scott-Hayward and
Henry F. Fradella.
Description: Oakland, California : University of
California Press, [2019] | Includes bibliographical
references and index. |
Identifiers: LCCN 2019009255 (print) | LCCN 2019012445
(ebook) | ISBN 9780520970496 (e-book) |
ISBN 9780520298309 (cloth : alk. paper) |
ISBN 9780520298316 (pbk. : alk. paper)
Subjects: LCSH: Bail—United States. | Arrest—United
States. | Equality—United States. | Criminal justice,
Administration of—United States.
Classification: LCC KF9632 (ebook) | LCC KF9632 .S36 2019
(print) | DDC 345.73/072—dc23
LC record available at https://lccn.loc.gov/2019009255

Manufactured in the United States of America

27   26   25   24   23   22   21   20   19
10   9   8   7   6   5   4   3   2   1

# CONTENTS

# ACKNOWLEDGMENTS

We would like to express our thanks to some of the people who helped make this book a reality. Our editor, Maura Roessner, encouraged us from the start and patiently guided us through the writing and publication process. Thank you to her and all of the staff at UC Press. Thanks also to the anonymous reviewers who provided thoughtful and helpful feedback on both the proposal and manuscript.

*Christine S. Scott-Hayward and*
*Henry F. Fradella*

I'd like to add my thanks to my colleague and friend Hank Fradella. I have long thought about writing a book about the injustices of the bail system, but without Hank, quite simply, it would not have happened. Hank has been my mentor and friend since he hired me at California State University, Long Beach, and words cannot express how much I value our relationship. Thank you for your patience and guidance throughout this project. I would also like to thank Sarah Ottone, a former graduate student at CSULB, now at Georgetown University Law Center. Sarah and I collaborated on a study of pretrial decision making in Southern California, and the research we conducted informs many of the arguments in this book. Finally, I thank my family, particularly my husband Mike and my children, James and Jack. You have listened to me rail about bail for years, and I dedicate this book to you. Thank you for your love and support.

*Christine S. Scott-Hayward*

CHAPTER ONE

# The Origins and History of Bail in the Common Law Tradition

## INTRODUCTION

In 1964 US attorney general Robert Kennedy testified before a sub-committee of the US Senate Judiciary Committee to advocate for legislation reforming the bail system in the United States. He began his remarks by saying that "the rich man and the poor man do not receive equal justice in our courts. And in no area is this more evident than in the matter of bail."[1] He illustrated this point with a number of poignant stories:

> Recently, in Los Angeles, a man was forced to stay in jail awaiting trial for a minor crime because he could not afford bail. His case came to trial after 207 days. He was acquitted.
>
> A Pennsylvania man who could not raise $300 spent 54 days in jail awaiting trial on a traffic offense—the maximum penalty for which was *five* days in jail.
>
> In Glen Cove, New York, Daniel Walker was arrested on suspicion of robbery and spent 55 days in jail for want of bail. Meanwhile, he lost his job, his car was repossessed, his credit destroyed, and his wife had to move in with her parents. Later, he was found to be the victim of mistaken identity and released. But it took him four months simply to find another job.[2]

In the more than half century since Kennedy shared these observations, little has changed in the United States, which remains one of only two countries in the world that continues to utilize an extensive system of money bail for those awaiting criminal trial that is dominated by for-profit commercial bail agents.[3] Consider the stories of Derek West Harris, Kenneth Humphrey, and Kalief Browder.

Derek West Harris was a well-dressed and well-liked barber from Newark, New Jersey. He was pulled over for a minor traffic violation in May 2009. Police arrested the fifty-one-year-old for failing to register and insure his new car, as well for having several unpaid traffic tickets. Unable to pay the $1,000 bail set for him, West Harris was placed in a halfway house, where he was robbed and killed for the $3 he had in his pockets.[4]

In May 2017, sixty-three-year-old Kenneth Humphrey was arrested and charged with robbery for going into his neighbor's room in a senior citizens' housing complex and allegedly stealing $5 and a bottle of cologne from that neighbor. Even though he posed no threat to society, he spent 250 days in the San Francisco County Jail because he could not afford to pay the $350,000 bail set in his case.[5] Not only did the California Court of Appeals order that Humphrey be released after finding that his bail had been unconstitutionally excessive, but also, as explained in chapter 2, it ordered all state judges to consider a defendant's ability to pay when making bail decisions rather than strictly relying on published bail schedules.[6] As of the writing of this book, review by the California Supreme Court is pending.

Perhaps the most well-known case of injustice in the contemporary bail context is that of Kalief Browder. In October 2014 the *New Yorker* published an article by Jennifer Gonnerman that detailed the sad series of events that led to Browder's suicide.[7] In May 2010, less than two weeks before his seventeenth birthday, Browder and a friend had attended a party in the Bronx. As they walked home in the early morning hours, a police car drove toward the two boys. A few minutes later a New York City police officer confronted the two teens, saying that a man had just reported that they had robbed him. Browder denied the accusation and invited the officer to check his pockets. The search revealed nothing. The officer returned to his squad car to talk with the alleged victim, at which time the man changed his story and said that the two boys had not robbed him that night, but rather had stolen his backpack two weeks earlier.

Browder and his friend were taken into custody. Browder, who maintained that he had not committed the crime, was charged with robbery. Because he was already on probation for a previous joyriding offense, the judge ordered that Browder be held in custody unless he posted $3,000 bail. Because his family could not afford to post bail, the young man was taken to Rikers Island. More than two months passed before Browder next appeared in court. During that time a grand jury indicted him for the alleged robbery. He entered a plea of "not guilty." But because Browder had been on probation at the time of the alleged offense, the judge remanded him into custody without bail.

As the weeks and months passed, Browder steadfastly refused to plead guilty, insisting on his innocence. This differentiates Browder from many pretrial detainees in the United States, who plead guilty to escape the conditions of their pretrial confinement. "Individuals who insist on their innocence and refuse to plead guilty get held[,] ... [b]ut the people who choose to plead guilty get out faster."[8]

More than two years went by, during which more than a half dozen requests for continuances by the prosecution resulted in postponement after postponement of Browder's trial date. During this time, Browder spent a significant amount of time in solitary confinement, largely as a result of minor infractions. He became depressed and twice attempted to commit suicide.

In the fall of 2012 prosecutors offered Browder a new plea deal. In exchange for a plea of guilty, he would be sentenced to two and one-half years in prison. Given the time he had already served, that meant Browder would be released in a matter of weeks. According to his court-appointed defense attorney, "Ninety-nine out of a hundred would take the offer that gets you out of jail.... [But Browder] just said, 'Nah, I'm not taking it.' He didn't flinch. Never talked about it. He was not taking a plea."[9] In March 2013 a judge offered Browder a most tempting opportunity: plead guilty to two misdemeanor offenses in exchange for immediate release on time served. Browder refused yet again, asserting that he had not done anything wrong. Just over two months later, the judge dismissed the case against Browder.

Ultimately, Browder spent three years in jail awaiting trial, including nearly two years in solitary confinement. Browder was never able to recover from the psychological damage caused by his ordeal, which included enduring repeated assaults by both guards and inmates, as well as months of isolation in twenty-three-hour-per-day lockdown. In June 2015 he killed himself at the age of twenty-two.[10]

Browder's case garnered intense media attention. Indeed, Mayor Bill de Blasio cited what happened to Browder as part of the impetus to reform New York City's court system to reduce or eliminate the excessive delays that had caused Browder to be kept in jail for more than three years for a crime he most likely did not commit.[11] Jay-Z and Harvey Weinstein produced a six-part documentary series on Browder's ordeal for Spike television, which aired in 2017.

What happened to Derek West Harris, Kenneth Humphrey, and Kalief Browder serves as extreme examples of the potential consequences of the unjust ways in which pretrial detention operates in the United States. Browder's single-parent family could not come up with money for his $3,000 bail. Although Browder's status as a probationer ultimately caused him to be held without bail, the overwhelming majority of pretrial detainees remain in custody because they cannot afford to pay for their release on bail—just like Derek West Harris and Kenneth Humphrey. In contrast, wealthy defendants, even those who might be a flight risk, can pay high bail amounts and are set free. Take Robert Durst as an example. Durst, who was profiled in the HBO documentary *The Jinx*, was arrested for the murder of a neighbor in 2001;

after bail was set at $250,000, he promptly paid the amount and then absconded.[12] As he admitted in the documentary, his intention was always to put up the money and then leave. His wealth enabled him to be released almost immediately.[13]

However, most defendants do not have that luxury. According to a research report issued by the Prison Policy Initiative, 60 percent of the people who cannot pay bail come from the poorest third of society.[14] But this figure does not even begin to capture the financial toll the US money bail system takes on people accused, but not convicted, of criminal offenses:

> In a given year, city and county jails across the country admit between 11 million and 13 million people. In New York City, where courts use bail far less than in many jurisdictions, roughly 45,000 people are jailed each year simply because they can't pay their court-assigned bail. And while the city's courts set bail much lower than the national average, only one in 10 defendants is able to pay it at arraignment. To put a finer point on it: Even when bail is set comparatively low—at $500 or less, as it is in one-third of nonfelony cases—only 15 percent of defendants are able to come up with the money to avoid jail.[15]

The effects of not being able to post bail go beyond the loss of liberty while awaiting trial. Indeed, being held in pretrial detention is the single best predictor of case outcome, even after controlling for other factors. For example, roughly half of all nonfelony cases in New York City end with an acquittal; in contrast, the conviction rate skyrockets to 92 percent for pretrial detainees.[16] The New York City Criminal Justice Agency interpreted these data as supporting the proposition that pretrial detention is so unpleasant that it pressures those accused of crimes to plead guilty in order to escape the conditions of confinement.

Although bail now serves as both a mechanism "for locking people up" prior to any criminal conviction and for inducing guilty pleas, neither could be further from the intended emancipatory purpose of bail when the concept first came into practice in England.[17]

## A PRIMER ON BAIL IN THE UNITED STATES

Bail is a guarantee.[18] In return for being released from jail, the accused promises to return to court as needed. The accused often needs to secure this promise by pledging money or property with the court. If the defendant appears in court when requested, the security is returned. If he or she fails to appear, the security can be forfeited.

### *Overview of Common Bail Procedures*

Bail procedures vary by jurisdiction and according to the seriousness of the crime. In the majority of states, those arrested for minor misdemeanors can be released fairly quickly by posting bail at the police station. In most communities, lower-court judges have adopted a fixed bail schedule that specifies an exact amount for each offense. Although bail schedules provide for quick and easy decisions regarding release after arrest, "they seem to contradict the notion that pretrial release conditions should reflect an assessment of an individual defendant's risk of failure to appear and threat to public safety."[19] Such concerns have led appellate courts in Hawaii and Oklahoma to reject bail schedules on due process grounds.[20] In jurisdictions that do not use bail schedules, bail determinations are made on a case-by-case basis, in much the same way that bail decisions for felonies have historically been made.

Depending on the jurisdiction, bail may be set during an initial appearance, a preliminary hearing, or a separate bail hearing. In all these situations, the arrestee appears before a commissioner, magistrate, or lower-court judge, who must determine whether the arrestee qualifies for release on bail and, if so, what the conditions will be. As frequently depicted on the television show *Law and Order*, these proceedings are often very quick, frequently lasting only a few minutes. But unlike their television counterparts, bail determinations in real life often do not involve defense counsel arguing on the arrestee's behalf. In jurisdictions that use a judicial proceeding to set bail, arrestees may

TABLE I
## Common Forms of Pretrial Release

| Type | Description |
|------|-------------|
| Release on recognizance (ROR) | Judges release a defendant without any bail if they believe the person is not likely to flee. Such personal bonds are used most often for defendants accused of minor crimes and for those with substantial ties to the community. |
| Cash bond | The accused must post with the court either the full amount of cash bail or a percentage of it in the form of a cash bond. All of this money will be returned when all court appearances are satisfied. |
| Property bond | Most states allow a defendant (or friends or relatives) to use a piece of property as collateral. If the defendant fails to appear in court, the property is forfeited. Property bonds are rare because courts generally require that the equity in the property be double the amount of the bond. |
| Bail bond | The arrestee hires a bail agent to post a bond for the amount required. The agent charges a nonrefundable fee for this service, typically set at 10% of the amount of the bond. |

SOURCE: Adapted from table 10.3 in Neubauer and Fradella's *America's Courts and the Criminal Justice System*, 13th edition, p. 293. © 2019 South-Western, a part of Cengage, Inc. Reproduced by permission. www.cengage.com/permissions.

remain in police custody for a number of hours—perhaps as long as two days—before they have the opportunity to make bail.[21]

### Common Forms of Pretrial Release

Once bail has been set, a defendant can gain pretrial release in four basic ways, which are outlined in table 1. Any of these types of release may be combined with nonfinancial conditions of pretrial release, such as supervision, drug testing, participation in counseling and rehabilitation services, electronic monitoring, residence restrictions, and no contact orders, just to name a few of the more common ones.[22]

Because many of those arrested lack ready cash, do not own property, or lack the needed social clout, the first three options for making bail listed in table 1 are often unavailable for them. As a result, nearly half of those granted financial bail have no choice but to resort to a commercial bail bond. Indeed, reliance on for-profit bail "is the most common form of release, doubling from 24 percent to 49 percent of releases from jail from 1990 to 2009."[23]

## Commercial Bail

Bail bonds are a commercial business that, like all for-profit businesses, are run for the purposes of making money. Defendants who utilize the services of a bail bond company are required to pay a nonrefundable fee, and in exchange for that payment, which is usually tied to a fixed percentage of the overall bail amount assessed by a court, the commercial bail entity guarantees that the defendant will appear in court, usually by posting a surety bond underwritten by an insurance company.[24] If the accused fails to appear as promised, the bail business is in theory responsible for paying the full amount of the bail to the court, although as explained in chapter 2, that rarely occurs in practice. In addition, bail agents are then often empowered to apprehend the defendant who failed to appear in court, either themselves or by using the services of a bounty hunter.[25] Although bail agents claim to play an important role in the criminal justice system, as described in more detail in chapter 2, the industry is known for its corrupt and predatory practices.[26]

## Preventive Detention

In the US system of monetary bail, those who are wealthy enough can often buy their freedom while awaiting trial. But the poor await trial in jail. On any given day, there are nearly 744,600 persons in jail (not prison), approximately 60 percent of whom have not been convicted of any crime.[27] Approximately 90 percent of these pretrial detainees "had a bail amount set, but were unable to meet the financial conditions required to secure release."[28] In contrast, just 4 to 6 percent of those held in pretrial detention have been denied bail on one or more of several grounds, including the risk that the person will flee; the risk that the accused may threaten, injure, or intimidate a prospective witness or juror; or because the charged offense involved serious violence or major drug distribution or is punishable by life imprisonment or death.[29]

## The Context of Bail Setting

Deciding whom to release and whom to detain pending trial poses critical problems for judges. The realities of the bail system in the United States reflect an attempt to strike a balance between the legally recognized purpose of setting bail to ensure reappearance for trial and the working perception that some defendants should not be allowed out of jail until the trial.

Trial court judges have a great deal of discretion in setting bail. Statutory law provides few specifics about how much money should be required, and appellate courts have likewise spent little time deciding what criteria should be used. Although the Eighth Amendment to the US Constitution prohibits excessive bail, appellate courts will reduce a trial judge's bail amount only in the rare event that flagrant abuse can be proved. In practice, then, trial court judges have virtually unlimited legal discretion in determining the amount of bail. That discretion is often guided by two primary factors: (1) the risk of flight or nonappearance in court, which often involves consideration of the arrestee's "ties to the community," such as stable employment, property ownership, marital status, number of close relationships, and length of presence in the community; and (2) the perceived risk the arrestee poses to himself or herself or others, which often involves consideration of the person's mental condition, the seriousness of the crime(s) for which the person was arrested, and the arrestee's prior criminal history.

At first blush, these factors might seem straightforward. But uncertainty abounds because typically few details of the alleged crime are available shortly after a warrantless arrest. Similarly, information about the defendant's mental status, ties to the community, financial resources, and even criminal history is often in short supply. In many courts, for example, police "rap sheets" (lists of prior arrests) are available but typically do not contain information about the eventual disposition of prior cases: dismissal, plea, or imprisonment. Moreover, each bail decision is risky. In the face of the uncertainty caused by a lack of complete information, judges must weigh risks such as whether a defendant released on bail will commit another crime and whether police groups, district attorneys, and the local newspapers may criticize a judge severely for granting pretrial release to defendants. In addition, judges must worry about jail overcrowding. If an arrestee is placed in pretrial detention, judicial officials might worry that someone else—perhaps someone more dangerous—will be released from a jail crowded beyond its capacity.

Bail decisions also depend on what scholars refer to as *situational justice*: a subjective series of factors such as how the defendant appears, acts, responds to questions, and the like. Note that the use of situational justice might lead judges to make certain judgments about defendants based on demographic characteristics, resulting in racial, ethnic, gender, and sexual orientation disparities in bail decisions.[30]

## THE COMMON LAW ORIGINS OF BAIL

The modern context and implications of bail decisions are examined in more detail in chapters 2, 3, and 4. In the balance of this chapter we explore the origins of bail and how it evolved into the pretrial release and detention systems now utilized in the United States.

### Bail in the Anglo-Saxon Period

The concept of bail can be traced back in England hundreds of years before the Norman Conquest. With the fall of the Roman Empire in the early fifth century CE, much of Western Europe fell under the control of the kings of Germanic tribes from what is now Scandinavia. Germanic tribal justice blended retributive and restorative justice.[31] The former embodied the same principle of *lex talionis*—"an eye for an eye, a tooth for a tooth"—found in the law of many ancient civilizations, including the Babylonians under Hammurabi.[32] Such an approach allowed aggrieved parties to become agents of retribution. In the case of homicide, the surviving kin of a victim could avenge the death of their family member. This often led to "blood feuds" in which long-standing disputes between groups led to killings to avenge killings, which in turn led to more killing.[33]

Over time Anglo-Saxons implemented a legal process to avoid blood feuds that involved the payment of restitution for a variety of transgressions, even for murder, rape, theft, and assault.[34] This system of compensation varied based on the value of someone's "life and bodily faculties in accordance with his rank in society."[35] These compensatory payments generally fell into three categories: *wergild*, paid to a family group as compensation for the death of another family member; *bot*, paid for injuries less serious than death, including compensation for the repair of houses and tools; and *wite*, a public fine payable to a lord or monarch as atonement for a crime.[36] If *wergild* could not be paid or was refused, then the blood feud was permitted in homicide cases.

By the second half of the seventh century Anglo-Saxon kings sought to bring order and consistency to dispute resolution by creating a rudimentary court system in which an aggrieved man could initiate a complaint and the accused was required to "give *borh* (surety) and make any retribution prescribed by the judicial officer."[37] *Borh* is a synonym for bail; in the same way that bail is supposed to act as a surety today, *borh*

was designed to ensure that the accused appeared before a judicial officer to participate in the judicial process.[38] This system avoided the
costs attendant on pretrial incarceration at a time when the "circuits of
the itinerant justices were irregular, and often a matter of years."[39] The
system also avoided numerous troubles associated with pretrial detention, most notably the ease with which escape from custody was often
accomplished.[40]

*Borh* also served another important function: providing assurance
that the applicable form of fine, whether *wergid, bot, wile,* or some combination thereof, would be paid if the accused were convicted. This
function became even more important after the system of *borh* was
extended from preadjudication surety to the time after trial.[41] The oath
of the *borh* was especially important to this latter function if a person
needed to pay *wergild* over time in installments.[42] Similarly, the oath of
the *borh* was important if the accused fled. In such a circumstance, he
was presumed guilty and the surety was expected to pay *wergild, bot,*
and *wile,* as applicable, on behalf of the person for whom *borh* was
pledged. Serfs were placed under the *borh* of their feudal lords, and for-
eign visitors were placed under the *borh* of their hosts.[43]

By the early 900s the Anglo-Saxon surety system permitted family,
friends, and acquaintances to act as *borh.* Moreover, property could
pledged in satisfaction of surety. But if the accused had neither property nor other forms of *borh,* then the law of England permitted that he
be held in custody until judgment.[44] By the mid-900s every person in
England was required to have a *borh,* thereby bonding "surety and prin-
cipal . . .'body for body.'"[45]

Importantly, the value of the *borh* pledge in the Anglo-Saxon surety
system was equal to the amount of the compensation to be paid as a
penalty upon conviction. "Thus, the amount of the pledge, that is, the
amount of bail, was identical to the penalty upon conviction."[46] As law
professor June Carbone noted, this system deterred flight: "By tying
bail to the potential penalty, the system necessarily linked the amount
of the pretrial pledge to the seriousness of the crime."[47]

### The Effects of the Norman Conquest on Bail

When William the Conqueror took control of England in 1066, he and the Normans brought with them very different views about the philosophy of justice. As a result, the administration of law in England changed dramatically.[48] Acts that today are considered to be crimes gradually came to be viewed as transgressions that required the intervention of the state.[49] By the time Henry II ruled England in the mid- to late twelfth century, crimes were no longer considered to be private matters, but instead were viewed as offenses against the Crown.[50] Partly as a result of this shift, the law of the land began to be harmonized into a "common law": one law that applied consistently throughout the king's lands.

As the common law developed, the criminal process of the state could be initiated in one of two ways. As had been the custom in the past, the alleged victim of a crime—or the next of kin in homicide cases—could swear, under oath, an accusation against the suspect.[51] But Henry II put in place a system of presentment by jury, a forerunner to the grand jury system, via the Assize of Clarendon in 1166. Pursuant to this mandate, twelve law-abiding men in each village were assembled and sworn under oath to "'present' those suspected of crimes to the royal courts."[52] Trials were often by water, ordeal, or combat.[53] Trial by water and ordeal gradually lost legitimacy, giving way to presenting to juries that determined guilt at trial. In 1215 the Fourth Lateran Council of the Roman Catholic Church banned clergy from participating in trials by water or ordeal.[54] This in turn cleared the way for trials to become adjudication processes before secular English tribunals.

A series of official abuses of state power relevant to criminal justice committed by three successive monarchs, such as curtailing the trial process, contributed to pushing England to the brink of civil war.[55] To avoid that consequence, King John signed Magna Carta in 1215. Article 39 of that document provided: "No free man shall be taken, imprisoned, disseised, outlawed, banished, or in any way destroyed … except by the lawful judgment of his peers and by the law of the land." The next clause stated: "To no one will We sell ... deny or delay right of justice." Originally, these protections were meant for noblemen, but they soon applied to all citizens. These statements came to form the basis of the due process guarantees in the US Constitution, including the right to trial by jury.

Punishments under early English common law also changed significantly under the Anglo-Saxons from the compensation system that had been applicable to most offenses. The concept of paying damages and fines was largely considered to be insufficient for having offended against the monarch for all but the most trivial of offenses; rather, harsh punishments—ranging from corporal punishment to loss of limbs or life—became commonplace.[56]

Collectively, these changes in the criminal process necessitated modifications to the system of pretrial surety that worked well when *borh* and compensatory punishments were balanced. As long as offenses were punishable through one or more types of compensation, all transgressors were "bailable" under the Anglo-Saxon *borh* system.[57] But the harsher penalties enacted after the Norman Conquest changed the calculus that had made *borh* sensible when restorative justice principles governed the punishment of offenses. "The accused threatened with loss of life or limb had a greater incentive to flee than the prisoner facing a money fine, and judicial officers possessed no sure formula for equating the amount of the pledge or the number of sureties with the deterrence of flight. At the same time, the growing delays between accusation and trial increased the importance of pretrial release and the opportunities for abuse and corruption. The determination of whom to release became a far more complicated issue than calculating the amount of the [financial punishment]."[58]

At first those accused of homicide lost the right to bail, primarily because the offense became punishable by death.[59] Other offenses were subsequently made nonbailable, especially those so deemed by local sheriffs.[60] But this tremendous discretion in the hands of local law enforcement officials not only led to widespread corruption concerning bail but also resulted in all but the most minor of offenses being non-bailable.[61] In an attempt to address both of these problems, Parliament enacted the Statute of Westminster in 1275.[62] It defined bailable and nonbailable offenses in a manner that lasted until 1826.[63]

### The Statute of Westminster

The Statute of Westminster specified that all offenses not punishable by loss of life or limb were eligible for bail. But since so many offenses carried some form of corporal or capital punishment, the class of nonbailable offenses nonetheless remained sizable, including murder, arson, treason, escape, and certain forestry offenses on royal lands. In addition, just because an offense was bailable did not automatically establish a right to bail. The Statute of Westminster required sheriffs to weigh the likelihood of conviction as part of the decision to grant release on bail. "The statute required the sheriffs to inquire, first, whether the evidence was reliable, i.e., was the accused caught in the act, had he confessed, had he been named by someone who had confessed, or had he been charged only on the basis of light suspicion; and, second, did the behavior of the accused indicate his guilt, i.e., had he attempted to escape, had he committed crimes in the past, or was he of 'ill fame.'"[64] As a result, persons "caught in the act" could be detained even for relatively minor offenses, whereas those accused of serious offenses without significant evidence to support the suspicion against them could be granted bail. Great discretion remained for intermediate offenses, especially when balancing the reliability of the evidence against a suspect's reputation in the community.

Given the modest nature of the reforms contained in the Statute of Westminster, it should come as no surprise that it largely failed to curb local corruption in the granting or denial of bail. Parliament repeatedly tweaked the Statute of Westminster in attempts to add protections for the accused in the bail process, most of which proved ineffectual.[65]

Parliament also enacted laws defining the bail eligibility of offenses not contained in the Statute of Westminster.[66] Finally, in 1486 Parliament took steps to dramatically change the bail process by requiring that two justices of peace make bail decisions in open judicial sessions at which the accused and the witnesses against him would testify.[67] This "marked the introduction of the preliminary hearing into English law."[68] Subsequent laws, such as the Habeas Corpus Act of 1679, added procedures to facilitate timely bail determinations but did not limit the amount of bail.[69] It was not until 1689 that Parliament addressed the problem of prohibitively high bail amounts when it enacted a Bill of Rights.[70] The importance of the Bill of Rights including a prohibition on "excessive bail" cannot be overstated, for two reasons. First, this law marked the first time that legislation expressed concern for the amount of bail, rather than whether bail was granted or denied.[71] Second, the "excessive bail" language used in the statute was subsequently used in the Eighth Amendment to the US Constitution.

### English Common Law in the United States

Many US colonies mirrored the Statute of Westminster in their approaches to bail.[72] And as in England, the amorphous approach to bail expressed in that statute led to many concerns that ultimately ushered in needed reforms. Some colonies, such as Massachusetts, enacted laws guaranteeing a right to bail for all noncapital crimes, even for many serious offenses.[73] Perhaps more important, after the Revolutionary War (1775–1783), some new US states incorporated in their constitutions a right to bail for all noncapital crimes. In states such as Pennsylvania, which limited capital punishment—for all people other than Black men—to cases of deliberate murder, "the effect was to extend the right to bail ... far beyond" that provided under English law and the law of most US colonies.[74] Nearly every state constitution adopted after 1776 incorporated a right to bail. Indeed, forty states currently guarantee a right to bail in their state constitutions for all or most noncapital offenses, and eight more do so in statutory law.[75] The overwhelming majority of these state constitutional guarantees employ some variation of the following language: "All persons shall be bailable by sufficient sureties, except for capital offenses when the proof is evident or the presumption great."[76] Notably, however, the right to bail in some jurisdictions is not as strong as such language suggests, because other constitutional provisions or state statutes carve out exceptions for those charged with certain felonies who are on probation, parole, or pretrial release on a different felony charge, or because the nature of the current charge suggests the accused is dangerous.[77]

## BAIL IN THE UNITED STATES

The Eighth Amendment to the US Constitution provides, "Excessive bail shall not be required, nor excessive fines imposed, nor cruel and unusual punishments inflicted." The first clause in this amendment is commonly referred to as the Excessive Bail Clause. Importantly, unlike in the constitutions of many US states, this provision in the federal constitution does not establish a right to bail. Rather, it merely states that if bail is granted, then it may not be "excessive."[78] In other words, the Eighth Amendment limits judicial discretion setting the amount of bail, but release on bail is wholly dependent on legislation setting forth the offenses for which bail might be available.[79] The scope of this limited right, however, is far from clear.

### Early US Cases Addressing the Purpose of Bail

The first important federal case to address the purpose of bail was *United States v. Feely*, decided in 1813.[80] The defendant had been indicted, and he and his surety entered into a recognizance agreement pending trial. (Note that unlike today, *recognizance* and a *bail bond* at that time were basically one and the same.[81]) When the defendant subsequently failed to appear when scheduled, he defaulted on his bond. But he subsequently appeared in court during the following term. Given his previous failure to appear, he was placed in pretrial detention.

The defendant then filed a stay arguing that the funds he had previously posted to guarantee his appearance in court should be returned to him. But the federal authorities argued that the forfeited bond had become a debt due to the United States in much the same way that a contractual debt might be due and therefore that the court lacked jurisdiction to consider the defendant's application for a stay. Chief Justice John Marshall, sitting as a circuit judge in Virginia, rejected that view:

> The object of a recognizance is, not to enrich the treasury, but to combine the administration of criminal justice with the convenience of a person accused, but not proved to be guilty. If the accused has, under circumstances which show that there was no design to evade the justice of his country forfeited his recognizance, but repairs the default as much as is in his power, by appearing at the succeeding term, and submitting himself to the law, the real intention and object of the recognizance are effected, and no injury is done. If the accused prove innocent, it would be unreasonable and unjust in government to exact from an innocent man a penalty, intended only to secure a trial, because the trial was suspended, in consequence of events which are deemed a reasonable excuse for not appearing on the day mentioned in the recognizance. If he be found guilty, he must suffer the punishment intended by the law for his offense, and it would be unreasonable to superadd the penalty of an obligation entered into only to secure a trial.[82]

Thus, bail forfeitures are not designed to enrich the state, but rather to ensure the appearance of the defendant at subsequent proceedings.

In 1835 the US Supreme Court decided *Ex parte Milburn*.[83] That case reaffirmed the principle that bail is "not designed as a satisfaction for the offense ... but as a means of compelling the party to submit to trial."[84] Thus, early jurisprudential views in the United States on the purpose of bail were more closely aligned with its functions after the Norman Conquest rather than with the earlier Anglo-Saxon approach, in which bail was closely tied to punishment for the crime. Nonetheless, early case law on bail clearly expresses a strong preference for pretrial release on bail, not only as a corollary to the presumption of innocence but also to facilitate the accused assisting counsel with his or her defense.[85] Put differently, nineteenth-century case law in the United States expressed several related principles concerning the purpose of bail: (1) partially as a function of the presumption of innocence, bail is not supposed to be used in a manner that keeps those accused of crimes in pretrial detention; and (2) bail is not supposed to prevent the commission of future crimes, but rather to assure appearance at trial.[86] These early jurisprudential perspectives, however, changed significantly over time. For instance, in the 1979 case *Bell v. Wolfish*, the US Supreme Court backed away from bail being tied, even in part, to the presumption of innocence.[87] On the contrary, the Court unequivocally stated: "Without question, the presumption of innocence plays an important role in our criminal justice system. . . . But it has no application to a determination of the rights of a pretrial detainee during confinement before his trial has even begun."[88] Moreover, the purposes of bail have evolved in ways that reduce the propositions articulated in cases such as *United States v. Feely* and *Ex parte Milburn* to little more than historical footnotes.

### The Evolution of US Jurisprudence on Bail

The purpose of bail in the United States morphed over time. Since at least 1984, and arguably longer, the denial of bail to protect the community from the accused committing further offenses has been one of the primary aims of this important pretrial determination. In light of this statutorily sanctioned aim, questions concerning the meaning and scope of the Eighth Amendment's Excessive Bail Clause have been largely relegated to academic discourse. Indeed, there has been precious little guidance from the US Supreme Court concerning this enumerated yet underdeveloped constitutional right.

### THE RIGHT TO BAIL

Whether the Eighth Amendment embodies a right to bail remained an open question until the mid-twentieth century. One of the most important cases to address this question was a 1943 case from New York, *People ex rel Shapiro v. Keeper of City Prisons.*[89] In that case, the defendant was denied bail pending trial for extortion because he had seven prior convictions. On appeal, the highest court in New York upheld the denial of bail. In so doing, the court rejected the notion that the Eighth Amendment implied a right to bail, reasoning that the history of bail at English common law supported the conclusion that legislatures were free to set rules regarding the determination of bail.[90]

Although some courts flirted with the logic that a right to bail was necessarily implied by the text of the Eighth Amendment, the position espoused in *Shapiro* was ultimately the one adopted by the US Supreme Court in the 1952 case *Carlson v. Landon.*[91] In that case, nonresident aliens who were facing deportation were denied bail because they were members of the Communist Party. They filed a petition for a writ of habeas corpus, arguing that their detention violated the Eighth Amendment. In rejecting their petition, and over the objections of strong dissenting opinions, the majority of the Court squarely held that the US Constitution does not guarantee a right to bail; it only prohibits excessive bail amounts.[92] As a result, legislatures are seemingly free to establish classes of bailable and nonbailable offenses, just as Parliament had done in the Statute of Westminster.

### FREEDOM FROM EXCESSIVE BAIL

In light of the holding in *Carlson v. Landon* that the Eighth Amendment does not guarantee a right to bail, the Court's 1951 decision in *Stack v. Boyle* assumed an even more important role in the criminal justice process than may have at first appeared.[93] In that case, a trial court set bail at a uniform $50,000 for each of twelve defendants charged with conspiring to violate the anticommunist Alien Registration Act (commonly known as the Smith Act), which criminalized membership in any group that advocated the violent overthrow of the US government.[94] The defendants moved to reduce their bail, arguing that it was excessive, in violation of the Eighth Amendment. After that motion was denied, the defendants—all of whom lacked the financial resources to secure bail in that amount—fielded a petition for a writ of habeas corpus, which ultimately was appealed to the US Supreme Court.

The Court began its analysis by stating that then-applicable federal law—including the Judiciary Act of 1789 and Rule 46(a)(1) of the Federal Rules of Criminal Procedure—established "that a person arrested for a noncapital offense shall be admitted to bail."[95] The Court described this approach as serving several important purposes, including permitting the defendant to assist in his own defense, preventing the infliction of punishment prior to conviction, and preserving the presumption of innocence.[96] The Court then stated that the Excessive Bail Clause guarantees that the amount of bail must be carefully fixed such that a particular defendant's subsequent participation in judicial proceedings could reasonably be guaranteed. Quoting the Federal Rules of Criminal Procedure applicable at that time, the Court explained that the judicial officer setting bail must take into account "the nature and circumstances of the offense charged, the weight of the evidence against [the defendant], the financial ability of the defendant to give bail, and the character of the defendant."[97] Because the amount of bail in the case was set higher than the bail amounts for other crimes punishable by similar penalties—and five times higher than the maximum fine upon conviction of a Smith Act violation—without there having been any evidentiary showing that such a high amount was necessary to ensure the appearance of the defendants in the case, the Court remanded the case to the district court "so that a hearing may be held for the purpose of fixing reasonable bail for each petitioner."[98]

*Stack v. Boyle* could be interpreted as standing for two related propositions. First, bail determinations are supposed to be customized with particularity not only with respect to the nature of the accused's alleged actions and the weight of the evidence on such charges, but also to the defendant's criminal history, character, and financial situation. Second, bail set at an amount higher than reasonably calculated to assure subsequent appearances in court is "excessive" and therefore constitutionally prohibited. But as explored in more detail in subsequent chapters, neither of these propositions would be a fair conclusion considering the way that bail determinations have been made in practice. In particular, the first proposition has been undercut by bail schedules, which have significantly minimized individualized consideration of bail. And the second proposition has never been operationalized in a meaningful manner. Indeed, as legal historian William F. Duker observed in 1977, "bail is not excessive because the defendant is unable to meet it."[99]

As should be evident, the language of Federal Rule of Criminal Procedure Rule 46(c) cited approvingly in *Stack v. Boyle* resembles strongly the directives in the Statute of Westminster, insofar as the strength of the evidence and the character of the accused are both part of the calculus for determining the likelihood of flight and subsequent nonappearance.[100] In 1946 the Federal Rules of Criminal Procedure were amended to specifically require consideration of the defendant's prior criminal record.[101] When courts reviewed that factor along with the other key criteria for determining bail eligibility—the nature of the offense, the weight of the evidence, and the character of the accused—the defendant's financial status was reduced in importance such that most courts considered it "only within the limits dictated by the seriousness of the offense."[102] Indeed, as a landmark 1954 study by Caleb Foote revealed, a defendant's lack of financial resources rarely played a significant role in the determination of bail.[103] This resulted in many defendants being held in pretrial detention because they could not afford to post bond.[104]

## DOES THE EIGHTH AMENDMENT'S EXCESSIVE BAIL
## CLAUSE APPLY TO THE STATES?

On numerous occasions the US Supreme Court has had the opportunity to address squarely which provisions in the Bill of Rights are incorporated via the Fourteenth Amendment so that they apply to the states.[105] But that cannot be said of the Eighth Amendment's Excessive Bail Clause. In the 1980s at least three federal circuit courts of appeal held that the Excessive Bail Clause applied to the states because a prohibition on excessive bail was integral to the concept of ordered liberty.[106] But the Supreme Court has never decided a case that required it to rule squarely on whether the Excessive Bail Clause restrains only the federal government or also applies to the states.[107]

However, in *McDonald v. City of Chicago*—a 2010 case in which the Court held the Second Amendment was incorporated and made applicable to the states by the Due Process Clause of the Fourteenth Amendment—the Court, in dicta, included a footnote in which it listed the provisions of the Bill of Rights that had previously been held to be incorporated against the states.[108] Curiously, the Court included the Excessive Bail Clause in its list, citing 1971's *Schilb v. Kuebel* as the case holding that the prohibition on excessive bail had been incorporated. But *Schilb v. Kuebel* also referenced the Excessive Bail Clause in dicta as having been incorporated, rather than as the central holding of the case: "Bail, of course, is basic to our system of law ... and the Eighth Amendment's proscription of excessive bail has been assumed to have application to the States through the Fourteenth Amendment.... But we are not at all concerned here with any fundamental right to bail or with any Eighth Amendment–Fourteenth Amendment question of bail excessiveness."[109] The Court cited two cases in support of its "assumed" incorporation dicta: an Eighth Circuit decision and a concurring opinion in *Robinson v. California*, which declared unconstitutional a statute criminalizing the status of being addicted to the use of narcotics.[110] Thus, this footnote announced that the Excessive Bail Clause has been incorporated by the Fourteenth Amendment to apply to the states, without citation to any US Supreme Court case that had ever squarely addressed that question—an "oddity" that "does not does not inspire confidence that the Justices had reached a momentous civil-rights decision."[111] Hence, law professor Samuel Wiseman argued that the *McDonald* case itself incorporated the Excessive Bail Clause.[112]

As law professor Scott Howe has suggested, assuming that the Eighth Amendment's Excessive Bail Clause applies to the states after the pronouncement in *McDonald*, it is unclear how that constitutional provision might restrain the authority of state courts and legislatures when it comes to bail decisions.[113] Howe posited two alterative interpretations:

> One view ... assumes that the Eighth Amendment does not limit the legislature and only requires that a judicial officer allow bail in accordance with any directions from the legislature. On that view, the clause is a mere reminder to judicial officers to honor the separation of powers on bail questions. The alternative view could make the clause an especially important safeguard for liberty and justice. This alternative view assumes that the Eighth Amendment limits the ability of both the legislature and judicial officers to deny bail or to set bail at a level designed to exceed the defendant's ability to pay and, thus, to incarcerate him.[114]

Because the first view renders the Excessive Bail Clause insignificant, Professor Howe concluded that the second view must be correct. As a matter of logic, it is difficult to dispute that conclusion. Constitutional rights are rarely, if ever, interpreted as mere reminders to judges to honor the separation of powers by following the mandates of legislative bodies. Nonetheless, the conclusion that the Excessive Bail Clause limits both legislatures and the judiciary is not easily supported in light of legislative bail reform efforts enacted in the 1980s and the sole US Supreme Court decision on the Excessive Bail Clause since the 1950s.

## THE FIRST WAVE OF BAIL REFORM EFFORTS IN THE UNITED STATES

In the wake of Caleb Foote's groundbreaking 1954 study on how bail decisions were made in Philadelphia, the Vera Foundation (now the Vera Institute of Justice) launched an experiment in New York City known as the Manhattan Bail Project.[115] Vera researchers developed a tool that used a point system to measure several dimensions of defendants' community ties as a way of predicting their subsequent appearance in judicial proceedings. Although the experiment did not include those charged with the most serious of violent crimes, it did include defendants' prior criminal records in the point system calculations. Defendants who were released on their own recognizance (i.e., without monetary bail) based on Vera's recommendations failed to appear in only 1.6 percent of cases, about half the 3 percent failure to appear rate for defendants who were released on bail.[116]

The results of the Manhattan Bail Project focused national attention on using ties to the community as a proxy for flight risk to make bail determinations, rather than for the potential outcome of trial. The results of the Vera study and similar experiments in other US cities led US attorney general Robert Kennedy to direct all federal prosecutors to release criminal defendants on their own recognizance, whenever feasible.[117] The failure to appear rate for federal defendants released on recognizance as a result of that directive was approximately 2.5 percent, roughly the same percentage as those required to post a bail bond.[118] Congress ultimately responded by enacting the Bail Reform Act of 1966.

### *The Bail Reform Act of 1966*

The Bail Reform Act of 1966 legislatively mandated that with the exception of those charged with a capital crime, all criminal defendants were to be released on their own recognizance unless there were some reason that such release would "not reasonably assure" the defendant's appearance at trial.[119] The act marked the first significant legislative reform of bail in the federal system since the Judiciary Act of 1789. Like its 1789 predecessor, the Bail Reform Act of 1966 established a statutory right to bail for noncapital offenses. But the act went even further, not only by creating a statutory presumption in favor of pretrial release (as well as release pending appeal), but also by setting forth a series of nonmonetary alternatives to bail bonds, including "placing the person in the custody of a designated person or organization which agrees to the supervision; restrictions on travel, association and/or residence; execution of a bail bond with a sufficient number of solvent sureties; and finally, the imposition of any other condition deemed reasonably to assure appearance as required, including a condition requiring that the person return to custody after specified hours."[120]

Importantly, the Bail Reform Act of 1966 incorporated the Manhattan Bail Project's notion of "community ties" as a statutory criterion to be considered as part of the pretrial release decision-making process.[121] As a result, magistrates were to consider factors such as family ties, the length of time that the defendant had resided in the community, employment, property ownership, and financial resources, along with the more traditional criteria of the nature of the offense, the weight of the evidence, and prior criminal history—including any past record of failure to appear.[122] Financial bonds were only permissible if a magistrate determined that no combination of nonmonetary conditions of release would sufficiently guarantee the defendant's appearance in subsequent judicial proceedings. After twenty-four hours, any defendant who was unable to meet the condition of release was entitled to have the magistrate review the bail determination and, if unchanged, the order became subject to appellate review.[123] Nonetheless, the seriousness of the offense remained the central question for decisions about whether to grant bail and the amount of bail.[124] In fact, magistrates approached bail determinations using the perceived dangerousness of the accused as a substitute for flight risk and set high bail accordingly.[125] Put differently, "federal courts were taking matters into their own hands, effectively denying bail in cases where they deemed defendants to be dangerous by setting inordinately high bail, albeit on stated grounds of risk of flight."[126]

### The Bail Reform Act of 1984

Just over a year into his first term, President Ronald Reagan sought congressional action on a wide range of anticrime proposals.[127] Bail reform was among the proposals advocated by Reagan and the US Department of Justice, albeit in a qualitatively different manner than the advocacy leading to the Bail Reform Act of 1966. Mirroring conservative calls for stricter criteria for releasing defendants on bail that started soon after the Bail Reform Act of 1966 went into effect, the Reagan administration sought to redefine the decision-making factors from flight risk to "prevent[ing] a dangerous defendant from returning to the streets to prey once again on innocent citizens."[128] Congress responded by amending the Bail Reform Act in 1984 to specifically sanction "the previously unspoken practice of considering the dangerousness of a defendant."[129] In fact, the 1984 act specified that defendants charged with certain felonies "shall" be denied pretrial release if a judicial officer is persuaded, by clear and convincing evidence, that "no condition or combination of conditions will reasonably assure the appearance of the person as required and the safety of any other person and the community."[130] As Professor Carbone pointed out, the explicit sanctioning of preventative detention is not the same as setting a high bail amount, because the former "guarantees incarceration and marks the first return to explicit remand after a century and a half of expansion of the right to bail."[131]

In 1987 the US Supreme Court upheld the constitutionality of the Bail Reform Act of 1984 in *United States v. Salerno*. As a result, judges to this day concern themselves not only with a criminally accused person's flight risk, but also with the danger that person poses to the community if released on bail.[132] This is true in both the federal and state systems.[133] Troublingly, however, predictions of future dangerousness typically amount to little more than unreliable prognostications.[134]

*Salerno*'s interpretation of the Eighth Amendment supports a denial of bail if a defendant "is likely to flee, impede the justice process, or pose a danger to others."[135] If bail can be denied for one of these reasons, it stands to reason that bail could also be granted in a high amount as a deterrent to a defendant subsequently failing to appear. But how high is too high? And to what degree must individualization occur?

The US Supreme Court has not provided sufficient guidance to lower court judges to answer these questions even though intermediate appellate court decisions have provided conflicting advice for decades. Here we consider two of these cases.

In 1987 the First Circuit decided *Wagenmann v. Adams*.[136] In that case, the defendant had threatened his daughter's boyfriend in an attempt to stop their impending wedding, which he objected to. To prevent possible violence, local law enforcement officers intercepted the defendant and arrested him on two minor offenses—one for paperwork infractions of the motor vehicle code and another for disturbing the peace. Bail was set at $500, an amount that the defendant could have paid with the cash he had on his person at the time of arrest. Yet that amount of bail was held to be excessive to ensure subsequent appearance at trial because the defendant "was a responsible citizen, gainfully employed, without any blackened past record" and the charges were "not particularly serious."[137]

The following year, the Fifth Circuit decided *United States v. McConnell*.[138] The defendant in that case had been charged with bank fraud. A magistrate set bail in the amount of $750,000 after determining that the defendant posed a flight risk. Even though there was no question that the defendant could not afford to post bond to satisfy bail in that amount, the court held that the bail amount was not excessive.

In a 2013 law review note, Michael Woodruff poignantly and pithily noted that "poverty alters the analysis" concerning excessive bail.[139] Despite this, courts have been reluctant to consider ability to pay as part of Eighth Amendment analyses. And in recent years advocates have moved away from bail challenges based on the Eighth Amendment. Instead, they have turned to the Fourteenth Amendment, relying on its dual guarantees of due process and equal protection to argue that bail systems that systematically discriminate against the poor without providing an individualized pretrial release decision violate the Constitution. As explained in chapter 2, although the Supreme Court has yet to rule on any of these challenges, the claims have met with some success.

PRETRIAL RELEASE AROUND THE WORLD

As in other areas of criminal justice, when compared with pretrial justice globally, some aspects of the American system are exceptional.[140] Not only is the United States one of only two countries (the other being the Philippines) with a commercial bail bond industry, but it has one of the highest rates of pretrial detention in the world, particularly when compared with other common law jurisdictions.[141] As of November 2016, the rate of pretrial detention in the United States was 146 per 100,000, compared with 50 per 100,000 in Australia, 40 per 100,000 in Canada, and just 16 per 100,000 in England and Wales.[142] That said, the United States is not alone in its overreliance on pretrial detention. Roughly one-third of prisoners around the globe are pretrial detainees, and that number has increased by about 15 percent since 2000.[143] On any given day there are about three million people in pretrial detention around the world, and as in the United States, most of these people "are poor, and economically and politically marginalized."[144] In addition, as law professor Shima Baradaran-Baughman explained, defendants in many countries often endure "excessively long" periods of pretrial detention in terrible conditions while awaiting trial.[145] For example, in Nigeria the average length of pretrial detention is 3.7 years.[146] Worse yet, in some nations those accused of crimes may also endure abuse and torture as part of attempts to induce confessions.[147] While a full detailing of pretrial justice issues around the world is beyond the scope of this book, it is important to remember that many of the issues that we identify are not limited to the United States.

CONCLUSION

As the case of Kalief Browder makes clear, pretrial detention can have tragic results, but even in more typical cases, pretrial release decisions and outcomes have significant consequences for all aspects of our criminal justice system. The contribution of pretrial detention to mass incarceration, in terms of both the numbers detained pretrial and its impact on sentencing, is substantial. Further, in its reliance on money bail, our current system of pretrial release does more than make it difficult for the poor to post bail; it punishes poverty and exacerbates racial, ethnic, and class disparities in the criminal justice system. As we demonstrate in the remainder of this book, the inability to post bail sets in motion a chain of events that stacks the deck against those without financial resources in ways that call into question not only the constitutionality of many bail decisions under the Eighth Amendment's Excessive Bail Clause, but also the constitutionality of the criminal justice process as a matter of both due process and equal protection.

Chapter 2 explains how pretrial release decisions are currently made and notes the disconnect that often exists between release decisions and outcomes. It describes how quickly release decisions are made and highlights two particularly insidious features of the US pretrial justice system—bail schedules and commercial money bond—as well as efforts (both successful and unsuccessful) to eliminate these features. We discuss both legal and legislative attempts at reform, as well as a recent grassroots alternative to commercial bail: community bail funds. Finally, we explore what is commonly thought to be the best alternative to money bail: pretrial supervision and monitoring. Chapter 3 turns to what is perhaps the most controversial issue in pretrial justice reform: actuarial risk assessment tools. We examine their history, use, and operation and address the question of whether these tools are systematically biased against minorities. We conclude that while actuarial risk assessment tools are not without problems, they have the potential to make pretrial decision making fairer, particularly when compared with the alternatives.

Chapter 4 describes in detail the consequences of the high rates of pretrial detention and emphasizes that these negative impacts fall heaviest on the most marginalized members of society. Although courts do not consider pretrial detention to be "punishment," we demonstrate that it is exactly that and show how the effects of pretrial detention go beyond confinement, with both short- and long-term consequences for defendants' cases, employment, and family relationships. Finally, we highlight the contribution of pretrial detention to mass incarceration, particularly through increases in guilty verdicts and more severe sentencing.

Chapter 5 concludes the book by looking forward. Using a series of recommendations issued by the Pretrial Justice Institute as a starting point, we suggest several ways to reduce unnecessary pretrial detention and mitigate the ways in which the current system negatively impacts the poor.

# CHAPTER TWO

# Pretrial Release Decisions and Outcomes

## INTRODUCTION

The pretrial release process consists of two primary components: release decisions and release outcomes.[1] Release *decisions* focus on whether a defendant will be released pending trial, and if so, what conditions of release, if any, will be imposed. Release *outcomes* are the consequences of these decisions.[2] Both elements of the process are important, and it is essential to consider each separately, as the factors that determine release decisions often differ from those that determine release outcomes.[3]

Release decisions are determinations made directly by judges or other judicial officers such as magistrates, commissioners, and justices of the peace.[4] Throughout this chapter we use "judges" as a catchall term for all types of judicial officers who are called upon to make pretrial release decisions.

As discussed in chapter 1, release outcomes refer to whether the defendant is ultimately released or held in pretrial detention.[5] Judges are sometimes unaware that there is often a disconnect between their decisions and outcomes. For example, in their study of felony bail hearings in Southern California, criminologists Sarah Ottone and Christine

Scott-Hayward found that while just 4.3 percent of defendants whose arraignments they observed were denied bail outright, 78 percent of defendants remained in custody at the conclusion of the study or had been in custody for the duration of their cases.[6] The researchers noted that judges did not appear to be aware of these high numbers. One judge they interviewed guessed that approximately three-quarters of defendants "on a regular daily basis are out of custody," when the opposite is actually true.[7]

At the initial hearing, or whenever the pretrial release decision is made, judges are asked to make four decisions.[8] First, the judge must determine whether a defendant will receive a release option or will be denied bail. As explained in chapter 1, although the US Constitution does not grant defendants a right to bail, approximately half of all states still guarantee defendants a right to bail in all noncapital cases.[9] Most other states follow the federal Bail Reform Act and allow defendants to be denied bail if they are determined to be likely to flee or to pose a danger to the community.[10] In practice, however, very few defendants are denied bail and ordered into preventative detention. In fact, in 2009 just 4 percent of defendants in the seventy-five largest counties in the United States were denied bail outright.[11]

Second, a judge must decide whether to release a defendant unconditionally—meaning on his or her own recognizance. Individuals granted release on recognizance simply promise to appear at designated court hearings. If they fail to do so, they may be charged with a new offense. For example, in California a defendant charged with a misdemeanor who is released on his or her own recognizance but then "willfully" fails to appear is guilty of a misdemeanor; similarly, a released defendant who is charged with a felony and who fails to appear is guilty of a felony.[12] In addition, if a defendant fails to appear at a scheduled court hearing, a judge may issue a bench warrant, allowing the defendant to be arrested and returned to court.[13]

Many jurisdictions guarantee defendants the right to be released pretrial under the least restrictive conditions necessary, which for

many individuals would be release on recognizance.[14] Indeed, the
American Bar Association's Pretrial Release Standards state that conditions should be imposed "only when the need is demonstrated by the
facts of the individual case reasonably to ensure appearance at court
proceedings, to protect the community, victims, witnesses or any other
person and to maintain the integrity of the judicial process."[15] However, in practice few defendants are released without conditions, and as
discussed in more detail in the second section of this chapter, it does
not appear that judges always engage in the individualized determination assumed by the ABA standards and the various state statutes that
guarantee release under the least restrictive conditions necessary.
Across the seventy-five largest US counties between 1990 and 2004,
20 percent of defendants were released on their own recognizance, and
that number declined over time; between 1990 and 1994, approximately
41 percent of releases were unconditional, but by 2009 the percentage
of defendants released on their own recognizance had dropped to
23 percent.[16]

If release on recognizance is not granted, the defendant may be
released conditionally. In such cases, the judge must decide what conditions to impose (the third decision). In more than two-thirds of cases,
the condition imposed will be a financial one: bail.[17] If a defendant who
has been released on bail fails to appear in court, typically the bail
amount will be forfeited, and a bench warrant can be issued for the
defendant's arrest.[18] In addition, defendants are eligible to be charged
with a new offense of failure to appear. For example, in West Virginia a
person who has been released on bail and who "willfully and without
just cause" fails to appear is guilty of an offense.[19] If the underlying
offense was a felony, the new failure to appear offense will also be a felony; if the underlying offense was a misdemeanor, then the new failure
to appear offense will be a misdemeanor.[20]

Usually the cash bond is secured, meaning that the defendant (or
a third-party surety, usually a commercial bail agent) must post the
full amount with the court. In a small number of cases (approximately

4 percent), however, the bond is unsecured, meaning that while a bail amount is set and can be forfeited if the defendant fails to appear, the defendant does not have to pay up front.[21] Judges can also impose non-financial conditions such as regular reporting, drug testing, and electronic monitoring. As discussed in more detail later in this chapter, defendants subject to these types of conditions are typically supervised by a pretrial services agency (PSA).

Finally, for the majority of defendants who are released conditionally on bail, the judge must decide what amount of bail to set (the fourth decision). There is significant variation among jurisdictions in how much bail is set. In their study of pretrial decision making in the seventy-five largest US counties, Cohen and Reaves found that the median bail amount was $9,000, while the average amount was $35,800. To determine at what amount to set bail, more than thirty states rely on bail schedules, which are guidelines that assign bail amounts for different offenses or offense types.[22] There are numerous problems with the use of bail schedules, from both policy and constitutional perspectives, and these are discussed in more detail in the third section of this chapter. In states without bail schedules, judges have the same discretion that they have in making other pretrial release decisions.

Judges have significant discretion in making all of these decisions. But as discussed subsequently in this chapter, the exercise of this discretion is guided by state constitutions, statutes, and rules of criminal procedure. We explain here the structure and process of bail decisions and examine the factors that judges typically rely on in making pretrial release determinations. We also discuss one particularly problematic feature of the pretrial process: reliance on bail schedules. The second part of this chapter examines the ways in which defendants who are granted release actually get out of jail. In particular we look at the roles that commercial bail, community bail funds, and PSAs play in the pretrial justice process. Actuarial risk assessments, which play an increasingly important role in determining release, are discussed in detail in chapter 3.

## THE BAIL HEARING

When defendants first appear in court, typically they will be arraigned, meaning that they are entitled to have the charges that have been filed against them read, they should be informed of their rights, and they will be asked to enter a plea.[23] In many jurisdictions, it is at this initial appearance that the judge will make the four decisions relating to pretrial release just described. In other jurisdictions, bail will be determined at a separate adversarial hearing.[24] Problematically, as we describe in detail in chapter 5, defendants are often unrepresented by counsel during this initial appearance even though bail determinations should be viewed as a "critical stage" of any criminal prosecution that triggers Sixth Amendment rights.

Regardless of when pretrial decisions are made, judges must follow state and local laws and rules; this puts some limits on the discretion that they can exercise. In California, for example, judges are guided by the state constitution, the state penal code, and the rules of court in making the pretrial release decision.[25] These laws require judges to consider a variety of factors, including the seriousness of the offense, prior criminal record, the likelihood that the defendant will appear in court if released, the safety of the public, the victim, and the victim's family. Although judges are supposed to make release decisions based on the totality of the circumstances, the penal code makes it clear that public safety should be the court's primary concern.[26] In addition, judges must consider the county bail schedule, which, as we discuss in detail later in the chapter, plays a disproportionately large role in release decisions.[27]

Other jurisdictions also ask judges to assess a wide variety of factors. In Arizona, for example, except for certain serious offenses, judges must decide whether to release defendants on their own recognizance or to set bail.[28] In doing so, they must consider twelve factors, among them the views of the victim, the nature and circumstances of the charged offense, the weight of the evidence against the accused, the defendant's criminal history, and factors related to drug use, residence, family ties, financial resources, and mental condition.[29] Several jurisdictions place more emphasis on risk assessment (discussed in chapter 3) and PSA recommendations (discussed later in this chapter). For example, as a result of the 1966 Bail Reform Act, explained in chapter 1, and later District of Columbia laws, judges in the District of Columbia are required to "order the pretrial release of the person on personal recognizance, or upon execution of an unsecured appearance bond in an amount specified by the court, subject to the condition that the person not commit a local, state, or federal crime during the period of release, unless the judicial officer determines that the release will not reasonably assure the appearance of the person as required or will endanger the safety of any other person or the community."[30]

In making this determination, judges rely heavily on the recommendations of the PSA, which conducts investigations, including interviews with defendants, and writes a report and recommendation for judicial consideration. In the District of Columbia, pretrial detention requires a finding that "no condition or combination of conditions will reasonably assure the appearance of the person as required, and the safety of any other person and the community," although in certain serious cases there is a rebuttable presumption in favor of detention.[31] In determining whether detention is the only option, judges are required to consider the nature and circumstances of the offense, the weight of evidence against the defendant, the history and characteristics of the defendant, and the nature and seriousness of any potential danger to the community.[32]

New Jersey began an overhaul of its bail system in 2014, and while it does not eliminate money entirely, it now only allows monetary bail to be set "when it is determined that no other conditions of release will reasonably assure the eligible defendant's appearance in court when required."[33] The PSA is required to complete a risk assessment and make release recommendations to the court within forty-eight hours of a defendant's commitment to jail. Judges are then required to consider this risk assessment and the release recommendation when determining whether and how to release the defendant.[34]

It is important to note, however, that even in jurisdictions where release is supposed to be the default position, detention rates remain high. For example, as Scott-Hayward explained, in the federal system judges are required to release defendants on their own recognizance or on an unsecured bond "unless the judicial officer determines that such release will not reasonably assure the appearance of the person as required or will endanger the safety of any other person or the community."[35] After viewing the release data for the period 2006 to 2015, Scott-Hayward concluded:

> [D]espite the apparent difficulty of detaining defendants pretrial, in reality a majority of defendants are detained, and this number has increased over time, even when immigration cases, which often involve non-citizens who are unlikely to be released, are excluded: In 2006, excluding immigration cases, over 47% of defendants were released pretrial, while in 2015, the most recent year for which data are available, fewer than 43% of defendants, excluding noncitizens, were released pretrial. Although the increase in the detention rate is slight, the raw numbers are striking. In 2006, more than 30,000 defendants were released pending trial, while in 2015, that number had dropped to less than 24,000.[36]

She agreed with Professor James Oleson and colleagues, who explained that today "pretrial detention for federal defendants is not the exception but the rule."[37]

Given the number of decisions that judges need to make and the multiplicity of factors that they are asked to consider when making these decisions, we might expect that bail hearings would be long and contested. However, there is little evidence that that is the norm. A study of over 1,600 misdemeanor arraignments in Florida in 2010 found that 82 percent of arraignments lasted less than three minutes, with many defendants pleading guilty or no contest during this time.[38] More recently, Scott-Hayward conducted an observational study of bail hearings in Southern California in 2015 and 2016 along with then graduate student Sarah Ottone. After observing more than 230 bail hearings in Los Angeles and Orange Counties, they concluded that bail hearings were extremely short and that arguments of any kind were rare.[39] They found that attorneys contested bail in just one-third of cases; defense attorneys usually asked for release on recognizance or a lower bail amount, while prosecutors asked for bail to be set according to the schedule or for higher bail. Regardless of the type of argument, "ensuing discussions were generally brief, and judges usually denied requests for lower bail or ROR without comment."[40] One judge acknowledged the speed of the hearings: "Well, you know, somebody will come through and you know, it's Costco justice. They're doing things really fast. But somebody comes through with a felony, he's he's [sic] not really gonna have too much time to consider bail in depth. So more often than not bail gets set at the bail schedule."[41]

Similarly, in their study of arraignment hearings in the Bronx, New York, and Union and Hudson Counties in New Jersey, Andres Rengifo, a criminology professor at Rutgers University, and his colleagues found that on average, bail hearings lasted about five minutes.[42] Data from another source suggest that bail hearings are shorter than one might expect. Court Watch NYC is a collaborative project aimed at providing "transparency and accountability from the criminal legal system."[43] As part of the project, volunteers sit in arraignment court and observe and track what they see. One of the things they record is the length of arraignment hearings, at which bail is decided. They have noted that almost two-thirds of hearings last between two and five minutes.[44]

Just as criminologists Alisa Smith and Sean Maddan found in Florida, Ottone and Scott-Hayward found that bail hearings in Southern California were typically routine and rarely individualized. For example, they describe one judge who typically "would call the case by name and number and then ask if the defendant waived further arraignment, full reading or charges, and advisement of rights, and plead not guilty."[45] They also observed a judge in a different courthouse "ask for the attention of all the public defenders and alternate public defenders, and then ask them all, as a group, to waive formal reading of the charges, enter a plea of not guilty, set a preliminary hearing (based on the statutory time) and submit on the county-wide bail schedule."[46] Although this increased the speed of proceedings, it certainly did not promote the idea that judges are making individualized decisions in each case.

It is of course possible—and even likely in some places—that judges have access to information that is not discussed at the bail hearing and on which they rely. Scholars have been examining the factors that predict bail decisions for years. These studies typically examine case-related or legal factors, such as offense severity, as well as extralegal factors, which are unrelated to the case, including demographic factors such as race, sex, and socioeconomic class. Although there is significant variation in the study findings, as discussed later in this chapter, most researchers conclude that the two most important factors, those that best predict the bail decision, are (1) the seriousness of the charged offense and (2) the defendant's criminal history.

### Factors Considered by Judges: Legal Factors

The earliest study of the bail decision process was conducted by Arthur Beeley during the 1920s. He found that bail amounts in Cook County, Illinois, were based only on the charged offense.[47] Decades later, in two separate studies, Professor Caleb Foote also found that in both Philadelphia and New York City, it was the nature of the charged offense that mattered most in determining bail.[48] Similarly, in his classic study of bail decision making in Philadelphia in the 1970s, criminologist John Goldkamp concluded that "bail decision-making, in its various facets, seems to operate almost exclusively on the basis of the seriousness of the charge."[49] As discussed in the next section, more recent research on decision making focuses on disparities and examines extralegal factors, primarily race, gender, and ethnicity. However, two recent studies show that charge severity remains of primary importance, albeit indirectly.

First, the New York Criminal Justice Agency, in a review of bail cases in Brooklyn and Manhattan, found that charge severity was important but noted that its impact was indirect, through the prosecutor's bail request.[50] The prosecutor's bail request was the best predictor of both whether the defendant would be released on his or her own recognizance and, if not, what the bail amount would be. However, "the amount of bail requested by prosecutors was heavily determined by charge severity, and this was also a crucial factor in their consent to [release on recognizance]."[51]

Second, in their qualitative study of bail decisions in Southern California, Ottone and Scott-Hayward found that the main factor determining the bail amount set appeared to be the county bail schedule, which is based almost exclusively on the severity of the charged offense. The importance of the schedule was routinely demonstrated in a variety of ways. In some cases, judges specifically said that they were setting bail according to the schedule. On one occasion, prior to conducting the individual arraignment hearings, a judge asked all the defense attorneys to "submit on the county-wide bail schedule."[52] Further, many of the arguments over the amount of bail imposed focused on whether it had been correctly calculated according to the schedule—for example, whether a prior offense had been correctly held to be a serious or violent felony that would increase the bail amount. In addition, all of the judges and attorneys interviewed acknowledged the importance of the bail schedule.[53]

Although we explore the implications of such reliance on bail schedules in the third part of this chapter, one point cannot be overstated. Recall from chapter 1 that the purpose of bail is to guarantee a defendant's appearance at trial. Put differently, within the context of financial conditions of pretrial release, judges are supposed to focus on imposing bail amounts that are just high enough to deter defendants from failing to appear. Conversely, bail amounts are not supposed to be set so high that defendants cannot afford to pay the required amount. But bail schedules subvert such individualization. In fact, in their observational study, Ottone and Scott-Hayward specifically examined whether the ability of a particular individual to pay the bail amount set was considered. They found that in the overwhelming number of cases, this factor was completely ignored. In just two of the eighty-two of cases in which the defendant's ability to pay the bail amount was even raised by defense counsel, judges rejected such arguments.[54]

Scholars typically ground research on pretrial decision making in the theory of focal concerns. This theory suggests that judicial decision making reflects consideration of three primary concerns: the blameworthiness of the offender, protection of the community, and practical constraints and consequences.[55] However, judges often lack the time and information needed to fully assess the focal concerns. These constraints imbue the decision-making process with ambiguity and uncertainty, prompting reliance on a patterned response, or "perceptual shorthand."[56] It is not surprising then that judges turn to factors such as offense severity and criminal history, which are associated with defendant blameworthiness and safety of the community. As sociologist Traci Schlesinger noted, as a result of the bail reform legislation that "generally mandates that judges base the denial of bail on the need to protect the community from the defendant[,] attributions concerning dangerousness—and the capacity for violence—are most likely to affect this decision."[57] Yet as we discuss in more detail in chapter 3, neither factor is a particularly good predictor of a defendant's failing to appear for a hearing or committing new criminal activity while on pretrial release.

### *Factors Considered by Judges: Extralegal Factors*

Although judges should only be relying on legal factors in making decisions, there is some evidence that certain extralegal factors influence pretrial decision making. For example, the third focal concern—practical constraints and consequences—usually refers to "organizational costs, such as court resources, and potential social consequences such as the defendant's familial obligations."[58] Although few studies have found support for this in the pretrial decision-making context, criminologist Marian Williams did find that in eight counties in Florida, overall the capacity of local jails, a practical constraint, played a role in bail decisions. She found that the higher the rated jail capacity (meaning the more beds that were used), the lower the bond amounts, the higher the likelihood of financial release, and the higher the likelihood of defendants receiving conditional or supervised release.[59]

As we discuss in detail in chapter 4, there is more support for the importance of select demographic factors—specifically ethnicity, race, and sex—in pretrial decision making. For example, female defendants are more likely to receive nonfinancial conditions of release as well as lower bail amounts.[60] Further, Black and Latino defendants are treated more harshly than White defendants in release decisions. Compared to White defendants, people of color are more likely to be denied release. Moreover, if granted bail, people of color are more likely to have bail amounts set higher and more likely to be ordered into pretrial detention.[61] For example, criminologist Meghan Sacks and colleagues found that defendants of color in New Jersey were more likely to have to pay a financial condition of release.[62] Black defendants were 36 percent less likely than White defendants to have nonfinancial bail set, while Hispanic defendants were 26 percent less likely than White defendants to be given a nonfinancial bail outcome.[63] A study of pretrial release decisions in New York found that when bail is granted, White defendants may receive lower bail amounts than non-White defendants.[64] Criminologists Charles Katz and Cassia Spohn also found that Black defendants were more likely to be detained than White defendants, although they did not find any racial disparities in the amount of bail set for defendants charged with violent offenses in Detroit.[65]

There is also evidence that defendants of color are less likely to be released than White defendants. Criminologists Stephen Demuth and Darrell Steffensmeier found that White males are more likely to post bail than Hispanic defendants.[66] Similarly, in New Jersey, regardless of prior criminal history, "Blacks and Hispanics are profoundly less likely than Whites to post bail in a given criminal matter."[67] Further, Megan Stevenson found that Black defendants in Philadelphia were 40 percent more likely to be detained than non-Black defendants.[68] Although some studies find that these effects disappear when they control for legal factors, such as offense seriousness and criminal history, others find that the racial disparities remain.[69] Criminologist John Wooldredge found that overall, legal factors explained most of the racial disparities in pretrial release outcomes for defendants in Ohio. However, even after statistically controlling for legal factors, African Americans between the ages of eighteen and twenty-nine were less likely to receive release on recognizance, were more likely to receive higher bond amounts, and were more likely to be sentenced to incarceration.[70] Other researchers have pointed to the relationship between race and socioeconomic disparities (discussed in more detail in chapters 3 and 4), noting that racial and ethnic minorities might be less likely to post bail because they are overrepresented among indigent defendants.[71]

Traci Schlesinger argued that the importance of race and ethnicity makes sense under the focal concerns perspective. She explained that lack of time and information—which explains why judges turn to apparent proxies for blameworthiness and community safety, specifically severity of the charges—also explains why judges might rely on "attributions of different racial and ethnic groups."[72] In particular, judges may rely on stereotypes, for example that Blacks are dangerous and violent, or that Latinos are likely to be involved in the drug trade and may not have legal status and thus are a flight risk.[73]

Consistent with the other studies, in her study of pretrial decisions involving over thirty-five thousand defendants arrested between 1990 and 2000, Schlesinger found that Black and Latino defendants were approximately 25 percent more likely to be denied bail than White defendants and also less likely to be granted nonfinancial release.[74] She also found that the racial and ethnic disparities were greater for defendants charged with violent crimes and drug crimes, supporting the theory that judges are relying on stereotypes. She concluded: "Judges use racialized attributions to fill in the knowledge gaps created by limited information on cases and defendants. Through this process, racial and ethnic stereotypes become pertinent 'knowledge' that direct criminal justice decisions. However, stereotypes are not always already salient. Rather, they need to be made salient by other criminal justice features. When criminal justice features—such as the type of crime a defendant is charged with—increase the salience of racialized attributions, racial and ethnic disparities in punishment outcomes are reproduced and magnified."[75]

A recent study by economists David Arnold, Will Dobbie, and Crystal Yang supports this theory.[76] Consistent with prior research, the authors identified racial disparities in the treatment of White and Black defendants and, by examining marginal defendants—that is, those defendants for whom the expected cost of release is equal to the perceived benefit of release—they concluded that racial animus did not explain the harsher treatment of Black defendants.[77] Instead they conclude that the existence of racial bias against these defendants exists because "bail judges rely on inaccurate stereotypes that exaggerate the relative danger of releasing Black defendants versus white defendants."[78]

Surprisingly, one factor that would seem to be important in the bail decision, a defendant's socioeconomic status, has not been the subject of much research. This is largely because much of the research in this area is quantitative, and there is rarely available data on socioeconomic status in official court records. However, as we describe in chapter 4, a few recent studies, which used defendant zip code as a proxy for socioeconomic status, did find that defendants from poorer neighborhoods had worse outcomes than those from wealthier neighborhoods.[79]

## BAIL SCHEDULES

One of the most criticized aspects of the bail system is its use of bail schedules. Bail schedules have existed since 1945, when California developed them for misdemeanor defendants; it later adopted felony bail schedules in 1973.[80] These schedules, as well as those in other jurisdictions, were initially intended to help people who were arrested get out of jail without having to wait potentially days before appearing in court for a formal bail hearing.[81] On paper, that is still the purpose of some bail schedules; for example, the 2018 Los Angeles County Bail Schedule states that its purpose "is to fix an amount upon which a person who is arrested without a warrant may be released from custody prior to appearance in court."[82] Typically, a bail schedule consists of a list of offenses or classes of offense, with a presumptive bail amount for each offense or offense class.[83] In some jurisdictions, including California, the schedule also includes a list of enhancements and prior convictions for which bail may be increased.[84] In California, county bail schedules are approved by the judges of the superior court, and then jail officers are authorized to release arrestees upon payment of the presumptive bail.[85] In addition to their use in release directly from jail, as discussed previously, the schedules are also used at a defendant's initial court appearance.

The use of bail schedules is widespread. A 2009 survey of 112 of the most populous US counties found that 64 percent relied on them.[86] This survey also found that more than half of the 68 counties in the study that reported using bail schedules did so both at jail and at the bail hearing.[87] A review of state laws governing bail and pretrial detention conducted in 2017 found that bail schedules are authorized in more than thirty states, either at the state level or at the judicial district/ county level. However, their use varies. For example, Georgia *allows* courts to establish bail schedules for most offenses, whereas California *requires* counties to establish bail schedules for both misdemeanor and felony offenses.[88]

Although most bail schedules are not binding on pretrial decision makers, there is evidence that "they often become de facto law."[89] As explained previously, Ottone and Scott-Hayward found that most judges seemed to reflexively follow the bail schedule, and evidence presented in several federal court cases supports the view that bail schedules interfere with individualized pretrial decision making. For example, in *O'Donnell v. Harris County* the court relied on the expert testimony of Professor Stephen Demuth, showing that hearing officers in Harris County "adhered to the prescheduled bail amount stated on the charging documents in 88.9 percent of all misdemeanor cases."[90] Similarly in *Jones v. City of Clanton*, District Judge Myron Thompson found that the city's municipal court relied on a bail schedule for misdemeanor arrests "from which it did not deviate."[91] There the court noted that defendants who could not pay the amount set, typically $500 or $1,000 per charge, "were required to wait in jail until the next court date, typically held on Tuesday afternoons."[92]

It is not surprising that bail schedules have been criticized since the early years of their use. Using money as the sole or primary mechanism for pretrial release poses two related problems. First, and as explained in more detail in chapter 4, overreliance on money bail leads to poor defendants remaining in custody even if they are neither dangerous nor a flight risk. Second, reliance on money bail can lead to dangerous defendants or defendants who pose a genuine risk of flight being released purely because they can afford to post bail.[93] These concerns led the American Bar Association (ABA) to recommend against the use of bail schedules in its Criminal Justice Standards: "Financial conditions should be the result of an individualized decision taking into account the special circumstances of each defendant, the defendant's ability to meet the financial conditions and the defendant's flight risk, and should never be set by reference to a predetermined schedule of amounts fixed according to the nature of the charge."[94]

The use of money bail to guarantee that released defendants will show up at trial and not commit new offenses assumes both that the threat of losing money is necessary to get defendants to come back to court for hearings and that money bail prevents crime. Bail schedules simply use offense seriousness as a proxy for both flight risk and dangerousness. As Judge Curtis Karnow noted in a 2008 article, there is, however, no evidence that tying bail amounts to the charge has any impact on either public safety or a defendant's likelihood to appear.[95] Karnow exhaustively reviewed the research on this question, including a series of studies on bail practices in Philadelphia, Pennsylvania, Florida, Arizona, and Massachusetts by criminologist John Goldkamp and colleagues. They concluded that "the seriousness of criminal charges was not a predictor of (was not systematically related to) flight or crime by defendants who gained pretrial release").[96]

Moreover, concern about the lack of individualized decision making is particularly significant when the use of bail schedules is not limited to preappearance release decision making. Bail schedules can be useful if they are used to facilitate quick release from jail before any court appearance. However, when they are employed at a defendant's bail hearing, there is a risk that they can be used to deprive defendants of an individualized release determination. As Professor Wayne Thomas cautioned in 1976: "As long as the defendant has not yet appeared, the schedule helps by making it possible to know immediately what bail is required and to secure release if he can afford the cost. Once the defendant appears in court, there is much less justification for determining the bail amount solely by the offense charged. The defendant is present, and the court can make an individual determination."[97]

Unfortunately, as explained previously, there is little evidence that when bail schedules are used, they allow for this individual determination. As we argue in the next section, this fact means not only that bail schedules are problematic as a policy matter, but also that they are unconstitutional, in violation of both the Eighth and Fourteenth Amendments to the US Constitution.[98]

### The Eighth Amendment

As discussed in chapter 1, there is no federal constitutional right to bail. The Eighth Amendment explicitly prohibits excessive bail, although due to the limited precedent in this area, it is unclear exactly what this means. In its 1951 decision in *Stack v. Boyle*, the Supreme Court noted that the purpose of bail was to assure "the presence of an accused" and that "[b]ail set at a figure higher than an amount reasonably calculated to fulfill this purpose is 'excessive' under the Eighth Amendment."[99] However, the Court's decision in *Stack* was complicated by its subsequent decision in *United States v. Salerno*, in which, upholding the 1984 Bail Reform Act, the Court held that bail could be denied if a defendant posed a danger to others.[100] In doing so, it emphasized the "number of procedural safeguards," including the right to testify at a hearing, provided to such defendants under the act.[101] But as explored in more detail in chapter 5, many of these procedural safeguards are illusory in everyday practice—especially in state proceedings.

Since *Salerno*, courts (including the US Supreme Court) have provided little guidance about what it means to be free from excessive bail, although the Court has recently stated that the right applies in both state and federal courts.[102] The Ninth Circuit, in *Galen v. County of Los Angeles*, made it clear that states "may not set bail to achieve invalid interests."[103] However, just because the bail amount is beyond a person's means does not mean that it is excessive. Instead, the Eighth Amendment requires "only that it not be greater than necessary to achieve the purposes for which bail is imposed." In *Galen*, the court rejected the defendant's argument that bail of $1 million, enhanced from the $50,000 listed in the county's bail schedule, was excessive, because the defendant failed to show that his bail was enhanced "for an improper purpose or that [it] was excessive in light of the purpose for which it was set."[104]

Scholars disagree on the meaning of the Excessive Bail Clause. Law professor Samuel Wiseman argued that "as interpreted by the Court, [it] has so little force that it simply does not matter very much whether it applies to the states or not."[105] Wiseman held that the clause places limits only on "the most extreme legislatures and courts, and the most careless."[106] On the other hand, law professor Scott Howe argued that the fact that the Supreme Court has incorporated the Excessive Bail

Clause, meaning that it has stated that it applies to the states, "conveys that the protection is viewed as exceptionally important in protecting liberty or justice by our society."[107] The Excessive Bail Clause would only have merited incorporation if it "confers a right to bail in some circumstances and regulates the permissible purposes of bail and, thus, the measure of excessiveness."[108] We agree. The Supreme Court has held that only guarantees in the Bill of Rights that are "fundamental to our scheme of ordered liberty and system of justice" should be incorporated.[109] It would make little sense for the Court to have incorporated a meaningless guarantee—even if, as explained in chapter 1—it did so in passing, without a formal holding in a case squarely presenting the question of whether the Excessive Bail Clause is incorporated by the Due Process Clause of the Fourteenth Amendment.

What restrictions the Excessive Bail Clause places on the use of bail schedules is unclear. The only circuit to explicitly address the issue found that "the mere use of a schedule does not itself pose a constitutional problem under the Eighth Amendment."[110] However, that court did note, "That is not to say that using a bond schedule can never violate the Excessive Bail Clause."[111] Thus we believe, consistent with Professor Howe's work, that when bail schedules are used in a way that systematically denies defendants an individual determination of bail, they violate the Excessive Bail Clause.

Howe correctly points out that the scope of the right to nonexcessive bail is unclear, but he convincingly argues that, at a minimum, "a defendant should receive non-excessive bail—which may sometimes mean release without bail—unless there are no conditions of release that could reasonably assure his appearance, his non-interference with the judicial process, and his compliance with the criminal law."[112] Nonetheless, Howe argues that bail schedules may be constitutional as long as defendants have a "prompt opportunity for individualized consideration of additional evidence that bears on whether he will reappear and the scheduled amount carries no presumption of correctness."[113] Unfortunately, as explained previously, the evidence that exists demonstrates that in practice, where bail schedules operate, most defendants do not receive individualized consideration of either dangerousness or likelihood of appearance, and further that the bail schedules do appear to operate presumptively.[114]

### *The Fourteenth Amendment*

Although the Fourteenth Amendment does not mention bail, it guarantees defendants two rights—the rights to due process and equal protection—that impact bail. Simply put, under the Due Process Clause, defendants are entitled to certain procedural protections before they are deprived of liberty. On the other hand, the Equal Protection Clause ensures that similarly situated individuals should not be treated differently. Although courts typically analyze practices that are alleged to violate the Fourteenth Amendment separately under each clause, bail is different. As the US Department Justice noted in its brief in *Walker v. City of Calhoun*, in cases, such as pretrial release, that involve "denying equal access to justice ... without consideration of ability to pay and possible alternatives ... the Court has recognized that the proper analysis reflects both equal protection and due process principles, and has rejected the use of the traditional equal protection inquiry."[115] In recent years, in a series of cases including *Walker*, numerous defendants have challenged money bail generally and bail schedules specifically as a violation of the Fourteenth Amendment, and as described later in this chapter, they have met with some success.[116]

The Supreme Court has consistently held that the Fourteenth Amendment prohibits states from discriminating against convicted defendants based on their poverty. For example, in *Griffin v. Illinois* the Court held that requiring defendants to provide a trial transcript in order to obtain appellate review unconstitutionally denied appellate review to indigent defendants.[117] More recently in *Bearden v. Georgia*, the Court held that a court may not revoke an individual's probation for failing to pay a fine or restitution if that individual genuinely lacks the resources to do so, noting that doing so is "little more than punishing a person for his poverty."[118]

Although the Supreme Court has not addressed the constitutionality of bail schedules, or indeed of money bail generally, the Fifth Circuit, in *Pugh v. Rainwater*, has suggested that there are problems with the use of bail schedules.[119] Although that court found the plaintiffs' claim moot, it noted that while "[u]tilization of a master bond schedule provides speedy and convenient release for those who have no difficulty in meeting its requirements ... [t]he incarceration of those who cannot, without meaningful consideration of other possible alternatives, infringes on both due process and equal protection requirements."[120]

More recently, in *ODonnell v. Harris County*, in granting a preliminary injunction Chief Judge Lee H. Rosenthal of the United States District Court for the Southern District of Texas held that the misdemeanor bail system in Harris County, Texas, was unconstitutional.[121] The case involved three named plaintiffs, all of whom were arrested for committing misdemeanors and were unable to pay the bail set in their cases. The facts of the named plaintiff, Maranda Lynn ODonnell, are illustrative:

Maranda Lynn ODonnell, a 22-year-old single mother, was arrested on May 18, 2016 at 5:00 p.m. and charged with driving with an invalid license. After she was booked into the Harris County Jail, she was informed that she would be released promptly if she paid a secured money bail of $2,500 set according to the County's bail schedule, but that she would remain in jail if she did not pay either the full bail amount to the County or a premium to a bail bondsman up front. Ms. ODonnell and her child struggled to meet the basic necessities of life. She received benefits from the federal government's Women, Infants, and Children program to feed her daughter. She could not afford housing, so she stayed with a friend. At the time of her arrest, Ms. ODonnell was working, but it was at a new job she had held for only seven days. She had no money to buy her release from detention. She was otherwise eligible for release.

Harris County Pretrial Services interviewed Ms. ODonnell at 11:52 p.m. on May 18. At 3:00 a.m., on May 19, Pretrial Services completed a risk-assessment report recommending her release on a personal bond—that is, an unsecured appearance bond requiring no up-front payment for release. Ms. ODonnell appeared before a Hearing Officer at 7:00 a.m., by videolink from the Harris County Jail. The Sheriff's deputies present ordered her not to speak. Without explanation, the Hearing Officer told her that she did not "qualify" for release on personal bond and imposed the $2,500 scheduled amount as secured bail, meaning that she had to pay the full bail amount or a bondman's premium to be released. When asked if she would hire her own lawyer or would be seeking help from a court-appointed lawyer, Ms. ODonnell responded, "Seeking help." These were her only words during her 50-second hearing.

On the morning of May 20, Ms. ODonnell appeared before a County Criminal Court at Law Judge. She completed an affidavit declaring her lack of assets and was found indigent for the purpose of appointing counsel. Her bail amount was not changed or set on an unsecured basis, even though she declared on her affidavit that she remained in jail. That same day, but after Ms. ODonnell filed this suit, an insurance underwriter for a commercial bondsman posted her bail amount. This third-party payment looks like an attempt to moot her claim. Ms. ODonnell was released from jail after three days in pretrial detention on the charge of driving with an invalid license.[122]

In reaching her decision, Judge Rosenthal held a series of hearings, which included testimony from hearing officers, county judges, representatives from the sheriff's department and pretrial services, as well as expert witnesses. In addition, in her almost two-hundred-page opinion, she exhaustively reviewed the pretrial decision-making process in Harris County as well as the history and practices of bail nationwide. Her factual findings were nicely summarized and affirmed by the Fifth Circuit Court of Appeals in its 2018 ruling, discussed here:

> When a misdemeanor defendant is arrested, the prosecutor submits a secured bail amount according to a bond schedule established by County Judges. Bonds are then formally set by Hearing Officers and County Judges. Hearing Officers are generally responsible for setting bail amounts in the first instance. This often occurs during the arrestee's initial probable cause hearing, which must be held within 24 hours of arrest. County Judges review the Hearing officers' determinations and can adjust bail amounts at a "Next Business Day" hearing.

The Hearing Officers and County Judges are legally proscribed from mechanically applying the bail schedule to a given arrestee. Instead, the Texas Code requires officials to conduct an individualized review based on five enumerated factors, which include the defendant's ability to pay, the charge, and community safety. The Local Rules explicitly state the schedule is not mandatory. They also authorize a similar individualized assessment using factors which partially overlap with those listed in the Code. Hearing Officers and County Judges sometimes receive assessments by Pretrial Services, which interviews the detainees prior to hearings, calculates the detainees flight and safety risk based on a point system, and then makes specific recommendations regarding bail.

Despite these formal requirements, the district court found that, in practice, procedures were dictated by an unwritten custom and practice that was marred by gross inefficiencies, did not achieve any individualized assessment in setting bail, and was incompetent to do so.[123]

Overall, bail hearings frequently did not occur in a timely fashion, they were usually very short, and defendants were usually not provided an opportunity to present any evidence of their ability to pay. Further, hearing officers rejected the recommendations of pretrial services to release defendants on personal bond more than two-thirds of the time and imposed the bail amount listed in the schedule about 90 percent of the time.[124] Judge Rosenthal concluded that neither hearing officers nor county judges were "making individualized bail assessments" and further, that the county had a "systematic policy and practice of imposing secured money bail as de facto orders of pretrial detention [against the indigent accused] in misdemeanor cases."[125] Relying on the Supreme Court's decisions in *Bearden* and related cases, as well as the Fifth Circuit's ruling in *Pugh*, Judge Rosenthal concluded that the county's bail system violated the Fourteenth Amendment. On appeal, the Fifth Circuit upheld Judge Rosenthal's ruling, highlighting the county's "current custom and practice, with their lack of individualized assessment and mechanical application of the secured bail schedule," and concluding that the lower court "had sufficient evidence to conclude that Harris County's use of secured bail violated equal protection."[126]

At least one state court has also highlighted problems with bail schedules. In 2018, in *In re Humphrey* (the facts of which are discussed in chapter 1) a California Court of Appeal found that a trial court's failure to inquire into and make findings as to the defendant's ability to pay, as well as alternatives to money bail, violated the Fourteenth Amendment. The court concluded that bail determinations "must be based on factors related to the individual defendant's circumstances."[127] Specifically, "[A] court may not order pretrial detention unless it finds either that the defendant has the financial ability but failed to pay the amount of bail the court finds reasonably necessary to ensure his or her appearance at future court proceedings; or that the defendant is unable to pay that amount and no less restrictive conditions of release would be sufficient to reasonably assure such appearance; or that no less restrictive nonfinancial conditions of release would be sufficient to protect the victim and community."[128] The court stopped short of holding that bail schedules are unconstitutional. However, it noted that they "represent the antithesis of the individualized inquiry required before a court can order pretrial detention."[129] Moreover, the court cautioned that "unquestioning reliance upon the bail schedule without consideration of a defendant's ability to pay, as well as other individualized factors bearing upon his or her dangerousness and/or risk of flight, runs afoul of the requirements of due process for a decision that may result in pretrial detention."[130]

At the time of writing, this case was pending before the Supreme Court of California, while other lawsuits challenging bail schedules are pending in a variety of jurisdictions.[131]

## OBTAINING RELEASE

Reliance on money bail in the United States means that most defendants need to come up with sometimes significant amounts of money in order to be released. When bail is set, the judge does not determine how it will be paid, but there are four ways in which defendants can post bail. A defendant can post the entire amount in cash with the court or post a property bond, such as the title to property the defendant owns. In this case, courts typically require collateral for double the amount of bail to be posted.[132] Some states, such as Illinois, allow a defendant to post a 10 percent deposit with the court. This is refundable.[133] Moreover, this approach was designed to cut out the final and most common way of making bail: the use of commercial bail bond services.[134] The role of commercial bail in pretrial decision making is discussed in the next subsection.

### Commercial Bail

> It is not so much that bondsmen are evil—although they sometimes are—but rather that they serve no useful purpose.
> —Floyd Feeney[135]

For defendants and their families who cannot afford to pay the bail set in their cases, the most common solution is to turn to a commercial bail bond company. Typically, defendants, their families, or their friends will pay 10 percent of the bail amount set by the court to the bail bond company. In addition to this nonrefundable payment, whoever signs the bail contract—the "guarantor"—also guarantees that if the defendant fails to show up in court, they are responsible for the entire amount. Sometimes the bail agent may require that collateral be posted. In return, the company posts the entire bail amount with the court, allowing the defendant to be released. If the defendant makes all court appearances, the bail company is able to recoup the posted bail amount from the court. If the defendant fails to appear, the bail amount is supposed to be forfeited, which in turn would prompt the bail company to turn back to the guarantor to pay the full bail amount. But it rarely works this way in practice, as we explain here.

The proportion of defendants utilizing commercial bail has increased significantly over time. Between 1990 and 1994, about a quarter of defendants used commercial sureties; by 2004, more than 40 percent of defendants did, and by 2009, roughly 49 percent of releases from jail were a result of the posting of commercial bail bonds.[136]

### A BRIEF OVERVIEW OF THE ORIGINS OF COMMERCIAL BAIL IN THE UNITED STATES

Bail bonds is a commercial business that, like all for-profit businesses, is run for the purpose of making money. Commercial bail has existed since the late nineteenth century.[137] It is believed to have originated in San Francisco, when brothers Peter and Thomas McDonough "began writing bonds as favors to lawyers who drank in their father's bar."[138] As researcher Timothy Schnacke explained: "When these brothers learned that the lawyers were charging their clients fees for these bonds, the brothers began to charge as well. By 1898, the firm of McDonough Brothers, established as a saloon, found its business niche by underwriting bonds for defendants who faced charges in the nearby Hall of Justice, or police court. The company, which became known as 'The Old Lady of Kearny Street,' rose and fell in only fifty years, leaving a legacy prototypical of the growing commercial surety industry."[139]

The modern business of bail uses a framework similar to the one employed by the McDonough brothers, insofar as defendants are required to pay a nonrefundable fee to a commercial entity. In exchange for that payment, which is usually tied to a fixed percentage of the overall bail amount assessed by a court, the commercial bail entity guarantees that the defendant will appear in court, usually by posting a surety bond underwritten by an insurance company.[140] If the accused fails to appear as promised, the bail business is responsible, in theory, for paying the full amount of the bail to the court, and the bail agent is then often empowered to apprehend the defendant who failed to appear in court, either herself or by using the services of a bounty hunter.[141]

When courts actually collect commercial bail money after a defendant fails to appear, the funds are then turned over to the jurisdiction housing the court as general fund income. But bail forfeiture is exceedingly rare; some states report that commercial bail companies actually pay only 1.7 to 12 percent of forfeitures they owe.[142] But even in the relatively uncommon circumstances when forfeiture payments occur, bail agents rarely pay the full bond amount when a defendant fails to appear. Some courts are willing to accept dramatically lower amounts in satisfaction of a bail bond.[143] Moreover, even after such payments, many states broadly authorize courts to remit all or a portion of the funds to sureties.[144] As a result, the insurance companies who back bail bonds tend to pay less than 1 percent of their bail-related revenue on forfeiture losses—a remarkably low figure in comparison to property and auto insurance companies, which usually pay between 40 and 60 percent of premium revenue on claim losses.[145]

The dirty secret of jurisdictions failing to collect on forfeited bonds pales in comparison to a far more significant problem with commercial bail: corruption. As noted by Schnacke when he quoted a *Time* magazine article on bail, "The Old Lady" was not alone; the corruption associated with the McDonough brothers' first bail company has seemingly continued to plague the commercial bail industry since its inception. In his 1976 book *Bail Reform in America*, Wayne Thomas cited numerous examples of collusion between judges and bond agents, including bribery, kickbacks, and the failure to pay off forfeited funds.[146] Just in New York City alone, there were four grand jury investigations of bond agents between 1939 and 1960.[147]

The bail bond industry has become more organized since the 1960s, forming a professional association, the American Association of Professional Bail Agents. Most states now require bail agents to be licensed, typically through state insurance departments.[148] However, licensing requirements tend to be relatively minimal. For example, in California, in order to be licensed a bail agent must be eighteen years old, a resident of California, take a twenty-hour prelicensing course, and then pass an exam.[149] Some states have even fewer requirements.[150]

Licensing and regulation have increased but not prevented corruption and other problems. Indeed, stories of corruption surface with some frequency from jurisdictions across the United States that continue to use commercial bail systems.[151] A 2017 report by Color of Change, a nonprofit civil rights advocacy organization, and the American Civil Liberties Union's Campaign for Smart Justice, entitled *Selling Off Our Freedom,* highlighted some recent issues in California, Minnesota, and New Jersey. For example, the California Department of Insurance, which regulates California bail agents, reports that complaints about bail, ranging from fraud and misrepresentation to theft, extortion, and kidnapping, increased fourfold between 2010 and 2015.[152]

Dissatisfaction with commercial bail led Illinois to eliminate the practice in 1963. Although it kept the money bail system, it replaced commercial bail agents with the court itself. Essentially the 10 percent fee that defendants previously paid to a bail agent would now be paid to the court, "which was now required to release the defendant on less than full bond." Further, unlike the fee paid to bail agents, this fee was almost entirely refundable.[153] As explained previously, commercial bail was also eliminated in the District of Columbia as a result of the 1966 Bail Reform Act. Only three other states—Kentucky, Oregon, and Wisconsin—disallow commercial bail.[154] And if SB 10, a recent bail reform law enacted in California, is supported by the voters in November 2020 that state may soon join the others.

## THE CONTEMPORARY ROLES OF COMMERCIAL BAIL COMPANIES

In the majority of states that retain commercial bail, its proponents—usually the bail agents and their advocates, including insurance companies who underwrite surety bonds—argue that they play an important role in the system. Many see themselves as "professional service providers."[155] One bail agent noted, "I can say that in the several years I've been writing bonds, most bonding agents, myself included, derive satisfaction in helping people. While there may be some bondsmen who care only about the money, there are many who take pride in performing this service well."[156] Similarly, Chris Blaylock, a bail agent from New Jersey, highlighted that he makes a "real connection with the clients."[157]

As Joshua Page, a sociology professor at the University of Minnesota who recently spent a year working as a bail agent, argues, "through engaging service activities (and invoking the service discourse) bondspersons imbue the job with meaning and construct it as morally right."[158]

Although Professor Page noted that some clients were angry and frustrated with the bail company, he was surprised at how many clients and their families expressed gratitude to him and other agents for their services. Accurately describing the pretrial process as "murky and intimidating," Page noted that it is "especially impenetrable to defendants' family and friends," who are usually the people with whom bail agents deal.[159] He cited numerous examples of agents providing information about the system to family who are "starved for information."[160] In our own observations of bail hearings, we have also seen how difficult it is for defendants' family members and friends to find out what is happening. Court officers and attorneys vary in how much information they can or choose to provide, and sometimes a family member will wait in court all morning only to find out that the defendant was not on the bus from the jail to the courthouse that day. It is not surprising then that "when bail agents provide even minimal help and treat clients with a modicum of respect, they likely exceed customer[s]' low expectations."[161]

Because bail agents and bounty hunters are private persons who are not state actors, they are not bound by the same constitutional constraints placed on law enforcement officers who track down those who fail to appear in court. As a result, bail agents and bounty hunters exercise broad authority to capture a fugitive from justice, wielding "the tools of arrest, foreclosure, and force in the course of regular business, with varied and often inadequate training, regulation, and oversight."[162] Although the drama of such actions is glorified in novels by Janet Evanovich and on television shows such as *Dog: The Bounty Hunter*, the reality of untrained bail agents sometimes manifests in "excessive use of force, false imprisonment, destruction of property, and arrest of innocent citizens."[163] Still, largely as a function of statutory and case law changes, the business of hunting bail jumpers is slowly finding itself subject to more state regulation and control. "Partly as a result of the threat of criminal prosecution, many states have bail bond societies and associations that are working to professionalize the industry. More jails, and the Sheriff's Offices that run them, require bail bond agents and bounty hunters to be licensed, are using technology to establish early warning systems to monitor potential misbehavior, and require criminal background checks to detect potential wrong-doing within the industry before it spirals out of control into a major scandal."[164]

Whatever constraints may be evolving to better control bail agents and bounty hunters, it is indisputable that the business of bail is thriving even though there are no reliable national data on something as fundamental as the number of people who fail to appear in court who are subsequently taken into custody by bail agents and bounty hunters. Indeed, a 2010 National Public Radio investigation into the bail industry presented anecdotal evidence from a Texas district attorney's office that most bail jumpers are not apprehended by bail agents or bounty hunters, but rather are rearrested by law enforcement officers.[165] Yet the commercial bail industry ostensibly acts a gatekeeper for more than two million of the defendants released on bail each year in the United States. Of course they do not do this out of magnanimity. The industry earns an estimated $2.4 billion annually.[166] And according to a 2017 report issued by Color for Change and the American Civil Liberties Union, the more than twenty-five thousand individual bail bond businesses in the United States are typically underwritten by "under-the-radar subsidiaries" of large multinational insurance companies.[167] Indeed, only nine large insurers underwrite a majority of the roughly $14 billion in bail bonds issued in the United States each year.[168] In exchange for underwriting these sureties, these companies charge bail agents 10 to 20 percent of the premiums that the latter charge directly to defendants and their families.

These premiums ostensibly cover the risk to companies of bail forfeiture. However, through their contracts the insurance companies put the risk of forfeiture back on the bail companies, who themselves, in their contracts, place the responsibility for losses on defendants and their families, who guarantee that they will pay the entire bail amount if it is forfeited. *Selling Off Our Freedom* gives the example of a contract between Bankers Surety, a bail insurance company, and an unnamed bail bond agency: "[The contract] required the agency to take 'all liability for any undertaking of bail,' including requiring full payment of all forfeitures, losses, costs, or expenses to the insurer, with interest. In the event that all those protections don't work, insurers have as backup the Build-Up Fund, paid into by the bail agent with a percentage of each bond. For the insurance companies, the system works: they collect hundreds of millions of dollars a year in their cut of the bail premiums and face virtually no risk."[169]

A recent study of a bail bond company in a large urban county illustrates the predatory practices of bail companies. Page and colleagues noted that bail agents tend to work mainly with the friends and families of defendants, particularly women, and highlight numerous examples showing that "poor women of color ... stand at the center of predatory bail targeting."[170] They described in detail the practice of "prospecting," whereby agents "cold-call potential co-signers without defendants' knowledge or permission."[171] In one case this led to a defendant's mother committing to pay $1,200 against his wishes: "The last thing he wanted was for his mother to lose hundreds of dollars just because of his 'bullshit case.'"[172]

Given how lucrative this enterprise is and how much money the industry stands to lose if states were to move away from money bail, it should come as no surprise that the commercial bail industry often fights to maintain the status quo.[173] In fact, the industry forms a significant obstacle to bail reform through lobbying efforts not only to secure the for-profit bail system, but also to quash virtually every effort to reduce the use of money bail.

Opposition to bail reform efforts from commercial bail companies is not new. For example, in the 1960s bond agents in New York City responded to the threat posed to their business by the Manhattan Bail

Project by limiting bonds, which "resulted in jail overcrowding and concessions on the part of city officials."[174] More recent lobbying efforts have been better funded and more coordinated. In the 1990s the National Association of Bail Insurance Companies worked with the American Legislative Exchange Council (ALEC)—the corporation-funded legislative action group formed to pass numerous statutes "to insulate and expand for-profit bail's role"—to create the "Strike Back" initiative, which advocated for the elimination of PSAs and the minimization of the use of release on personal recognizance.[175] And since that time, the American Bail Coalition and ALEC have spent millions of dollars annually to fight bail reform efforts and to help elect politicians who promise to maintain the commercial money bail system.[176] Such advocacy efforts in Broward County, Florida, serve as a poignant example of their successful influence in perpetuating the industry's stranglehold on pretrial justice. As then law student Thanithia Billings explained in a 2016 article, the Broward County Commission increased the use of PSAs in 2007 to avoid building a new jail. Notwithstanding the success of the program, two years later their use was scaled back, largely as a result of pressure by the bail bond industry: "In the year preceding the vote to scale back PSAs, bail bond companies donated thousands of dollars to county commissioners' campaigns. Additionally, they hired a lobbyist to push the commissioners to decrease funding for PSAs and to encourage them to pass an ordinance decreasing the categories of prisoners for release through PSAs."[177]

Despite these efforts, some signs of progress have been made. Most notably, New Jersey successfully passed large-scale bail reform in 2014 that virtually eliminated money bail and the corporate bail industry. Reforms were supported by legislators, judges, and the governor, and voters approved an amendment to the state constitution to help implement them. The New Jersey Constitution now provides: "Pretrial release may be denied to a person if the court finds that no amount of monetary bail, non-monetary conditions of pretrial release, or combination of monetary bail and non-monetary conditions would reasonably assure the person's appearance in court when required, or protect the safety of any other person or the community, or prevent the person from obstructing or attempting to obstruct the criminal justice process."[178]

Similarly, in Alaska bail reform that virtually eliminated cash bail, and that will likely significantly impact the use of commercial bail, went into effect on January 1, 2018.[179] The impetus for reform was the high cost of incarcerating defendants pretrial. Now, instead of bail bonds, the state has switched to a system based on risk assessment. The state created a Pretrial Enforcement Division, which will administer the risk assessment and make release recommendations to judges. Secured bail bonds are still an option, but only for defendants with high risk scores or those charged with violent offenses. Release on recognizance is required for all defendants with low risk scores charged with nonviolent misdemeanors and class C felonies. For those in between, there is a presumption of release.[180]

Moreover, in 2017 the Maryland Court of Appeals unanimously amended its court rules to "promote the release of defendants on their own recognizance, or when necessary, unsecured bond."[181] As in New Jersey, the new rules require that defendants be released either on their own recognizance or an unsecured bond, unless a judge finds that "no permissible non-financial condition attached to a release will reasonably ensure (A) the appearance of the defendant, and (B) the safety of each alleged victim, other persons, or the community."[182] Since the rules went into effect in January 2018, there has been "a dramatic decline in the use of money bail" and an increase in the number of defendants released from custody.[183]

### Community Bail Funds

A growing alternative to commercial bail services is community bail funds. These are nonprofit funds typically run by local organizations which believe that pretrial detention is overused and that poor defendants charged with low-level offenses should not have to stay in jail just because they cannot afford to get out.[184] The oldest bail fund is the Bronx Freedom Fund; founded in 2007 by the Bronx Defenders, a public defense organization, it describes its goal as "to keep people in their communities while they await trial—and to fight for a system that no longer criminalizes poverty."[185] Community bail funds post bail for certain defendants, typically those charged with misdemeanors. For example, the Massachusetts Bail Fund posts bail of up to $500.[186]

It is not always clear how the funds determine who receives bail. As Jocelyn Simonson, a law professor at Brooklyn Law School, explained, while some funds do not reveal the criteria they use, others list the factors they consider, which include "a defendant's community connections, their warrant history, their connection to populations disproportionately affected by mass incarceration, or their vulnerability to violence in jail."[187] Other differences among the funds are the level of involvement with the defendant once bail has been posted.[188] For example, the Brooklyn Community Bail Fund provides a range of services, including reentry support and legal assistance.[189] Although the effectiveness of the funds has not been independently assessed, they report high levels of success; the Bronx Freedom Fund reported that 96 percent of clients return to court for their hearings. It also highlighted that 55 percent of clients' cases are ultimately dismissed. In part this is probably because their clients are usually represented by attorneys from the Bronx Defenders, one of the most respected public defense organizations in the country, whose model of "holistic defense" was recently shown to have cut pretrial detention by 9 percent.[190] This outcome illustrates the importance of defendants being represented by counsel at their initial appearance in court—a reform recommendation we explore in more detail in chapter 5.

Simonson cited examples from Brooklyn, New York; Nashville, Tennessee; and the state of Connecticut to show that the number of community bail funds is growing.[191] The first bail fund, the Bronx Freedom fund, is now part of a larger organization, The Bail Project, which has the goal of expanding bail funds to more than forty jurisdictions around the country. It currently operates community funds in Queens, New York; Tulsa, Oklahoma; and St. Louis, Missouri. Community bail funds have received national attention over the last two years through the support that some of them have provided to national bail out efforts. In particular, in May 2017 and 2018 the National Bail Out collective organized Black Mama's Bail Out Day, with the goal of bailing out mothers so they could spend Mother's Day with their children; they also provide supportive services to help the individuals whom they are able to get released.[192]

Community bail funds have been subject to pushback, but surprisingly, not from the commercial bail industry. This is because most of the bail amounts are smaller than those typically guaranteed by bail companies, so the community bail funds are not true competitors. Instead, in New York City, as Simonson explained, it was judges who resisted. In February 2009 Judge Ralph Fabrizio arraigned William Miranda on two misdemeanor assault charges and set bail at $3,000. When Miranda showed up out of custody for his next court hearing, Judge Fabrizio was surprised.[193] Moreover, Fabrizio became "irate" when he learned that Miranda's bail had been paid by the Bronx Freedom Fund even though, as Simonson points out, "bail had served its purpose—the defendant appeared in court voluntarily and had harmed no one in the interim."[194] Over the next four months, Judge Fabrizio held a series of hearings into the practices of the Bronx Freedom Fund and eventually concluded that it was an unlicensed bail bond business and shut it down.[195] It ultimately took a series of amendments to New York law to allow charitable bail funds to become legal.[196]

## PRETRIAL SUPERVISION AND MONITORING

In addition to financial conditions of pretrial release (i.e., money bail), there are numerous nonfinancial conditions of release that judicial officers can impose on defendants to mitigate the risks of pretrial failure either through failure to appear or through reoffending while on pretrial release. These nonfinancial conditions have played an important role in pretrial release decisions since the Bail Reform Act of 1966.

As summarized in chapter 1, the Bail Reform Act of 1966 mandated that with the exception of those charged with a capital crime, all criminal defendants were to be released on their own recognizance unless there were some reason that such release would "not reasonabl[y] assure" the defendant's appearance at trial.[197] Importantly, this first statutory bail reform effort created a presumption in favor of pretrial release with conditions crafted to reduce failures to appear.[198] Within five years, thirty-six states had enacted similar bail reform laws, and by 1999, "virtually every state [had] established by statute or case law the practice of pretrial supervised release."[199] Pretrial services agencies play critical roles in supervising and monitoring defendants granted pretrial release on a range of nonfinancial conditions.

### An Overview of Pretrial Services Agencies

As the notion of pretrial supervised release grew, pretrial services programs began to play an important role in determining the pretrial risks posed by individual defendants. Dozens of US jurisdictions implemented programs modeled after the Vera Foundation's Manhattan Bail Project (see chapter 1).[200] The first of these was in the District of Columbia, begun in response to the Bail Reform Act of 1966's requirement that specific factors be used by judges in determining whether to detain a defendant.[201] The then D.C. Bail Agency and other PSAs were formed to gather, verify, and report the information judicial officers needed to make informed pretrial release decisions. They quickly became integral to supervising those defendants granted pretrial release in an attempt to mitigate the risks of failure to appear and pretrial reoffending.[202]

At the federal level, PSAs began in 1975 as demonstration projects in ten federal districts to "help reduce crime by persons released to the community pending trial and to reduce unnecessary pretrial detention."[203] The

Pretrial Services Act of 1982 expanded the demonstration projects to all federal districts. After reviewing the case file of a defendant, and sometimes after interviewing the person, pretrial services officers make recommendations to judges about whether the defendant should be released with conditions or be detained.

Incorporating standards from various justice advocacy organizations, including the American Bar Association, the National Association of Pretrial Services Agencies identified "six core functions of pretrial services programs":

- Impartial universal screening of all defendants, regardless of charge;
- Verification of interview information and criminal history checks;
- Assessment of risk of pretrial misconduct through objective means and presentation of recommendations to the court based on the risk level;
- Follow-up reviews of defendants unable to meet the conditions of release;
- Accountable and appropriate supervision of those released, to include proactive court date reminders; [and]
- Reporting on process and outcome measures to stakeholders.[204]

Most of these functions are not controversial; certainly, one would expect pretrial justice agency officials to be impartial, conduct thorough investigations, and report to relevant stakeholders. But even such seemingly straightforward criteria are not always achievable. For example, PSAs are often underfunded and lack information systems that are as fully developed as those available to police.[205] As a result, the ability to conduct thorough pretrial investigations and criminal history checks may be impeded as a function of limited human resources or poor data infrastructure.

Some of the other core functions listed pose ethical conundrums or empirical challenges. For instance, as explained in chapter 3, risk assessment "through objective means" might rely on tools that perpetuate systemic inequalities on the basis of race, ethnicity, and socioeconomic status. And as explained in the remainder of this part of the chapter, identifying and implementing "accountable and appropriate supervision" are far more challenging tasks than they might appear at first blush.

## Pretrial Supervision Options

At the outset, it is imperative to note that certain blanket conditions—such as those mandating universal drug testing, curfews, and even forbidding possession of firearms—not only violate the principle of release on the least restrictive conditions, but also are likely to run afoul of constitutional guarantees of due process.[206] Yet research suggests that blanket conditions are often imposed in more than 90 percent of cases "despite individual differences in risk levels."[207] To avoid potential constitutional violations, it is important to match the risks posed by a particular defendant and the conditions of pretrial release that should be imposed to minimize those risks.

The nonfinancial conditions of pretrial release typically fall into one of four categories:

- *Status quo conditions* require that defendants maintain their residence, school, or employment status.
- *Problem-oriented conditions* address specific defendant problems that affect future court appearance or rearrest. Release is conditioned on a defendant, for example, enrolling in substance abuse monitoring or treatment, vocational or educational training, counseling, or a social services program.
- *Contact conditions* require defendants to report by telephone or in person regularly to pretrial services or another entity.
- *Restrictive conditions* limit defendants' associations, movements, or actions. These include conditions to remain in the jurisdiction,

avoid contact with the complainant, observe curfews, and stay away from certain areas, such as those where drug sales are common.[208]

Technology, beyond telephone calls, is rarely used as part of the process of verifying status quo conditions. Pretrial services officers usually verify residence, school, or employment status through in-person visits. In addition, officers often maintain relationships with select businesses, agencies, and community organizations in order to help people granted pretrial release find or maintain a job.[209] Compliance with the typical status quo requirements may not pose a problem for arrestees with stable housing and employment (or enrollment in school). In contrast, status quo requirements can be incredibly challenging for people on the lower end of the socioeconomic spectrum—especially for people who are unemployed.[210] And as criminologist Nicole Myers found in her study of conditional pretrial release in Canada, the imposition of "numerous restrictive conditions of release for extended periods of time, may be setting people up to fail."[211] In addition, certain restrictive conditions on contact (sometimes referred to as "stay-away conditions") might require arrestees to vacate their housing and relocate away from family members with whom they have been ordered to refrain from having any contact.[212] To address such concerns, some PSAs have developed job training and housing placement programs, but other agencies are without the resources to offer such services.[213]

The Pretrial Justice Institute reported that technology plays an increasingly important role in supervising many other conditions of pretrial release. For example, integrated information and telecommunications systems can be used to substantiate contact conditions through automated calls that "verify the identity of the defendant through voice recognition" or using forms of biometric identity verification, such as computer-aided recognition of fingerprint, facial, and iris scanning.[214] Similarly, technology is often used to enforce restrictive conditions, such as "to detect alcohol or drug use ..., to monitor house arrest or curfew conditions through electronic monitoring, and to monitor the movement of defendants in the community through the use of global positioning system (GPS) technology."[215] But do such supervision conditions actually work to reduce pretrial failures? The scant research aimed at answering this question is mixed, but the best answer appears to be that we simply do not yet know.

## Which Options Work?

Empirical research has long struggled to identify "what works" in terms of pretrial release conditions, largely because programs and practices for pretrial supervision vary dramatically across the United States. "The frequency and types of contacts ranged from monthly phone contacts with an automated calling system to daily in-person reporting by defendants. Some agencies utilize face-to face contacts while others do not. The same is true for home contacts, collateral contacts, court date reminders, and criminal history checks—some agencies provide them and others do not."[216] Due in large part to the extensive variability in pretrial supervision practices, there is remarkably little research about the efficacy of different pretrial supervision practices. In fact, there are only two randomized controlled evaluation studies that have examined this question, both of which are more than twenty years old as of the writing of this book.

A three-site evaluation sponsored by the National Institute of Justice in the early 1980s involving 3,232 felony defendants reported several notable findings.[217] First, the use of pretrial supervision reduced local jail populations, at least in the short term. Second, defendants who were supervised while on pretrial release had slightly better appearance rates than those defendants granted unsupervised pretrial release. Third, pretrial supervision did not meaningfully reduce reoffending rates; in fact, defendants placed under supervision because they were charged with more serious crimes posed no higher risk of reoffending while on pretrial release than those charged with less serious offenses.

And fourth, neither type of pretrial failure was meaningfully reduced by providing social services to defendants on pretrial release.[218]

A study in Philadelphia conducted in 1996 involving 845 defendants reported several interesting findings. First, having a pretrial services officer meet face to face with a defendant, explain applicable expectations, and provide written instructions did not reduce either failure to appear or reoffending rates for defendants granted pretrial release.[219] Second, defendants who were placed on pretrial supervision demonstrated higher success rates in terms of court appearances and reduced reoffending than three different baseline samples of defendants who were granted unsupervised pretrial release.[220] But too much supervision—especially involving threats of sanctions that do not materialize—can be counterproductive. Thus, the researchers concluded that *some* supervision for defendants granted pretrial release is better than *no* supervision, but that graded increases in the levels of restrictions imposed on defendants granted pretrial release do not result in meaningful improvement in the numbers of pretrial failures.[221]

In their 2017 meta-analysis of pretrial research, criminologist Kristin Bechtel and colleagues bemoaned the paucity of high-quality research on pretrial release, which made it difficult to draw unqualified conclusions through reanalysis of data across studies.[222] They reported their conclusions regarding the level of restrictiveness associated with pretrial release conditions:

> It appears that more restrictive bond types are associated with lower [failure to appear] rates. Of the nine effect sizes generated, seven favored more restrictive bond types and two favored less restrictive bond types. These findings should be interpreted with caution, however, as we do not know how the groups may have differed [due to a] lack of demographic and criminal history information.... Any number of mitigating factors could have influenced our conclusion regarding more restrictive bond types, and therefore we must acknowledge that selection bias may be at work within the studies reviewed.[223]

These researchers did note, however, that court notification programs appear to be a reliable method of reducing failures to appear.[224]

For example, a study in Jefferson County, Colorado, found that a phone call reminder reduced the rate of failure to appear from 21 to 12 percent.[225] Similarly, Multnomah County, Oregon, saw a 31 percent reduction in failures to appear when it implemented an automated reminder system.[226] Despite these promising findings, we still know very little about which types of program work best and whether there are certain types of defendants who might benefit most from court appearance reminders.

Multiple evaluation studies have been unable to conclude that pretrial drug testing effectively reduces pretrial failures, even when used with a corresponding system of sanctions.[227] Similarly, multiple evaluation studies have been unable to conclude that electronic monitoring effectively reduces pretrial failures.[228] One study from 1991 even found that failure to appear rates were higher for those electronically monitored than for their unmonitored counterparts, although that study suffered from numerous methodological shortcomings, including a lack of statistical controls for offense types and risk levels, among other important factors.[229] A more recent study, which was limited to interpersonal violence offenders, found no differences in either failure to appear rates or pretrial reoffending rates between arrestees placed on pretrial electronic monitoring and those released without such a condition.[230] Nearly all summaries of research on pretrial electronic monitoring emphasize that more research is needed to demonstrate the possible efficacy of this technology for pretrial defendants.[231] Most studies also point to problems with the technology itself, including "signal loses, frequent equipment failures, limited battery life, and frequent 'nuisance alerts,' such as can occur when a subject is inside a building and the GPS signal is blocked."[232] Other problems associated with global positioning system monitoring include "loss of GPS satellite service, loss of cellular or landline telephone service, loss of electricity, vendor software problems, and loss of data."[233] Still, because the costs associated with implementing a pretrial electronic monitoring program, although not insubstantial, nonetheless offer significant savings compared to pretrial detention, commentators generally recommend exploring such an option for defendants who post a high risk of nonappearance.[234]

## *Potential Pitfalls*

In addition to the increased costs associated with supervised pretrial release in comparison to unsupervised release on recognizance, there are three drawbacks associated with active supervision of pretrial releasees: net widening, overkill, and invasion of privacy.

First, net widening is a theoretical position that posits that as a sanction becomes less punitive, it will be applied to more people.[235] Applying the theory to the use of pretrial supervision suggests that as supervision becomes easier and more cost effective (especially through the use of technology), judges may impose pretrial supervision conditions on defendants who might otherwise have been released on their own recognizance without any corresponding pretrial supervision conditions.[236] A research study of the supervised released program in Brooklyn, New York, found no support for the net-widening hypothesis in this context.[237] On the contrary, the study concluded that pretrial supervision conditions reduced the use of pretrial detention and were imposed on people who otherwise would have received high amounts of monetary bail, rather than widening the net to include offenders who otherwise would have been released on their own recognizance.[238] In addition, those granted supervised release were less likely to be convicted and less likely to be sentenced to a term of incarceration than those people in a matched comparison group who were held in pretrial detention.[239] But the study also revealed that arrestees placed in pretrial supervision did not fare any better in terms of pretrial failure rates than defendants released without supervision.[240]

Second, lower-risk defendants experience higher levels of pretrial failure when they are placed on supervision conditions than do lower-risk counterparts who are not placed on any special release conditions.[241] As Marie VanNostrand explained, "Despite the appealing logic of involving low-risk individuals in intensive programming to prevent them from graduating to more serious behavior, numerous studies show that certain programs may actually worsen their outcomes."[242] In other words, oversupervision is counterproductive. With the exception of defendants with mental health treatment needs, lower-risk defendants should be released on the least restrictive conditions possible, namely on their own recognizance.[243] Pretrial supervised release should be reserved for arrestees who pose a moderate to high risk of pretrial failure.

Finally, some critics of pretrial supervision—especially the use of electronic location monitoring technologies—express concerns about the attendant invasion of privacy for arrestees who have yet to be convicted of a crime. As law professor Samuel Wiseman has noted, such concerns are significantly outweighed by the benefits associated with avoiding pretrial detention: "Even the most thorough observation—even if it causes defendants to carefully monitor and restrict their behavior in order to limit the government's knowledge of their lives—would for most defendants almost certainly be preferable to imprisonment."[244]

### Summary

Telephonic, mail, and text-message reminders about upcoming court dates seem to be effective means of decreasing the rates of failure to appear. Release on supervision also yields benefits for most defendants in comparison to having high bail amounts set that they cannot pay, resulting in pretrial detention with all of its associated negative outcomes. But whether special conditions of pretrial release involving supervision of defendants actually produce systematic improvements in pretrial failure outcomes compared to release on recognizance remains an open empirical question. Given that methodologically sound research has yet to demonstrate the efficacy of pretrial supervision and monitoring as a means of reducing pretrial failures, it seems that widespread implementation of this recommendation is quite premature.

## CONCLUSION

We began this chapter by noting the plethora of factors that judges are typically required to consider when making pretrial release decisions. Unfortunately the evidence suggests that judges are not giving defendants the individualized attention to which they are entitled. Instead they rely on tools such as bail schedules or simply look at the severity of the charged offense as a proxy for the risk posed by the defendant. Indeed, there is some evidence that they base their decisions, either unconsciously or due to reliance on inaccurate stereotypes, on the race or ethnicity of the defendant. As a result, by setting monetary bail at amounts higher than most defendants can pay, judges are both forcing defendants to turn to for-profit bail companies and effectively detaining many people who likely do not pose any risk. It is not surprising then that the current system has been criticized. In response, many commentators, and indeed many states, have turned to actuarial risk assessment tools to help judges make better decisions. In the next chapter we discuss the development and use of these tools and conclude that while they do have some potential to make pretrial decision making fairer, they are not without their own problems.

# CHAPTER THREE

# The Problems with Risk-Assessment-Based Bail Determinations

## WITH MEGAN VERHAGEN

### INTRODUCTION

At the turn of the twenty-first century, a host of voices called for reforms to address a multiplicity of concerns associated with the pretrial detention of arrestees, who are presumed innocent under the law. Several advocacy groups, including the American Bar Association, the National Association of Pretrial Services Agencies, and the National Institute of Justice, recommended the adoption of more objective criteria to assist in making pretrial release or detention determinations.[1] Underlying these recommendations was the belief that the bail process could and should be improved to release more arrestees facing criminal charges while simultaneously improving public safety, decreasing unnecessary jail expenditures, and reducing demographic disparities in pretrial decisions.[2] In the decade that followed, a number of tools were developed to replace subjective decision making in pretrial release processes with structured and more objective assessments. By 2017 several states had either replaced their money bail systems with formal risk assessment systems or, alternatively, had revised their pretrial laws to adopt risk assessment instruments.[3]

The term *risk assessment* means different things in different situations. In the context of legal decision making, forensic risk assessment has traditionally involved the use of behavioral science, primarily psychiatry and psychology, to predict whether someone "poses a particular type of recognized threat," such as whether a person presents a risk of danger to self or others.[4] In 1928 sociologist Earnest Burgess published what is widely considered to be the first study of violence risk assessment using a group of parolees.[5] Since that time, several hundred articles and dozens of books have been written on a range of forensic risk assessment practices and instruments.[6]

Researchers have generally sorted risk assessments into four "generations" marked by different levels of empirical sophistication. In the second part of this chapter we trace the evolution of risk assessment, provide definitions of important terms, and evaluate the strengths and weaknesses of some of the more popular risk assessment instruments. Before doing so, however, we present a shorthand way of differentiating the four generations of risk assessment instruments. First-generation risk assessments are unstructured and are determined by subjective professional judgments.[7] Second-generation risk assessments are largely atheoretical, but they consist of static variables that are empirically derived through statistical tests.[8] Third-generation risk assessments are more grounded in theory and include dynamic risk factors.[9] Fourth-generation risk assessments resemble third-generation scales, but include dimensions relevant to ongoing case management, including intervention strategies for risk reduction.[10] This chapter explores the four generations of forensic risk assessment and critiques how validated forensic risk assessment instruments might be used to improve decision making relevant to pretrial detention.

## THE EVOLUTION OF RISK ASSESSMENTS

At the outset, it is important to note that the overwhelming number of risk assessment instruments devised over the past fifty years were not designed for use during pretrial stages of the criminal justice process. Indeed, most risk assessment instruments were designed for purposes completely unrelated to predicting the risk of nonappearance at future judicial proceedings, even though that is one of the primary purposes of bail. Nonetheless, because many risk assessment instruments were designed to predict a person's risk of future violence, albeit for use in sentencing or security classification upon intake in correctional facilities, some have been used in the processes related to making pretrial detention decisions.

### First-Generation Risk Assessment

Forensic risk assessment has been primarily concerned with making predictions about future dangerousness.[11] For most of the twentieth century these predictions were based on unstructured clinical assessments by psychiatrists and psychologists.[12] These clinical interviews were considered "unstructured" because there was no standardized protocol or even a checklist for completing these assessments. Rather, they were "grounded in the clinician's background and experience and affected by his or her ability to make inferences from interviews, case histories, current mental status, and performance on tests that were not designed to predict dangerousness, such as intelligence tests and a variety of personality tests: e.g., the Minnesota Multiphasic Personality Inventory (MMPI), the Rorschach inkblot test, the Thematic Apperception Test, and the Children's Apperception Test."[13] Because these largely subjective methods "were prone to error and bias," it is unsurprising that several studies found that unstructured clinical predictions of future dangerousness "were incorrect two out of three times, yielding an error rate worse than that predicted by chance."[14] Nonetheless, these evaluations of first-generation risk assessment provide a base rate of violence prediction against which subsequent risk assessments may be measured.[15]

### Bringing Structure to Risk Assessment Processes

The abysmal error rates associated with unstructured risk assessment led behavioral scientists to seek some standardization in the processes in the hopes of improving the reliability and validity of predicting the risk of future reoffending. Over time they developed two different structured approaches to risk assessment, one based on actuarial methods and the other on structured professional judgment.[16] These approaches, individually and in combination with each other, spawned three new generations of risk assessment instruments that significantly improved the process of predicting future violence in comparison to unstructured clinical risk assessment.

## ACTUARIAL RISK ASSESSMENT

Actuarial risk assessment instruments (ARAIs) estimate the likelihood or probability that people will engage in future behavior, such as violence, based on an algorithmic formula.[17] The equations ARAIs employ to predict risk are developed using items that have been statistically correlated with specific behavior (e.g., violent recidivism) and then statistically normed against a particular group of people—sometimes referred to as a *development sample* or *construction sample*—over a specific timeframe.[18]

Typically, ARAIs score the presence or absence of certain *risk factors* that are positively correlated with an increased probability of reoffending (e.g., age, sex, number of prior criminal offenses, history of substance abuse).[19] Less frequently, ARAIs may also score items indicating the presence or absence of certain *protective factors* that are positively correlated with a decreased probability of reoffending (e.g., family history of having lived with both biological parents until at least age sixteen).[20]

ARAIs are generally easy, straightforward, and quick to administer. In addition, ARAIs are largely objective, insofar as little if any subjective judgment is needed to rate items and calculate risk scores, leading to high levels of inter-rater reliability. Perhaps most important, ARAIs offer far greater accuracy than unstructured clinical assessments.[21] These benefits notwithstanding, ARAIs are not without their drawbacks.

First and foremost, ARAIs that calculate risk based only on *static* factors, such as demographic and historical factors, cannot take into account changes in personal and social circumstances that may increase risk (e.g., loss of employment) or decrease risk (e.g., getting married), which are referred to as *dynamic* risk factors. Second, risk scores on ARAIs represent probabilities based on statically normed group data. Psychologists Sarah Desmarais and Jay Singh offered an example in which a particular offender is assessed using an ARAI that yields a score associated with a 60 percent chance of violent reoffending over a ten-year period. This score means that 60 percent of the people in the original study who received the same score recidivated within the given timeframe, but it does not mean that the particular person being assessed with that specific ARAI has a 60 percent chance of recidivating over ten years. Moreover, 40 percent of the people in the original study did not recidivate within the timeframe. There is no way of knowing "where any given offender falls within a risk bin"—in the 60 percent or the 40 percent.[22]

## STRUCTURED PROFESSIONAL JUDGMENT

Structured professional judgment (SPJ), sometimes referred to as structured clinical judgment, incorporates statistically validated risk and protective factors into individualized clinical risk assessments. These risk assessment instruments are structured in a manner designed to guide trained assessors "to estimate risk level (e.g., low, moderate, or high) through consideration of a set number of factors that are empirically and theoretically associated with the outcome of interest."[23] In addition to the inclusion of a series of static risk factors, SPJ approaches allow assessors to consider individual factors that are affecting the particular person undergoing risk assessment.

The SPJ approach grew out of the work of a team of noted psychologists led by John Monahan and Henry Steadman in the MacArthur Violence Risk Assessment Study.[24] That study was conducted between 1992 and 1995 on a sample of 951 psychiatric patients. "Overall, the MacArthur research identified four different parameters that should be used to structure any examination of risk factors. This new perspective included: (1) Demographic features, such as age and gender; (2) Historical factors, including prior mental hospitalization and/or history of violent behavior; (3) Contextual variables, such as the degree of social support an individual has, the extent of disinhibiting influences, the degree of inhibiting influences; and (4) Clinical traits, including a broad array of factors having to do with diagnosis and specific symptoms."[25]

Unlike their purely actuarial risk assessment counterparts, SPJ approaches that incorporate the demographic, historical, contextual, and clinical domains identified in the MacArthur research can offer the benefit of specific case factors being considered as part of the process of forming particularized opinions regarding risk. But SPJ risk assessments also have drawbacks, most notably that they take longer and are often more expensive to administer than ARAIs. Another important limitation of SPJ approaches is that they potentially allow decision-making biases to affect the overall assessment of risk. Nonetheless, like ARAIs, SPJ instruments offer far greater predictive accuracy than unstructured clinical interviews. Indeed, researchers report that ARAIs and SPJ risk assessments both produce equally valid predictions of recidivism.[26] Perhaps that explains why the second, third, and fourth generations of risk assessment draw on one or both of these approaches.

### Second-Generation Risk Assessment

The second generation of risk assessment instruments represented the first use of actuarial risk assessment methods.[27] These tools "focused on standardized assessment of static risk factors that had been statistically demonstrated to predict future violence, such as sex, age, criminal history, psychopathy, low socioeconomic status, family criminality," and clinical diagnoses met the criteria in the so-called Bible of mental illnesses, the American Psychiatric Association's *Diagnostic and Statistical Manual of Mental Disorders*.[28] Select examples of second-generation risk assessment tools are the Salient Factor Score (SFS), Statistical Information on Recidivism (SIR), and Violence Risk Appraisal Guide (VRAG).[29]

### TRUE SECOND-GENERATION RISK ASSESSMENT INSTRUMENTS

The US Parole Commission originally developed the SFS in 1973 to assess parole applications. Although the instrument has been revised on a number of occasions, it nearly exclusively consists of criminal history variables.[30] Earlier versions included variables related to employment and education, but these factors were phased out as a "just deserts" model of criminal justice became more popular in the 1980s and 1990s.[31] Despite these limitations, the SFS has been found to hold predictive validity for general recidivism over a three-year period for both male and female parolees.[32]

At approximately the same time that the SFS was developed, Canadian researchers developed the SIR.[33] It uses fifteen items to predict recidivism within three years of release from custody.[34] Each item measures either a demographic or a criminal history characteristic. Its revised version reliably predicts general and violent recidivism among male offenders who are not of First Nation background.[35]

The VRAG was designed to predict recidivism by inmates released from penal institutions. It consists of twelve variables that have been found to be significantly correlated with violent recidivism, including factors such as elementary school maladjustment, prior criminal history, never having been married, age, a history of substantive abuse, and the presence of personality disorders.[36] Weighted responses on the items contained in the VRAG yield a score that has been found to predict recidivism among several differing offender populations, although its predictive validity is lower for sex offenders and offenders with schizophrenia or personality disorders.[37]

Second-generation risk assessment instruments offered much more reliable prediction of recidivism than unstructured clinical assessments.[38] Nonetheless, they were criticized for several important reasons. For example, in spite of being empirically derived, second-generation risk assessment instruments were constructed of items "selected with little regard for their theoretical or rehabilitative value."[39] Moreover, because these instruments relied on static risk factors, they did not account for changes in individual functioning and life circumstances that affect a person's risk for recidivating over time, nor did they identify areas of potential intervention for risk reduction.[40] As a result, corrections officials usually had to perform separate needs assessments of an offenders' life circumstances that were amenable to change through rehabilitative and reentry social services.[41] Third-generation risk assessment instruments addressed this need, in part, by integrating dynamic variables into the process of assessing risk.

### THE HARE PSYCHOPATHY CHECKLIST

In the nineteenth century, psychiatrists began to write clinical accounts of a personality disorder that came to be known as *psychopathy*. Truth be told, the discussion of psychopathic traits dates back centuries. "In fact, researchers have found references to psychopathic individuals in biblical, classical, and medieval texts."[42] Across the centuries, psychopathy has been referred to as *manie sans délire* ("insanity without delirium"), "innate, preternatural moral depravity," "moral insanity," and "moral colorblindness," and people with psychopathic personalities were referred to as "unscrupulous," "moral imbeciles," and "criminals by impulse."[43] In the wake of World War I, psychiatrist Hervey Cleckley published *The Mask of Sanity*, in which he detailed his clinical observations of psychopaths as "automatons" who do not experience normal human emotions.

In much the same way that researchers sought to bring some empirically validated measurement tools to the psychological assessment of risk for criminal offending, Canadian psychologist Robert Hare developed a checklist in 1980 to bring some standardization to diagnosing psychopathy. After more than thirty years of refining the assessment of traits associated with psychopathy, Hare published the Psychopathy Checklist–Revised (PCL-R) in 2003.[44] Administered as a semistructured interview that takes approximately two to three hours to complete, the instrument contains twenty items that are scored on a scale of 0 to 2, resulting in a maximum score of 40. A score of 30 or higher represents the threshold for a psychopathy diagnosis. Largely as result of Hare's work, traits such as glibness/ superficial charm, pathological lying, manipulativeness, lack of remorse or guilt, callousness, promiscuity, impulsivity, irresponsibility, and criminal versatility are now hallmarks of the disorder.[45] To be fair, however, many psychologists continue to debate the nature and scope of the "psychopathic personality," in terms of both its essential or core features and whether there are subgroups with discrete personality features.[46] Nonetheless, the PCL-R has become the "gold standard" for assessing psychopathy.[47]

Although the PCL-R was not developed to assess the risk of reoffending, dozens of studies have evaluated the instrument as a predictor of recidivism. A series of meta-analyses on these studies generally support "an association between measures of psychopathy and criminal reoffending, across contexts and types of people."[48] Numerous studies have documented significant correlations between a diagnosis of psychopathy and general recidivism, violent recidivism, and sexual recidivism, leading some researchers to conclude that the PCL-R performs as well as, and sometimes even better than, actuarial violence risk assessment instruments.[49] Perhaps because of such findings, "PCL-R measures of psychopathy continue to play a prominent role in contemporary risk assessment instruments and have demonstrated comparatively more predictive power than other recidivism-related variables, such as substance abuse, early behavioral problems, age, number of convictions, elementary school maladjustment, early separation from a parent, never having been married, and failure on prior conditional release."[50]

Even though the PCL-R is an exceptionally well-respected instrument for diagnosing psychopathy, it has it shortcomings. First, it takes a trained examiner several hours to administer and score the instrument, making it cost prohibitive in many forensic settings.[51] Second, the reliability of the instrument may be questionable because different examiners may score the subjective elements on the checklist differently, "which renders a diagnosis [of psychopathy] a delicate, if not futile task."[52] Third, because the PCL-R ignores the neuroscientific components of behavior, the test may be fatally outdated.[53] Fourth, the PCL-R was developed and validated on adult male offenders from Canada.[54] Although a sizable body of research has validated its use for diagnosing psychopathy in other populations, that does not necessarily translate into the tool's predictive validity for assessing violence risk generally or in other populations, such as females and adolescents.[55] Finally, and arguably most importantly, the PCL-R can be misused in forensic settings. Even its creator, Robert Hare, has cautioned against its misuse in the criminal justice system.[56] Because it was not designed as a risk assessment instrument, its results, as far as revealing the "presence or absence of psychopathy[,] can be misinterpreted and misrepresented—both by the prosecution and by the defense—as it relates to violence potential in criminal proceedings."[57]

### Third-Generation Risk Assessment Instruments

The third generation of risk assessment instruments, often referred to as *risk-needs instruments*, are empirically derived, but unlike earlier ARAIs, they are theoretically informed and include a combination of both static and dynamic risk factors. Dynamic risk factors account for changing criminogenic needs over time, such as financial stress, education level, employment status, housing needs, alcohol and drug use, interpersonal conflicts, social support, anxiety and other emotional problems, and antisocial attitudes.[58] Due to their inclusion of dynamic risk factors, most (but not all) research on the validity of third-generation risk assessment instruments concludes that they offer better prediction of violent recidivism than their second-generation counterparts.[59] The most commonly used third-generation risk assessment instruments are the Level of Service Inventory-Revised (LSI-R), the Historical, Clinical, and Risk Management Violence Risk Assessment Scheme (HCR-20), the Self-Appraisal Questionnaire (SAQ), and the Violence Risk Scale (VRS).[60]

## THE LEVEL OF SERVICE INVENTORY-REVISED

The LSI-R is one of the most widely used risk assessment instruments in the United States, especially in the community corrections setting.[61] It is an actuarial tool consisting of fifty-four items across ten subscales that include both static and dynamic factors that are scored during a semistructured interview administered by trained personnel. Higher scores indicate higher risk for engaging in either antisocial or violent behavior. Among the general populations, not only has the LSI-R been shown to demonstrate predictive validity of recidivism, but also, changes in LSI-R score are associated with changes in recidivism risk.[62] Other validation studies have noted, however, that the LSI-R struggles to predict risk at equivalent levels between White and non-White persons and that there are differential indicators of risk between men and women for which the LSI-R does not completely account.[63] Also, some research suggests that the overall predictive validity of the fifty-four items on the LSI-R could be higher with a more parsimonious model.[64]

## THE HISTORICAL, CLINICAL, AND RISK MANAGEMENT VIOLENCE RISK ASSESSMENT SCHEME

The HCR-20 was first developed in the mid-1990s in an attempt to design an SPJ risk assessment tool that integrated empirical research on violence prediction and the clinical practice of assessment. It was revised in 1997, and the third version of the test was released in 2013. It consists of twenty questions intended to evaluate violent behavior through clinical and actuarially derived risk-factor items that when scored yield low, moderate, or high levels of risk.[65] The HCR-20 is considered to be equally or more effective at predicting future violence than the PCL-R and second-generation risk assessment instruments such as the VRAG.[66] In some settings, however, such as forensic hospitals, the HCR-20 failed to predict future violence except in extreme cases.[67] These results suggest the need to have both properly trained assessors as well as instruments that are developed for particular populations.

### SELF-APPRAISAL QUESTIONNAIRE

As its name implies, the SAQ relies on self-reported data. It contains seventy-two true/false questions concerning criminal history, antisocial behavior, substantive abuse, and antisocial associates. It also contains a validity index and an anger subscale. The SAQ takes approximately fifteen minutes to complete. For a self-report instrument, the SAQ scores surprisingly high for predictive ability in both institutional and recidivist violence, although it appears to predict violence less accurately for certain populations of women.[68]

### VIOLENCE RISK SCALE

The VRS was developed to assess violent offenders other than those who commit sex crimes. It is also used to identify specific treatments that can be used to reduce risk of recidivism and measure changes in risk.[69] The VRS consists of six static and twenty dynamic items that have been linked to changes in recidivism and violence. Higher scores on the scale indicate a high likelihood of violent offending. The VRS has shown consistent predictive validity, inter-rater reliability, and internal consistency and has predicted both violent and nonviolent recidivism in both the short and the long terms.[70]

Third-generation risk assessment instruments tend to be most commonly used in a variety of criminal justice contexts even though some researchers question the empirical validity of dynamic risk factors as predictors of recidivism risk.[71] In addition, some researchers have cautioned against the use of third-generation risk assessment instruments for sentencing purposes because of their inclusion of dynamic risk factors. Specifically, although the classification of risk related to certain criminogenic needs is highly relevant to the development of rehabilitative and reentry treatment plans, the inability to meet certain social and psychological needs should not increase an offender's sentence.[72] Collectively, these shortcomings have led some researchers to conclude that risk-needs assessment tools are well-suited for correctional classification and treatment purposes, but not for the purposes of predicting risk for judicial procedures.[73]

Apart from the questionable usage of third-generation risk assessment instruments as tools in judicial processes, there is little doubt that the inclusion of dynamic risk factors is very important for the purpose of managing an offender's risk after sentencing. But these instruments lack some key measures relevant to case planning and other aspects of risk reduction with regard to the goals of enhancing treatment, improving supervision, and measuring changes that might allow for preventative interventions.[74] This has led researchers and practitioners—especially those involved in rehabilitation and reentry—to create the fourth generation of risk assessment instruments.

### Fourth-Generation Risk Assessment

Fourth-generation risk assessments mirror third-generation instruments insofar as they include both static and dynamic risk factors for recidivism that are grounded in both theory and empirical research. However, fourth-generation instruments are more comprehensive in that they can be used to guide case management and supervision.[75] For example, fourth-generation instruments include questions related to treatment barriers, such as low intelligence, reading and writing limitations, lack of transportation, child care needs, and language/cultural barriers to participation in rehabilitative programming. "These items are not directly related to recidivism, but instead have the potential to restrict the efficacy of treatment."[76]

Because these instruments include responsivity dimensions that allow for matching services "with personality, motivation, and ability," they are commonly referred to as *risk-need-responsivity* tools.[77] Consistent with their case management aims, fourth-generation risk assessment instruments are designed to be administered on multiple occasions so that corrections personnel can track changes in each offender's particular criminogenic needs and modify treatment plans to meet those changing needs.[78] Some fourth-generation instruments even integrate "community context indicators" because social ecology research strongly indicates that local-level variables (e.g., crime rates, poverty, unemployment levels, treatment availability options, and other contributing factors to cumulative neighborhood disadvantage) contribute to recidivism risk.[79] Two fourth-generation assessment instruments, the Correctional Assessment and Intervention System (CAIS) and the Ohio Risk Assessment System (ORAS), have not been studied as much as two other, more popular fourth-generation instruments, the Level of Service/Case Management Inventory (LS/CMI) and the Correctional Offender Management Profiling for Alternative Sanctions (COMPAS).[80]

### CORRECTIONAL ASSESSMENT AND INTERVENTION SYSTEM

The CAIS is a fourth-generation tool based on the Wisconsin Risk and Need Instrument (WRN), which was developed in the mid- to late-1970s.[81] The WRN had separate risk assessment and needs assessment components that were designed primarily to determine custody level for offenders upon intake to Wisconsin prisons. The CAIS updated and integrated the risk and needs assessments, along with case management items. It consists of between eighty-two and eighty-eight items (depending on whether it is being administered to a male or female respondent) that are scored by a trained interviewer.[82] Further study is needed to establish its reliability and predictive validity.

### OHIO RISK ASSESSMENT SYSTEM

The ORAS was created by researchers at the University of Cincinnati in partnership with Ohio's department of corrections.[83] Unlike many other risk assessment instruments of any generation, ORAS offers a range of risk assessment instruments, including two brief screening tools for use with prison and community supervision populations, as well as four full assessment tools "each designed for use at pretrial, at prison intake, with community supervision populations, or with reentry populations."[84] The ORAS assessment instruments are designed to be completed through structured interviews in combination with a review of official records, although ORAS tools also use self-report data. As with CAIS, further study is needed to establish the reliability and validity of the full range of ORAS assessment instruments.

### LEVEL OF SERVICE/CASE MANAGEMENT INVENTORY

The LS/CMI is a revision of the third-generation LSI-R scale that is gender and culturally informed to address criticisms about the generalizability of the LSI-R. The LS/CMI is an actuarial instrument consisting of forty-three items that include static and dynamic risk factors. But inclusion of responsivity items differentiates the LS/CMI from its predecessor, such that it fits within the risk-needs-responsivity model of assessment that emphasizes treatment and proactive interventions. The LS/CMI was developed in Canada and has been normed there as well as in the United States, the United Kingdom, and Singapore. The US data were normed from nine geographically diverse jurisdictions on both male and female inmates and community-based offenders. Validity studies suggest that the LS/CMI not only is a valid predictor of recidivism generally, but also successfully differentiates between males and females better than the LSI-R.[85] In addition, the LS/CMI has been validated across various community and institutional settings with racially and gender diverse samples.[86]

### CORRECTIONAL OFFENDER MANAGEMENT PROFILING FOR ALTERNATIVE SANCTIONS

The COMPAS is a software package that criminal justice actors and clinical personnel can use to assess risk and needs, make sentencing decisions, develop treatment plans, do case management, and assess recidivism outcomes.[87] Originally developed by the Northpoint Institute for Public Management in 1998, the current version has been normed for both males and females in three correctional settings—probation, jail, and prison—as well as among a composite group of offenders. The auto-mated system contains "42 separate scales that may be selected and com-bined for use with various offender populations (jail, prison, parole, probation) and at different decision points in the criminal justice process (pretrial release, case management)."[88] Evaluation studies suggest that the COMPAS possesses high levels of predictive validity concerning the risk of recidivism.[89]

Importantly, and unlike most other general risk assessment instru-ments, the COMPAS has been validated for use as a tool for pretrial release decisions based on a defendant's likelihood to reoffend in gen-eral, likelihood to reoffend with a crime of violence, and likelihood to fail to appear at trial.[90]

### Specialty Risk Assessment Instruments

In addition to the general risk assessments previously summarized, which are meant to be used on general populations of defendants or offenders, several specialty tools have been developed for use with par-ticular populations who may have unique risk characteristics that are not accounted for within the general risk assessment instruments, such as sex offenders, intimate-partner violence perpetrators, and juveniles. As with their general risk assessment counterparts, specialized risk assessment instruments can be classified into generations based on their inclusion of static, dynamic, or responsivity items. Generally speaking, second-generation specialty assessments—such as the Static-99, a ten-item tool for assessing the risk of sexual reoffending using the person's age and static factors (e.g., the number and characteristics of victims)—demonstrate moderate levels of predictive validity for future sexual reoffending.[91] Third-generation assessment instruments that include dynamic risk factors, such as the Violence Risk Scale-Sexual Offender Version (VRS-SO), have demonstrated even higher levels of predic-tive validity in terms of sexual offense recidivism.[92] Fourth-generation scales, such as the Youth Level of Service/Case Management Inventory

(YLS/CMI), have the greatest predictive accuracy across largely diverse youth offender groups.[93]

## PRETRIAL RISK ASSESSMENT

As discussed in previous chapters, pretrial release decisions involve balancing the rights of a particular defendant against public safety concerns. Accordingly, the processes associated with making pretrial release decisions require judges to consider two factors: the risk of flight/nonappearance in court and the perceived risk the accused poses to himself or herself or others. Law professor Lauren Gouldin notes that flight risk and the risk of nonappearance are often used interchangeably even though they are distinct concepts. The risk of what she calls *true flight* (fugitives fleeing a jurisdiction) is not the same as the risk of being either *local absconders*—"defendants who remain in the jurisdiction but actively and persistently avoid court"—or *low-cost nonappearers*—defendants who fail to appear in court for a myriad of reasons having little to do with attempting to avoid adjudication.[94] To date, no pretrial risk assessment instruments differentiate among these three types of defendants even though different interventions are needed to target each form of nonappearance.

Overwhelmingly, the determination of a defendant's pretrial risk—both for flight/failing to appear or for reoffending while on pretrial release—has been based on judicial discretion.[95] Concerns over judicial objectivity, however, have led to increased calls for processes that curb unbridled judicial discretion through the use of standardized guidelines, such as bail schedules, or the use of validated risk assessment instruments. As discussed in chapter 2, bail schedules suffer from a number of problems, not the least of which might be their unconstitutionality.[96] But there are also serious concerns about "objective" risk assessment instruments.

For example, most second- through fourth-generation ARAIs were "derived from statistical analyses of aggregate (primarily White) male correctional population data" and, as a result, "their predictive reliability for women and racialized populations is unclear."[97] Another important limitation of general violence risk assessment tools is that they were not developed and validated to assess the risk of flight/nonappearance in court, but rather to assess the long-term risk of violent behavior for convicted offenders either serving periods of incarceration or being supervised in the community on probation or parole; fourth-generation risk assessment instruments even seek to assess convicted offenders' ongoing treatment needs. Thus, although some of the instruments described in the second section of this chapter may appear at first blush to be of some limited use for helping judicial officers make decisions concerning a particular arrestee's risk of reoffending if granted pretrial release, they are actually ill-suited for this purpose because they do not "assess unsentenced defendants' short-term pretrial risk to public safety and/or nonappearance in court."[98]

Of all the risk assessment instruments mentioned in this chapter thus far, only the ORAS and the COMPAS have scales that were designed for use in the pretrial decision-making stage, and only the latter has been externally validated for that purpose, albeit only in a single study as of the writing of this book.[99] There are, however, a few risk assessment instruments that have been specifically developed and validated for pretrial processes, including the Manhattan Bail Project's tool, the Urban Institute of Justice Policy Center tool, the Virginia Pretrial Risk Assessment, the Ohio Risk Assessment System's pretrial screening tool, and the Arnold Foundation's Public Safety Assessment.

### The Manhattan Bail Project/Vera Point Scale

The Vera Foundation (now the Vera Institute of Justice) sponsored the Manhattan Bail Project during the 1960s.[100] Part of this effort involved the development of a pretrial risk assessment screening tool, commonly referred to as the Vera Point Scale, that incorporated static factors related to the likelihood that a defendant would fail to appear at a court date if released prior to the trial. Defendants who were released on their own recognizance (i.e., without monetary bail) based on Vera's recommendations failed to appear in only 1.6percent of cases, about half the 3 percent failure to appear rate for defendants who were released on bail.[101] One of the Manhattan Bail Project's important conclusions was that most defendants would appear for trial without the use of financial bail. This conclusion was bolstered for defendants with strong ties to the community.[102] Although revolutionary at the time, the Vera Point Scale was fairly simplistic by today's standards. Moreover, the Manhattan Bail Project's finding concerning community ties has been questioned by subsequent research. Specifically, a number of studies have reported that strong ties to the community do not accurately predict failure to appear, especially when residential stability is used as a measure of ties to the community.[103]

### Contemporary Pretrial Risk Assessment Instruments

According to the Pretrial Justice Center, only about a dozen local jurisdictions were using actuarial pretrial risk assessment instruments (APRAIs) by the turn of the twenty-first century.[104] But in the years since then, many jurisdictions have begun using APRAIs. "Some of these tools are still applicable to only a single local jurisdiction, but others have been developed for multiple localities or for statewide use. For example, there are empirically-derived statewide tools in Virginia, Ohio, Kentucky, Colorado, and an empirically-derived tool used nationwide in the federal courts.... Jurisdictions that have implemented these tool [sic] have reported that released defendants' actual success rates match very closely to the predicted success rates."[105]

Although APRAIs vary considerably, most classify a defendant's risk on a three-point (low, moderate, high risk) to five-point (lowest to highest risk) scale.[106] APRAIs serve two important goals. First, they help to standardize the process of assessing risk. Not only does standardization improve transparency by setting forth the factors that are taken into account at bail hearings, but standardization also promotes consistency across judicial officers, thereby reducing disparate and potentially arbitrary decisions concerning pretrial release or detention.[107] Second, APRAIs maximize successful decision making in pretrial processes insofar as they facilitate the release of people who do not need to be held in pretrial custody pending trial. Conversely, they identify those who pose the highest levels of risk of nonappearance or short-term reoffending so that they may be held in pretrial detention, thereby promoting community safety.[108]

Most APRAIs rely on a number of validated static risk factors, the six most common of which include prior failures to appear, prior criminal convictions, a present felony charge, being unemployed, a history of drug use, and having other criminal charges pending in addition to the ones for which a pretrial release or detention decision must be made.[109] Others are age, the number of prior incarcerations, education level, and community ties (often measured through residential stability), even though ties to the community do not appear to add to the empirical prediction of pretrial risk.[110]

Several APRAIs are summarized in the following subsections. First, however, it is important to note why there are so many different assessment instruments. Put simply, research suggests that APRAIs need to be validated on the specific populations being served because risk factors may vary by geographical location.[111]

### DISTRICT OF COLUMBIA

In 2001 the Pretrial Services Agency of the District of Columbia contracted the Urban Institute to develop a pretrial risk assessment instrument. Two years later, Urban Institute researchers released their final report, assessing the tool they had created to predict both the risk of failing to appear and the risk of rearrest while on pretrial release.[112] The instrument was validated on more than 7,570 cases in the District of Columbia.

The Urban Institute's APRAI for the District of Columbia employed twenty-two items that yield two subscale scores, one for failure to appear and the other for rearrest while on pretrial release. Nineteen of the twenty-two items concern factors related to criminal history, substance use, and the nature of current criminal charges. The other three items are age, citizenship, and whether the offender shares a residence with other family members. Scores range from 0 to 100, with statistically established cutoffs for five levels: low (release on recognizance), condition monitoring (release with mostly nonrestrictive conditions, such as passport surrender), moderate (release with restrictive conductions, such as a curfew, alcohol or drug treatment, or pretrial services supervision), high (release on highly restrictive conditions, such as intensive supervision, house arrest, or halfway house residency), and severe (pretrial detention recommended).[113] The instrument demonstrated moderate predictive power for both types of pretrial risks, with correlations of .21 for predicting failure to appear and .16 for predicting reoffending, although the instrument did achieve a maximum accuracy rate of predicting both types of failure for nearly 80 percent for certain defendants.[114] Overall, the moderate correlations between scores and pretrial risk outcomes may have been a function of where the cutoff values were set because nearly half the sample was classified at moderate risk levels.

Over time the District of Columbia Pretrial Services Agency worked with the Urban Institute and others to refine its pretrial risk assessment tools. The instrument developed in 2009 was validated in 2012 and now examines more than seventy static and dynamic risk factors across five domains, including demographic characteristics, criminal history, instant offense details, drug and alcohol use, and current criminal justice status.[115] The tool offers even better predictive validity than its predecessor and provides specific types of reoffending risks for violent, property, and domestic violence offenses.[116] According to the most recent data made available by the District of Columbia Pretrial Services Agency (covering fiscal year 2015):

- Ninety-one percent (91%) of released defendants remained arrest free while their cases were being adjudicated.
- Ninety-eight percent (98%) of released defendants were not rearrested on a crime of violence while in the community pending trial.
- Ninety-percent (90%) of released defendants made all scheduled court appearances.
- Eighty-eight percent (88%) of released defendants remained on release at the conclusion of their pretrial status, without a pending request for removal or revocation due to noncompliance.[117]

## VIRGINIA

In 2003 the Virginia Department of Criminal Justice Services began to develop the Virginia Pretrial Risk Assessment Instrument (VPRAI).[118] Based on data collected from the late 1990s through 2001 from 1,971 adults, researcher Marie VanNostrand and her team used multivariate logistic regression—a statistical technique that can control for a range of factors to show which variables can predict a dichotomous outcome, such as whether or not someone reoffended while on pretrial release— to analyze fifty variables concerning arrestees in seven different municipalities in the state of Virginia.[119] Nine of these variables emerged as significant predictors of the risk of failing to appear and the risk of rearrest while on pretrial release:

1. Primary Charge Type—Defendants charged with a felony are more likely to fail pending trial than defendants charged with a misdemeanor.
2. Pending Charge(s)—Defendants who have pending charge(s) at the time of their arrest are more likely to fail pending trial.
3. Outstanding Warrant(s)—Defendants who have outstanding warrant(s) in another locality for charges unrelated to the current arrest are more likely to fail pending trial.

4. Criminal History—Defendants with at least one prior misde-meanor or felony conviction are more likely to fail pending trial.

5. Two or More Failure to Appear Convictions—Defendants with two or more failure to appear convictions are more likely to fail pending trial.

6. Two or More Violent Convictions—Defendants with two or more violent convictions are more likely to fail pending trial.

7. Length at Current Residence—Defendants who have lived at their current residence for less than one year are more likely to fail pending trial.

8. Employed/Primary Child Caregiver—Defendants who have not been employed continuously at one or more jobs during the two years prior to their arrest or who are not the primary caregiver for a child at the time of their arrest are more likely to fail pending trial.

9. History of Drug Abuse—Defendants with a history of drug abuse are more likely to fail pending trial.[120]

Each of these variables is assigned either 0 or 1 point, other than the failure to appear variable, which is weighted more heavily with either 0 or 2 points, given the predictive power of that variable. Thus, the final score on the VPRAI ranges from 0 to 10 points. Five levels of risk (low, below average, average, above average, and high) were normed based on the participants in the research sample. Only 10 percent of defendants with a low risk assessment score of 0 or 1 (which accounted for 24 percent of the participants in the original validation study) either failed to appear or reoffended. In comparison, 53 percent of the defendants who were given a high-risk score of five or higher failed to appear or reoffended while on pretrial release. The figure rose to 80 percent for the six arrestees (< 1 percent) with a risk score of 8 or higher. The were no statistically significant differences based on sex, race, income levels, or the arresting community type (i.e., rural, small urban, large urban, mixed).[121]

By 2005 all of Virginia's PSAs were using the VPRAI. The state contracted with Luminosity, Inc., to conduct a revalidation study using nearly ten thousand defendants across two data sets. The research team determined that the VPRAI could be improved by omitting the "outstanding warrants" variable, thereby reducing the instrument to eight risk factors with a maximum score of 9 points. Only 7 percent of defendants with a low risk assessment score of 0 or 1 either failed to appear or reoffended. In comparison, 32 percent of the defendants who were given a high-risk score of five or higher failed to appear or reoffended while on pretrial release. Overall, the revised instrument correctly predicted success while on pretrial release for 82 percent of arrestees.[122]

The VPRAI was adapted for use in Lake County, Illinois. Cooprider's 2009 case study of the use of that adapted tool supported the validity of the VPRAI.[123] Specifically, Cooprider reported that Lake County succeeded in releasing more people on recognizance or under supervised release conditions while simultaneously reducing pretrial release disparities. At the same time, the county was able to reduce supervisory field contacts while keeping violation rates stable and in some cases even reducing them.[124]

Virginia has continued to refine its pretrial assessment instrument. Since September 2017 the state has used the VPRAI-R, which added a "Praxis tool," a type of supervision matrix. Developed in 2016, the VPRAI-R is scored on a scale of 0 to 14; other refinements include differentiation of the current charge as a felony drug charge, a theft charge, or a fraud charge; the "history of violence" category being scored based on whether there are two or more violent convictions; "employment stability" being measured as being unemployed at the time of the present offense; and removal of the length of time at the present residence as a risk factor. The VPRAI-R now uses six risk levels.[125] Although a comprehensive validation study had not yet been performed at the time of the writing of this book, an internal study by the Virginia Department of Criminal Justice Services found that the VPRAI-R predicted success for roughly 94 percent of arrestees classified as low risk (with scores of

0 to 2 points) and 63 percent of those classified at the highest levels of risk (with scores of 11 to 14 points).[126]

As previously discussed, researchers at the University of Cincinnati developed ORAS in partnership with the state department of corrections.[127] ORAS includes a range of assessment tools designed for use at different stages of the criminal justice process, one of which is the ORAS Pretrial Assessment Tool (PAT).[128] Original data collection involved sixty-three items for 342 adult offenders. These items included several variables across eight different risk and need domains, including "criminal behavior history, pretrial supervision history, drug/alcohol abuse, employment and attitudes about employment, residential stability, mental and medical health, criminal attitudes and orientation, and criminal associations."[129] From those, a scale was constructed using six statistically significant items: age at first arrest, the number of prior failures to appear, three or more incarcerations, any drug of use history, the severity of problems associated with substance abuse, and employment status at the time of arrest. Two additional items were included even though they did not reach statistical significance in the original models: residential stability and the number of failures to appear in court within a two-year period of time.[130] Scores range from 0 to 10 and were normed such that scores of 0 to 3 indicate low risk, scores of 4 to 7 indicate medium risk, and scores of 8 or higher are classified as high risk. The instrument successfully predicted failure to appear such that only 2.1 percent of low-risk arrestees failed to appear and 4.3 percent reoffended while on release, compared to 19.6 percent of medium-risk and 33.3 percent of high-risk defendants for both types of failures.[131]

The ORAS-PAT underwent some modifications that resulted in its being reduced to seven items with scores ranging from 0 to 9. That version was field tested on 452 arrestees in seven Ohio counties. The overall correlation between risk level classification and outcome failure was

.22.[132] Only 5.4 percent of the low-risk arrestees failed to appear or were rearrested while on pretrial release, compared to 17.8 percent of the medium-risk and 29.5 percent of the high-risk arrestees. While the ORAS-PAT appears to have moderate predictive validity, the authors could locate no other validation studies of the instrument.

### CORRECTIONAL OFFENDER MANAGEMENT PROFILING FOR ALTERNATIVE SANCTIONS: PRETRIAL RELEASE RISK SCALE

As previously discussed, the COMPAS is a fourth-generation risk assessment instrument that includes scales specifically created for use during pretrial processes. The COMPAS Pretrial Release Risk Scale (PTRS) was developed using a "large sample" of felony defendants in Kent County Michigan.[133] Specific details about the items included in the COMPAS-PTRS are not contained in the online "Practitioners' Guide" to the COMPAS or in any scholarly sources. This raises transparency concerns about this proprietary instrument.[134]

The COMPAS-PTRS yields three risk scores—one for failing to appear, another for general reoffending (i.e., any crime), and another for violent reoffending. Each scale ranges from 1 to 10, resulting in classification into one of three groups—low risk (1 to 4), medium risk (5 to 7), and high risk (8 to 10) for each of the three categories.

In 2010 Florida State University researchers conducted a study in Broward County, Florida, that validated the COMPAS-PTRS.[135] Using data from 5,575 cases, these researchers found that the instrument successfully predicted rearrests for general offenses, rearrests for violent offenses, and failures to appear, although predictive power was strongest for general rearrests and failure to appear. Specifically, over a one-year period, 18.1 percent of arrestees classified as low risk reoffended, 38.4 percent of medium-risk defendants reoffended, and 61 percent of the high-risk arrestees reoffended.[136] The researchers therefore concluded that the COMPAS-PTRS "is very predictive of actual recidivism among offenders released from jail, it is particularly accurate in identifying high-risk offenders."[137] But the instrument had poorer predictive validity concerning violent recidivism and failure to appear. For example, twelve-month nonappearance rates varied among 11.7 percent (low risk), 18.0 percent (medium risk), and 17.2 percent (high risk), suggesting that the COMPAS-PTRS is not effective at predicting the risk of failure to appear.[138] And the researchers noted that their analyses were inconclusive regarding whether the instrument demonstrated sufficient predictive validity for arrestees of varying demographic characteristics, especially sex, race/ethnicity, and age.[139]

### THE LAURA AND JOHN ARNOLD FOUNDATION PUBLIC SAFETY ASSESSMENT

In 2013 the Laura and John Arnold Foundation (LJAF) funded research to develop the Public Safety Assessment (PSA) to be used as a pretrial risk assessment tool. Unlike most other APRAIs, the LJAF-PSA is meant to be used anywhere. In other words, it is designed to be a universal instrument to assess pretrial risk—one that is not dependent on where it is used. Since the PSA is a tool developed by academic researchers in partnership with a nonprofit foundation, the LJAF provides the instrument free of charge to any US jurisdiction that adopts it.[140]

The LJAF's research team developed the PSA using data from 746,526 cases from more than three hundred US jurisdictions. It is comprised of nine static items that can be obtained without a client interview: age at current arrest, current violent offense, other pending charges at the time of the current alleged offense, prior misdemeanor conviction, prior felony conviction, prior conviction for a crime of violence, prior failure to appear within a two-year period, prior failure to appear beyond a two-year period, and a prior sentence to a period of incarceration. These nine factors are weighted, and raw scores are then converted to one of six risk levels that predict failure to appear and new criminal activity (general recidivism). The PSA also "flags" people at risk for new violent criminal activity (violent recidivism). Notably, the PSA does not include any dynamic/criminogenic needs variables, nor does it include demographic characteristics such as gender, race/ethnicity, education level, employment status, or history of substance abuse.

By the beginning of 2018 the LJAF-PSA had been adopted in thirty-eight US jurisdictions, including statewide use in Arizona, New Jersey, and Kentucky. But validation data are incredibly difficult to come by. At the time this chapter was researched and written, no final reports for the original validation study were anywhere to be found on the LJAF website. No peer-reviewed validation studies were indexed in *Criminal Justice Abstracts* or any similar research databases. One commentary appearing in the *Federal Sentencing Reporter* authored by the cocreators of the PSA stated that the tool helped judges in Kentucky grant pretrial release to more defendants while reducing the amount of crime committed by people on pretrial release "by up to 15 percent."[141] In addition, they stated that the PSA helped to identify the approximately 8 percent of arrestees at "elevated risk" for committing other violent crime while on pretrial release, as evidenced by the fact that those defendants were rearrested "at a rate 17 times higher than that of other defendants."[142]

In a recent article published in the *Yale Journal of Law & Technology*, law professors Robert Brauneis and Ellen P. Goodman praised the fact that the PSA fully disclosed its algorithms, but criticized the fact that the LJAF had "not revealed how it generated the algorithms, or whether it performed pre- or post-implementation validation tests and, if so, what the outcomes were."[143] The authors attempted to obtain validation data from courts where the PSA was used, but most refused to provide data, citing memoranda of understanding with the LJAF that prohibited disclosure about its PSA programs. Undeterred, Brauneis and Goodman contacted LJAF directly. Representatives from the LJAF responded with much of the same general information that was already on the foundation's website, but added that independent validation studies were being prepared or conducted by at least three external research agencies. The LJAF also disclosed the following:

To date, the preliminary results are encouraging. The most recent data is from Lucas County, Ohio, which encompasses the greater Toledo area. The percentage of pretrial defendants released by the court on their own recognizance, meaning they did not have to post bail, jumped from 14 percent before the county began using PSA to almost 28 percent today. Pretrial crime is down. The percentage of pretrial defendants arrested for other crimes while out on release has been cut in half—from 20 percent before the county began using the PSA to 10 percent today. In addition, the percentage of pretrial defendants arrested for violent crimes while out on release has decreased—from 5 percent before the county began using the PSA to 3 percent today. More defendants are returning to court. The percentage of pretrial defendants who skipped their court date has been reduced—from 41 percent before the county began using the PSA to 29 percent today. Other jurisdictions have reported decreases in the jail population or pretrial detention without reported increases in crime. Mecklenburg County, North Carolina, for instance, saw a 20 percent decrease in the jail population over the first year they were working toward implementation of the PSA.[144]

Clearly, more independent research is needed to establish the validity of the PSA.

After this chapter was initially drafted, the first independent validation study of the PSA was posted on SSRN in May 2018 by researchers affiliated with RTI International and the University of California, San Francisco.[145] That study used a Kentucky data set of more than 164,500 defendants and concluded that the tool "meets standards for criminal justice risk assessments" because there were "small positive correlations" between case outcomes and PSA scores indicating failure to appear ($r = 0.188$) and new criminal activity ($r = 0.171$), but weaker correlations for new violence criminal activity (0.067).[146] All three types of PSA scores resulted in "good" predictive accuracy levels using more sophisticated "area under the curve" analyses, a statistical method for identifying the best threshold for separating positive and negative examples (with receiver operating characteristic [ROC] scores ranging from 0.646 for the failure to appear scale to 0.664 for the new violence criminal activity scale).[147]

Although the researchers did not find significant differences in the PSA's predictive validity by gender, they did find significant differences in the predictive validity of PSA scores by race. Specifically, they determined that failure to appear scores were far more accurate predictors of case outcomes for White defendants (ROC = 0.655) than for Black defendants (ROC = 0.612), while other scales did not reveal statistically significant differences by race.[148] The RTI researchers also found "intercept differences" in all three PSA scales by race. "These findings suggest that an average PSA score of $X$ is not associated with an average" pretrial failure rate for failing to appear, new criminal activity, and new violent criminal activity rates for Black and White defendants.[149] Perhaps even more troubling is that the researchers found extreme "slope differences" by race on the failure to appear scale, meaning that the same score on that PSA scale does not mean the same thing for White and Black defendants. Of course these results come from a single state, so they may not be generalizable to other jurisdictions. Moreover, because the paper was self-posted on SSRN by the researchers who authored it, the results were not subjected to peer review as of the time this book went to press. With those caveats in mind, the results of this first independent validation study of the PSA suggest that more independent research is needed to validate and properly norm the PSA for people of different racial backgrounds. Indeed, these racial differences in APRAI scores are one of several challenges associated with using pretrial risk assessment instruments. In the next part of this chapter we explore that concern and others in greater detail.

## THE CHALLENGES ASSOCIATED WITH PRETRIAL RISK ASSESSMENTS

The widespread adoption and implementation of APRAIs pose numerous challenges. First and foremost, APRAIs need to target pretrial risks associated with the two relevant outcomes of pretrial release, namely whether the defendant appears or fails to appear at subsequent court proceedings and whether the defendant commits another crime while on pretrial release. Two points deserve reiteration. First, the risks of failing to appear differ markedly for defendants who pose either a risk of flight from the jurisdiction or a risk of purposeful evasion of court appearance while remaining within a local jurisdiction, and those who fail to appear due to inadvertence, illness, emergencies, or logistical challenges.[150] Second, many risk assessment instruments were designed to predict recidivism and general criminogenic factors and therefore are ill-suited to the prediction of pretrial outcomes failures. But even instruments that were designed specifically to predict pretrial risks need to be valid and reliable instruments. Moreover, such tools need to be administered and scored by properly trained justice system officials and then appropriately interpreted and used by judicial actors. Certainly the costs of adopting proprietary APRAIs, as well as the expense associated with providing adequate training for the use of any APRAI, might prevent some jurisdictions from adopting such instruments. But monetary concerns aside, there are still several important issues that need to be considered even though the use of "objective" APRAIs is largely considered to be a "best practice."

### Methodological Shortcomings

As this chapter should make clear, APRAIs are often validated within the context of two pretrial risk outcomes: the risk of failing to appear and the risk of reoffending while on pretrial release. But neither type of pretrial outcome is universally defined and measured.

First, many US jurisdictions differ not only in how they define failure to appear, but also in how they measure nonappearance rates. Nearly four out of five jurisdictions calculate failure to appear rates only for defendants granted pretrial release and placed under the supervision of pretrial services departments or agencies, whereas only 10 percent calculate nonappearance rates for all defendants.[151] Jurisdictions also differ on the circumstances under which failure to appear rates are formally recorded. Some immediately enter that status into their data systems upon any nonappearance, whereas nearly two-thirds of jurisdictions make an effort to contact the defendant or the defendant's family and grant the person on pretrial release a second chance to appear before recording the failure and issuing a bench warrant.[152]

Second, the same types of variation in definitions and practices also exist for determinations of reoffending while on pretrial release. Fewer than 40 percent of all jurisdictions even calculate the rate of reoffending by defendants on pretrial release, and of those that do, 87 percent only include defendants placed under the supervision of pretrial services departments or agencies.[153] Moreover, even when reoffending rates are calculated, what "counts" varies across jurisdictions. Some jurisdictions use rearrests as a measure of reoffending even though rearrests are a poor measure for that purpose.[154] Further, some jurisdictions include all rearrests, while others exclude traffic or misdemeanor arrests.[155]

Third, many PSAs are understaffed and have limited financial resources.[156] As a result, their information systems tend to be "underdeveloped."[157] Some PSAs rely on manual information systems, and even those that use automated systems may not be integrated with data systems of other criminal justice agencies.[158] As a result, there are significant data quality limitations in some jurisdictions, especially with regard to data cleaning and analysis.[159] Even the Bureau of Justice Statistics has warned against using data from the national State Court Processing Statistics project for assessing the effectiveness of particular programs, on account of data limitations.[160]

Fourth, the samples on which APRAIs are validated differ significantly. Samples might include "defendants who have never been detained, those who have never been released, those who have been detained at arraignment and subsequently released prior to disposition, or those released at arraignment and subsequently detained prior to disposition."[161] The numbers of arrestees drawn from different groups might be too small to achieve robust statistical power—a problem that is exacerbated by the low rates of reoffending during the relatively short period of time during which many offenders are on pretrial release. Researcher Cynthia A. Mamalian explained the shortcoming in this manner: "The reality is that low-risk defendants are typically released, high-risk defendants are typically detained without bail, and there is a large group of defendants—low risk, low offense, low release—who remain incarcerated. When we look at failure rates of released defendants and they are low, this is primarily a function of the types of defendants that were released (i.e., low risk). In testing risk assessment instruments, we are usually studying whatever sample of defendants has been released. Our population of study is typically the lowest risk group."[162] In addition, because some validation studies for APRAIs were performed on small samples, there are concerns about the representativeness of the construction sample.[163]

The problem of measuring reoffending rates is complicated even further by so-called suppression effects. When arrestees are released and placed under the supervision of PSAs, their activities are often monitored. The conditions of pretrial release mitigate the risk of reoffending, yet APRAIs do not measure the risk of pretrial failure as offset by the suppression effects of pretrial supervision. Rather, APRAIs are designed to measure the "unsuppressed risk" of an aggregate class of people whose characteristics align with those of a particular defendant. In other words, the evaluation of various APRAIs frequently suffers from the very real confounding variable that large swaths of the research sample "may be contaminated with some combination of complete or partial suppression."[164]

Fifth, the aforementioned definitional and measurement concerns aside, the predictive validity of many APRAIs has not yet been adequately evaluated. A meta-analysis published in 2017 reported that of sixteen published and unpublished validation studies of APRAIs, more than two-thirds were in the form of reports, whereas only four were published in peer-reviewed journals.[165] Most of these studies did not include descriptive statistics about the validation samples. When the data from the studies that provided sufficient data for meta-analysis were reanalyzed in 2017, the researchers found that the "r-value for the random effects model is 0.23. This effect size falls between the cutoffs for small- and medium-effect sizes ... or in the 'fair' range."[166] They cautioned, however, that because so much of the original validation research lacked sufficient methodological rigor, no "concrete conclusions" could be drawn.[167]

Sixth, the reliability of APRAIs may be even more questionable than their validity. Few validation studies provide information to "ensure reliability in scoring across staff" beyond implementation descriptions. Indeed, the authors of the previously mentioned 2017 meta-analysis on the predictive validity of APRAIs noted that when reviewing the individual validation studies, not one "reported inter-rater agreement rates across staff who score the instrument, making it unclear if inter-rater agreement was being evaluated at all."[168]

### The Limits of "Statistical Justice"

Regardless of whether a risk assessment instrument is used for pretrial, sentencing, or correctional purposes, all actuarial tools for estimating the potential for someone to commit an act of violence involve some risk of prediction error. Like any type of empirical analysis, risk assessment instruments are capable of producing two types of mistakes. Type I error is associated with a *false positive*, the prediction of risk when there isn't any, whereas Type II error involves a *false negative*, the prediction of no risk when the risk of violence is actually present.

Given the risks associated with making either a Type I or Type II error, scholars have cautioned against *statistical justice*—the overreliance on statistically normed instruments—because such tools rely on how closely a particular defendant or offender matches an actuarial profile, rather than on other factors relevant to the individual and the case.[169] Indeed, "[c]ategorizing individuals as risky in comparison with an aggregate group contradicts the jurisprudential value of individualism"— especially because many risk assessment instruments were developed and normed on a population of offenders instead of on the general population.[170]

Many justice practitioners also misinterpret probability scores. Even if the predictive validity and reliability of an APRAI were well established (and to be clear, that is not yet the case), the end users of risk scores would still need to interpret those scores correctly. "Instead of understanding that an individual with a high risk score *shares character-istics* with an aggregate group of high-risk offenders, practitioners are likely to perceive the individual *as* a high-risk offender."[171] That misunderstanding can be especially problematic because, as the next section explores, the label "high risk" is fraught with ambiguity.

### Overestimation of Risk

What does it mean when someone is classified as being "high risk?" Clearly there are qualitative differences in the risks associated with different types of failures to appear and the risks associated with reoffending—especially for violent crimes. But do judges concern themselves with making fine distinctions in the types of risk? Research suggests the answer to this question is "no." In states where judges are supposed to consider both a defendant's flight risk and whether the defendant is dangerous (and thereby poses a high risk of violent reoffending if granted pretrial release), it appears that judges focus on the latter factor of dangerousness "almost to the exclusion of flight risk."[172] And even in the small minority of states where judges are not supposed to consider the dangerousness of an arrestee, they nonetheless seem to do so anyway.[173]

#### INFERRING RISK OF DANGEROUSNESS FROM THE SERIOUSNESS OF THE CURRENT CHARGE

A number of studies conducted from the 1950s through the early 2010s collectively establish that judges overwhelmingly make pretrial release decisions based on the seriousness of the present charge.[174] In other words, judges make a prediction about a person's dangerousness based on their perceptions of the seriousness of the crime for which the defendant is currently charged at the time of the bail determination. Scholars have criticized this approach because being charged with one crime, even a serious one, is not necessarily predictive of future conduct.[175]

The overall pretrial release reoffending rate for all types of crimes committed by misdemeanor and felony defendants combined is quite low—generally between 8 and 16 percent, although some studies from the 1980s reported rearrest rates as high as 20 percent.[176] Importantly, the overall rearrest rate drops to between 2 to 6 percent for those rearrested for a violent offense.[177] But some of these studies might not be generalizable because they relied on data from a single jurisdiction, used small sample sizes, or suffered from other methodological limitations. To address these shortcomings, law professor Shima Baradaran and economist Frank L. McIntyre analyzed a nationally representative sample of more than 116,000 cases drawn from the seventy-five largest counties in the United States between 1990 and 2006. In their comprehensive study published in 2012, they found that for nearly every type of crime charged, the likelihood of rearrest for crimes of violence while defendants were on pretrial release ranged between 1 and 3 percent.[178] There were three exceptions to this finding, each relating to a particular violent criminal charge. Specifically, murder, robbery, and rape defendants had pretrial release violent crime rearrest rates of 6.4 percent, 5.8 percent, and 3.2 percent, respectively.[179] The relatively high rearrest rate for defendants facing murder charges affirms "much of what has historically existed as a presumption against release of murder defendants."[180]

Although judges primarily use the perceived seriousness of the current charge as a proxy for dangerousness in terms of reoffending, it should also be noted that using this criterion for assessing the pretrial risk of failing to appear is similarly misplaced. Empirical studies repeatedly have "demonstrated that those charged with more serious crimes were actually more likely to appear in court."[181] For example, a 2009 study conducted in New York City replicated Caleb Foote's findings from 1954 (see chapter 1) insofar as the likelihood of pretrial failure was much lower for defendants charged with felonies, whereas both failure to appear and criminal reoffending while on pretrial release were overwhelmingly associated with defendants charged with misdemeanor offenses.[182]

### INFERRING RISK OF DANGEROUSNESS FROM PRIOR CONDUCT

Given how few people reoffend while on pretrial release, it should be self-evident that not all defendants predicted to be "high risk" are actually dangerous. As criminologists Franklin Zimright and Gordon Hawkins opined, the concept of *dangerousness* is "peculiarly seductive" because it embodies "a personal characteristic of the offender . . . [and] if dangerousness is viewed as a personal trait, this leads inevitably to the confusion of dangerousness and desert when both are animating purposes of punishment."[183]

Clearly, judicial determinations of "just desert" are part and parcel of sentencing, but as explained in chapter 1, about half of US jurisdictions retain remnants of the Statute of Westminster, insofar as judicial officers are permitted to consider both the defendant's character and reputation as well as the likelihood of conviction, based on the totality of the circumstances known at the time of a bail determination, when making pretrial release or detention decisions.[184] And roughly thirty-seven states permit judges to consider an arrestee's prior conduct as part of the bail decision-making process, which may include the defendant's prior convictions or even the defendant's full criminal record.[185]

Presumably the logic of using a defendant's prior record stems from the oft-cited behavioral scientific maxim that the best predictor of future conduct is past conduct.[186] But that saying is misleading because prior behavior predicts future behavior only under certain conditions.[187] A 2013 article in *Psychology Today* qualified the "gross oversimplification" of predicting future behavior from prior behavior by explaining that the rule of thumb works best for short-time intervals concerning "high-frequency, habitual behaviors" that have not been "extinguished by corrective or negative feedback."[188] Moreover, the actor must have remained "essentially unchanged" and then be faced with a situation that is "essentially the same as the past situation that activated the behavior."[189] Certainly being arrested and subjected to pretrial release under supervised conditions undercuts a number of these preconditions for the maxim to hold true, at least for the majority of defendants with pending criminal charges.

Researchers have long argued about whether past conduct is a valid predictor of future criminal offending.[190] Baradaran and McIntyre's 2012 study found that past crime was indeed a predictor of future crime, but not necessarily while a defendant was on pretrial release. Specifically, when using the number of prior criminal convictions to predict rearrest for a crime of violence while on pretrial release, they found that

> even those with many prior convictions are still unlikely to be rearrested for a new violent crime while on release.... About 1.5% of those with no prior record were rearrested, a number that rose only slightly for defendants with one conviction. On the other end of the spectrum, about 2.5% of those with four or more prior convictions were rearrested. Thus, the rearrest rate was not quite twice as high for those with many convictions as for those with none. A single past conviction, though, hardly appears to predict any increased dangerousness. Repeat offenders—those who have four prior convictions—were only arrested for pretrial violent crime in about 1 in 30 instances.[191]

Baradaran and McIntyre reported nearly identical findings if the number of prior arrests were used to predict reoffending while on pretrial release.[192]

## THE PSYCHOLOGY AND POLITICS OF RISK

Pretrial services personnel and judicial officials alike undoubtedly strive to balance both the real and perceived risks associated with pretrial failure. But given that the real risks associated with pretrial failure are so low, the perceived risks associated with pretrial release may be what drive many judges to order defendants they perceive as dangerous into pretrial detention.

Research demonstrates that judges, like other people, often rely on *heuristics*—intuitive, subconscious shorthands that allow them to make quick and efficient decisions that are often subject to unconscious biases.[193] Importantly, these unconscious biases are particularly likely to manifest themselves in bail hearings because the facts are often in dispute and judges exercise broad amounts of discretion.[194] This in turn can lead judges to overestimate both types of pretrial risk, but most especially the risk of violent reoffending, because they easily call to mind "worst-case scenarios" of people on pretrial release "who commit horrific and highly-publicized acts of violence."[195] By neglecting the very low probability of such an event occurring and focusing instead, even if unconsciously, on the potential harm associated with a worst-case scenario, "judges may overestimate the likelihood that a defendant on pretrial release will commit a violent crime."[196]

But the overestimation of risk is not limited to the operation of psychological heuristics in the subconscious mind. Public fear of crime can predispose judges to err on the side of caution rather than release someone who may be potentially dangerous. Indeed, fear of releasing a defendant who will go on to commit a serious offense while on pretrial release is among judges' "biggest fears."[197] Such a decision often makes headlines that cause headaches for any judge, but such a scenario is particularly precarious for elected judges.[198] Considering that the overwhelming number of state court judges are either elected or subject to retention votes, the safer route for most judicial officers is to detain a potentially dangerous defendant because such a decision does not engender "negative reputational consequences."[199]

Might it be that pretrial reoffending rates are so low because judges are in fact detaining the highest risk defendants so that they cannot reoffend while awaiting trial? Again, the answer appears to be "no." Baradaran and McIntyre estimated that 25 percent more of the people ordered into pretrial detention could be released while decreasing the level of crime committed by people granted pretrial release.[200]

### Oversupervision

Separate from the overestimation of risk that results in too many defendants being held unnecessarily in pretrial detention, APRAIs can also lead to the oversupervision of defendants who are granted pretrial release. A study of APRAIs in the federal court system published in 2009 revealed a paradox associated with the type of pretrial supervision that is judicially ordered when relying on actuarial risk classifications.[201] The study used data from 565,178 federal criminal cases in all federal districts (other than the District of Columbia) decided over the six-year period between 2001 and 2007, a time when the federal pretrial detention rate rose from 53 to 64 percent of federal criminal defendants.[202] The study attributed 60 percent of this increase to pretrial services personnel classifying greater numbers of defendants as "high risk."[203]

The researchers employed a nine-item APRAI that classified the risk of pretrial release failure (i.e., failure to appear or reoffending while on release) on a five-point scale from low risk to high risk.[204] The nine predictors included "(1) whether there were other charges pending against the defendant at the time of arrest, (2) the number of prior misdemeanor arrests, (3) the number of prior felony arrests, (4) the number of prior failures to appear, (5) whether the defendant was employed at the time of the arrest, (6) the defendants residency status, (7) whether the defendant suffered from substance abuse problems, (8) the nature of the primary charge, and (9) whether the primary charge was a misdemeanor or a felony."[205] These factors were validated in that as risk classification increased, so did the rate of pretrial detention, suggesting that the APRAI's scaled classification system "mimic[ed] judicial practice."[206] Similarly, when defendants were released, failure rates increased in tandem with risk level. But one of the study's more curious findings suggests that simply classifying offenders according to actuarial risk is insufficient. Rather, the importance of judicial decisions concerning pre-trial release and supervision cannot be overstated. Here's why.

Roughly three-quarters of the federal defendants granted pretrial release were required to participate in at least one "alternative to detention" supervision condition, such as drug testing, drug treatment, location monitoring, or release under the supervision of a third-party custodian.[207] As would be expected, these programs successfully kept moderate- to high-risk defendants (levels 3 to 4) from experiencing pretrial failure compared to those who were similarly ranked in terms of risk level but were not placed under any supervision condition. Not surprisingly, given what we know about oversupervision of people on probation or parole, lower-risk defendants (levels 1 and 2) experienced higher levels of pretrial failure when placed under supervision conditions than other lower-risk defendants who were not placed under any special release conditions.[208] In other words, too many people with lower levels of risk experienced oversupervision. The researchers therefore recommended that with the exception of defendants with mental health treatment needs, lower-risk defendants should be released without special supervision conditions. Conversely, many moderate- to high-risk defendants do not necessarily need to be held in pretrial detention; rather, many such defendants could benefit from supervision conditions tailored to address their specific risks of pretrial failure.[209] Put differently, pretrial release should utilize the least restrictive conditions possible.[210]

### Are Risk Assessment Instruments Biased?

The final and perhaps most important concern surrounding risk assessment instruments is whether they are biased. In 2017 the National Institute of Corrections and the Community Corrections Collaborative Network issued a report entitled *Myths & Facts: Using Risk and Needs Assessments to Enhance Outcomes and Reduce Disparities in the Criminal Justice System.*[211] The report listed the following statement as a myth: "Use of standardized risk and need assessments increases racial and ethnic disparities within the criminal justice system."[212] To counter this statement, the report cited several studies of general ARAIs that concluded the predictive accuracy of most risk assessment instruments does not vary on the basis of race or ethnicity.[213] This assertion requires close examination.

## THE PROPUBLICA ARTICLE

In 2006 a study on a relatively small convenience sample of 532 male inmates in a work-release program reported significant racial and ethnic disparities between LSI-R scores and subsequent recidivism.[214] Specifically, that study found that Blacks were significantly overclassified as high risk (42.7 percent) compared to Whites (27.7 percent).[215] A larger study in 2014 also examined racial differences in the predictive validity of LSI-R scores and reported that in the United States, much more so than in Canada, "ethnic minorities have higher [risk] scores than nonminorities."[216] In light of studies reporting racial disparities in risk assessment scores, US attorney general Eric Holder called for more research on whether risk assessment instruments were potentially biased.[217] In response to his calls for research, ProPublica, an independent, nonprofit, nonpartisan investigative journalism consortium, conducted its own investigation.

A team of investigators published an article in 2016 on the ProPublica website, "Machine Bias: There's Software Used Across the Country to Predict Future Criminals and It's Biased Against Blacks."[218] They obtained risk scores on the COMPAS assigned to seven thousand defendants in Broward County, Florida, and compared those scores to rearrest records over a two-year period. ProPublica provocatively summarized its findings as follows:

> The [risk] score proved remarkably unreliable in forecasting violent crime: Only 20 percent of the people predicted to commit violent crimes actually went on to do so.
>
> When a full range of crimes were taken into account—including misdemeanors such as driving with an expired license—the algorithm was some-

what more accurate than a coin flip. Of those deemed likely to re-offend, 61 percent were arrested for any subsequent crimes within two years.[219]

In addition to the lack of predictive validity of the risk scores overall, the researchers found that the scores indicated false positives for Black defendants being at "high risk" (45 percent) for reoffending at nearly twice the rate of White defendants (23 percent); conversely, White reoffenders were incorrectly classified as "low risk" 70 percent more often than Black reoffenders (48 percent vs. 28 percent).[220] Moreover, even when controlling for prior criminal history, sex, and age, Black offenders' COMPAS scores were 77 percent more likely to classify them at high risk for violent reoffending than White offenders. Stated differently, the ProPublica study claimed that the COMPAS instrument has racially disparate rates of both Type I (false positive) and Type II (false negative) errors.

ProPublica's results have been criticized by both the Northpointe Corporation, which owns the COMPAS, and academic researchers.[221] The criticisms center primarily on ProPublica's sampling and data analyses. First and foremost, ProPublica used a sample that excluded people on probation or parole, leaving only pretrial defendants in the sample that was statistically analyzed using COMPAS recidivism scores designed to predict reoffending among probationers and paroles— offenders under correctional supervision after conviction and sentencing.[222] Second, ProPublica excluded failure to appear arrests as an outcome measure in its study even though failure to appear risk scores are the ones relevant for a sample of pretrial defendants.[223] Third, the ProPublica analyses collapsed medium- and high-risk categories into a single "high-risk" category when calculating false positives and false negatives.[224] Fourth, the ProPublica study did not use "well-established and accepted standards" to test for bias in the COMPAS.[225] When other researchers reanalyzed the ProPublica data in ways that were designed to correct for these shortcomings, they "failed to find evidence of predictive bias by race in the COMPAS."[226]

## BEYOND THE PROPUBLICA STUDY

In 2010 psychologist Jay Singh and forensic psychiatrist Seena Fazel published a review of eight different meta-analyses that had examined the predictive validity of various risk assessment instruments across races and ethnicities. Importantly, these meta-analyses are limited to general ARAIs, not to APRAIs that were designed and validated for use during pretrial processes.[227] Nonetheless, their findings may be instructive. Singh and Fazel reported that five meta-analyses concluded there was no evidence of racial bias in the prediction of risk, although several of these focused on the PCL-R rather than on true ARAIs.[228] Three studies, however, reported significantly higher rates of predictive validity for Whites than Blacks, Hispanics, or Native Americans on the PCL-R and ARAIs such as the LSI-R and the SFS, although these studies did not employ the types of statistical procedures that would be needed to contextualize their findings.[229]

What is to be made of these confusing findings? Although as previously mentioned the National Institute for Corrections concluded that racial bias in risk assessment is largely a myth, it did offer two caveats: "First, any risk and need assessment should still be validated on the target population to ensure that it predicts accurately across groups and that it does not contribute to disparities in criminal justice decision-making. The application of a risk and need assessment, even with good intentions, can have adverse effects on minority groups if this step is ignored or overlooked.... Second, while risk and need assessments may not be inherently biased, their results reflect the reality that bias exists within the criminal justice system."[230]

With regard to the first point, it is clear that many ARAIs have been subjected to numerous, peer-reviewed validation studies. But as the third section of this chapter should make clear, the same cannot be said of APRAIs—those designed for pretrial use. It therefore remains an open question whether APRAIs are comparable to their general violence risk assessment counterparts in terms of their predictive validity across racial, ethnic, and gender lines.[231]

With regard to the second point, there is little doubt that both general and pretrial risk assessment instruments rely on static risk factors that are statistically associated with race and ethnicity. For example, many ARAIs incorporate socioeconomic variables such as age, sex, marital status, education level, employment history, and financial status. These variables are included because they are statistically correlated with reoffending by other offenders in the past who share similar characteristics:

> For example, the weight a risk instrument assigns to unemployment would be loosely based on the strength of the association between unemployment and average recidivism rates in some past sample, holding other measured variables constant.
>
> When the government instructs judges to consider risk scores based on factors like these, it is explicitly endorsing sentencing discrimination based on factors the defendant cannot control. It is embracing a system that is bound to worsen the intersectional racial, class, and gender disparities that already pervade our criminal justice system. The risk assessment instruments commonly in use do not consider race.... But the socioeconomic, family, and neighborhood-related factors that the instruments do consider are highly race-correlated.[232]

Put differently, when judges make decisions about pretrial detention or postconviction incarceration using ARAIs, they do so using variables that are proxies for poverty. And because poverty disproportionately affects racial and ethnic minorities, these factors significantly correlate with both race and ethnicity.[233] Thus, ARAIs reproduce socioeconomic marginalization in the criminal justice system as it exists in society by relying on social factors that appear to be race-neutral even though they are not.[234] ARAIs thereby yield risk scores that classify people as dangerous "because of who they are, not what they have done."[235] As a result, some legal scholars argue that risk assessments that include socioeconomic and demographic variables violate the constitutional guarantees of due process and equal protection.[236] Although the US Supreme Court "has generally rejected proxy arguments absent proof of discriminatory intent," the possibility that poverty proxies nonetheless may be held to violate the US Constitution technically remains an open question.[237]

Criminal history serves as another example of how ARAIs perpetuate systemic discrimination. Nearly all risk assessment instruments—both general and pretrial tools—include items related to a defendant's prior criminal history. As with some of the aforementioned social factors on ARAIs, criminal history is yet another seemingly race-neutral variable that is statistically correlated with race.[238] Indeed, law professor Bernard Harcourt has persuasively argued that the inclusion of criminal history in ARAIs "produces a 'ratchet effect'" by oversampling from minority populations who are already disproportionately represented in the criminal justice system.[239] But does that correlation mean that criminal history is being used unconstitutionally as a "proxy" for race, as Harcourt, asserts?[240] At least one recent study suggests the answer is "no," but the matter is far from clear-cut.

Psychologist Jennifer Skeem and criminologist Christopher T. Lowenkamp tested the federal Post Conviction Risk Assessment (PCRA) on a sample of more than thirty-five thousand prisoners. They found that "Black offenders tend to obtain higher scores on the PCRA than do White offenders," which can lead to a disparate racial impact for "some applications" of the PCRA.[241] Moreover, they attributed nearly two-thirds of the racial differences to "criminal history—which strongly predicts recidivism for both groups."[242] Because criminal history plays such an important role in sentencing, this finding helps to explain racial disparities in incarceration rates.[243] Nonetheless, the researchers concluded that "criminal history is *not* a proxy for race" because "criminal history partially mediates the weak relationship between race and a future violent arrest."[244] They based this conclusion on the fact that their data analyses found that criminal history equally predicts a future arrest for a violent offense for Blacks and Whites and therefore such rearrests are not an artifact of overpolicing in areas with higher concentrations of racial minorities.[245] Even if that were true, however, criminal history also reflects biased prosecutorial practices.[246] In addition, and notwithstanding issues concerning the constitutionality of using variables as a proxy for race, the legal dimensions of risk assessment are not the be-all and end-all of the debate. There are serious moral and public policy questions about using tools that rely on variables so closely correlated with race and ethnicity.

Those who advocate for the use of ARAIs and APRAIs rarely dispute that sociodemographic biases underlie key prediction variables. Rather, they argue that the algorithms used to develop and norm risk scores represent a marked improvement over decision making by criminal justice personnel whose "biases are opaque and unknown."[247] Three statisticians wrote in a *New York Times* commentary when defending the use of APRAIs in the wake of the ProPublica article: "Algorithms are powerful tools for combating the capricious and biased nature of human decisions."[248] They pointed to the fact that harsh judges in New York City criminal courts are two times more likely to impose bail than lenient judges. It is undoubtedly true that some judges are stricter than others. And it is also undoubtedly true that there are some judges whose biases color their decision making in ways that ought not to exist. But such arguments do not change the notion that seemingly "objective" risk assessment variables simply are not objective, and therefore risk scores themselves contribute to unjustified assumptions about neutral decision making when in fact the scores mask the same biases that exist in the "black box" of some judges' minds.[249]

Science and technology may yet make it possible to develop more accurate prediction tools than the current generation of checklist-style APRAIs. Indeed, "a more advanced methodology [is] on the horizon: forecasting through machine-learning technologies."[250] A team of economists from Cornell University, Stanford University, the University of Chicago, and Harvard University analyzed more than 758,000 pretrial releasees in New York City and concluded that properly designed algorithms that utilize machine learning—a more powerful and complex tool for prediction than current APRAIs—"can be a force for racial equality."[251] Specifically, they devised their own machine-learning algorithms using different econometric strategies and determined that both violent and property crime rates could be reduced by "up to 24.7% with no change in jailing rates" and that the rate of pretrial detention could be reduced by "up to 41.9% with no increase in crime rates."[252] Moreover, "these gains can be achieved while simultaneously reducing racial disparities."[253] Such desirable outcomes may be a function of the fact that evolving algorithms that utilize machine learning avoid racially biased prediction errors that judges may make as a function of racial animus, racial stereotypes, or unconscious implicit biases—concerns that appear to be magnified when inexperienced or part-time judicial officers make pretrial release determinations.[254] Then again, the complexities of algorithms developed using machine learning present even more problems with transparency than the often opaque algorithms employed by current APRAIs.

Moreover, there are reasons to doubt whether even the most advanced machine-learning technologies can make predictions of future risk that are not tied to structural inequalities of the past. Law professor Sandra Mayson summarized this concern as "bias in, bias out" (a modification of the computer science idiom "garbage in, garbage out").[255] "If the thing that we undertake to predict—say arrest—happened more frequently to black people than white in the past data, a predictive analysis will project it more frequently for black people than white in the future. The predicted event, called the target variable, is thus the key to racial disparity in prediction."[256] Thus, there are reasons to question whether valid, reliable, and transparent risk assessment tools can be developed to promote public safety while reducing social inequalities.

## CONCLUSION

Are risk assessment instruments fair? The answer appears to depend on one's conceptualization of fairness. Krishna Gummadi, director of the Networked Systems Research Group at the Max Planck Institute for

Software Systems in Saarbrücken, Germany, explained that the Pro-Publica investigators and both Northpointe and the academic researchers who challenged the ProPublica findings are all "correct" because they use different measures of fairness. Indeed, statistician Richard A. Berk and colleagues argued that there are least six different types of fairness embedded in different risk assessment strategies, some of which are incompatible with others and with the notion of predictive accuracy.[257]

At one end of the spectrum, algorithms might be optimized to maximize the true positives and thereby serve public safety goals by identifying "as many people as possible who are at high risk of committing another crime."[258] The result of such an algorithm, however, would be a higher number of false positives than would be identified if the algorithm were optimized to minimize the number of people who might falsely be identified as presenting a risk of public safety. But a system designed to minimize false positives could result in more defendants being granted pretrial release who ought to be detained. As a different study that reanalyzed the Broward County data concluded, optimizing for public safety can produce "stark racial disparities," whereas satisfying predictive parity across groups would mean "releasing more high-risk defendants, adversely affecting public safety."[259] Which is more "fair"?

Beyond abstract questions of fairness in terms of optimizing to reduce Type I or Type II error, even risk assessment instruments that have been independently validated nonetheless incorporate biases. There is no such thing as a bias-free actuarial risk assessment, because all of them use algorithms to make predictions using aggregate statistics.[260] The individual data points underlying such group statistics undoubtedly reflect the biases of criminal justice actors—socioeconomic, racial, ethnic, sex, and otherwise—that already account for disparities in the criminal justice system.[261] The *Harvard Law Review* succinctly summarized these concerns as follows: "Risk assessments depend upon criminal justice data that is neither neutral nor objective. American criminal justice has been shaped by our country's legacy of slavery and racial discrimination, by decades of mass incarceration, by preventative polic-ing and profiling that targets minority communities, by a gulf between those who vote on criminal justice and those who are affected by it, and by the explicit and implicit biases of people working in the system."[262]

It is also important to keep in mind that some risk scores depend on scoring by pretrial services personnel. Those evaluators bring their own biases—both implicit and overt—to the assessment process, including moral judgments and individualized perceptions concerning a particular defendant's risk for factors that involve some discretionary decision making.[263]

Risk assessment scores also need to be interpreted. Pretrial services agency personnel and judicial officers alike need to be properly trained concerning how to interpret APRAI scores. But that does not always occur; indeed, it may not even occur often.[264] Criminologist Mona Danner and her colleagues conducted a study to determine whether training and implementation guidelines increased the correct use of the VPRAI-R.[265] They found that when pretrial services officers received training on the instrument (including the Praxis supervision matrix), they were 2.3 times more likely to recommend that defendants be released than those who were not trained on the Praxis component of the instrument.[266] This led to an increase in pretrial release because judges in Virginia were more likely to follow pretrial services officials' recommen-dations than they were to deviate from them. Unfortunately, though, the guidelines included in VPRAI-R and the associated training are not always included with pretrial risk assessment instruments, which in turn can decrease the overall effectiveness of even a well-validated tool.[267] In addition, the Virginia judges in that study may be quite different from those in other jurisdictions. The *Chicago Sun Times* reported, for example, that judges in Cook County, Illinois, "depart from risk assessment recom-mendations 85% of the time."[268] And law professor Megan Stevenson similarly found a 60 percent gap between the percentage of arrestees granted nonmonetary pretrial release (29 percent) and those recom-mended for such release using APRAI risk scores (90 percent).[269]

In sum, it is clear that ARAIs and APRAIs alike demonstrate predictive power based on aggregate data, but they do not predict the future behavior of any particular defendant. Nonetheless, their actuarial identification of people who share characteristics with other "high-risk" or "low-risk" defendants is clearly better than chance—which is really all *statistical significance* means. But as law professor Sonja Starr explained, chance is not the outcome to which risk assessments should be compared.[270] Rather, the proper comparison point is how risk assessments perform when compared to individualized determinations of risk that judges have made for time immemorial without the assistance of risk scores, which, as previously explained, are often racially biased. Professor Starr explained that very little research has ever conducted such comparisons, and the handful of studies that have done so are seriously methodologically flawed.[271] For example, Professor Starr critiqued a study of the federal pretrial risk assessment instrument that evaluated pretrial officers' assessments of "a single fictitious case" that had "no actual case outcomes with which to measure 'accuracy.'"[272] Even advocates of ARAIs admit that they "have not found a single credible study in which empirical comparisons are actually made."[273] Surely more research is needed to discern which APRAIs are both valid and reliable. Similarly, we need more empirical research on whether, and to what extent, particular risk assessment algorithms can increase public safety while mitigating, rather than perpetuating, racial, ethnic, and socioeconomic disparities.[274] Algorithms honed by machine learning may help to actualize such a goal one day. For now, however, it seems clear that current checklist-style APRAIs fall short of this goal, and therefore we believe the rush to implement them in pretrial decision making is premature—especially in light of the lack of transparency attendant on most of the checklist-style APRAIs currently available. Still, we respectfully disagree with those who suggest abandoning actuarial risk assessments altogether, because doing so does nothing to combat the underlying racial, ethnic, and socioeconomic disparities that exist in the criminal justice system.[275]

But even if we get to a point at which we have great confidence in the ability of an instrument to predict pretrial risk accurately while simultaneously reducing racial, ethnic, and socioeconomic inequalities, the tools themselves cannot be used mechanistically. Rather, their roles must be limited to providing data that are considered as only once piece of the puzzle for reforming pretrial decision-making processes. As the editors of the *Harvard Law Review* eloquently stated, "Independent of risk assessment's limitations, errors, and biases, safeguards are needed to prevent manipulation of these tools toward carceral and unequal ends."[276] Put differently, "only humans can perform the critical function of making sure that, as our social relations become ever more automated, domination and discrimination aren't built invisibly into their code."[277]

# CHAPTER FOUR

# The Impact of Pretrial Detention

## INTRODUCTION

Of the estimated three million people in pretrial detention around the world on any given day, almost half a million are in the United States, and that number has been growing.[1] Between 2000 and 2015 the growth in the number of jail inmates detained pretrial—meaning *before* being convicted of the offenses for which they were charged—accounted for 95 percent of the growth in the overall jail population.[2] Across the United States, approximately one-third of all criminal defendants are detained pretrial, resulting in the remarkable fact that 65.1 percent of jail inmates are incarcerated awaiting trial, with the remaining 35 percent serving sentences of incarceration following criminal convictions.[3] Yet only around 10 percent of defendants enduring pretrial detention are denied pretrial release and ordered into preventative detention for public safety reasons.[4] Nine out of ten defendants in jail awaiting trial are there because they either cannot or choose not to meet the release conditions set in their cases. Most likely they cannot afford to pay the bail that has been set.

A 2015 analysis of defendants in New Orleans found that one-third of all felony defendants remained in jail for the duration of their cases because they couldn't afford to pay the bail that was set. This is not surprising given the low income of people in jail. A 2015 report showed that the median annual income prior to incarceration for people in jail was approximately $15,000.[5] The median bail amount for felony defendants was $10,000, an amount that "the typical detained defendant would need to spend eight months' income to cover."[6] While misdemeanor bail amounts are usually much lower, data from the Federal Reserve reveal that the average American cannot come up with $400 in an emergency without borrowing it or selling something.[7] Indeed, a survey conducted in New Orleans, Louisiana, in 2015 found that two-thirds of respondents "reported that it was 'difficult' or 'very difficult' to raise the money required to post bail."[8]

In some cases, pretrial detention provides benefits to society, primarily by preventing crimes that might be committed by people awaiting trial and ensuring that defendants show up for court appearances. However, as we explain in this chapter, the negative impacts of detention on both defendants and society are huge and appear to outweigh any positive impacts. In addition to depriving individuals of their liberty and subjecting them to harsh conditions of confinement before they are convicted of the crime(s) with which they are charged, pretrial detention negatively impacts case outcomes, increasing both conviction rates and sentence severity and contributing to mass incarceration in the United States. In addition, as the US Supreme Court noted in 1975, "pretrial confinement may imperil the suspect's job, interrupt his source of income, and impair his family relationships."[9] Moreover, the fact that pretrial release is usually obtained by paying a financial bond can impose a significant financial burden on defendants and their families, even if they do manage to avoid detention. Finally, the consequences of pretrial detention fall overwhelmingly on the poor and minorities, exacerbating existing inequalities in the criminal justice system.

## CONSEQUENCES OF CONFINEMENT

The most immediate consequence of pretrial detention is, of course, deprivation of liberty and the associated pains of confinement.[10] Pretrial

detainees can spend from days to years awaiting trial or release. In
Harris County, Texas, for example, which includes the city of Houston, more than half of all misdemeanor defendants spend more than a
week in pretrial detention.[11] In New York City between October 2003
and January 2004, the average defendant spent fifty-one days in detention for a felony and eighteen days for a nonfelony; roughly half of all
defendants in cases in which bail was set were detained until case disposition.[12] Some defendants arrested for minor offenses end up spending longer periods of time in pretrial detention than are authorized
as the maximum possible sentences for the associated crimes in their
cases. An example is what occurred in Atlanta to twenty-four defendants arrested for traffic violations during a single month in 2003: "They
had spent anywhere from three to twelve days in jail without seeing a
lawyer or receiving anything more than a perfunctory court appearance (in a jailhouse courtroom) where they were informed of the
charges, bond amount and, court date. Many were charged with minor
violations that would normally result in only a fine; indeed, nine were
pedestrians, not motorists, charged with such offenses as 'Pedestrian
Obstructing Traffic' or 'Pedestrian in Road' (jaywalking) and 'Pedestrian Soliciting a Ride' (hitchhiking)."[13]

Some defendants spend far longer in detention. For example, as we
describe in more detail later in this chapter, defendants such as Kalief
Browder, Tung Nguyen, and Tyrone Tomlin spent long periods of time
in pretrial detention, only to see the charges against them ultimately
be dismissed. But even those who are eventually convicted of serious
crimes can spend inordinate amounts of time in pretrial detention, typically in facilities that were not designed for the purpose of long-term
confinement. An example is Carlos Montero, who spent almost seven
years awaiting trial on a murder charge before accepting a plea offer
from prosecutors.[14] Similarly, Kharon Davis spent more than ten years
in jail in Alabama before he was convicted of murder.[15]

Lengthy periods of pretrial detention are not limited to the United
States. For example, at the time this chapter was written a defendant

in a murder case in Swaziland had been locked up for more than nine years, unable to afford the $4,070 bail set in his case.[16] Although some defendants in the United States receive sentence credit for the time they spend detained pretrial, that is not always the case.[17] Further, it is important to remember that pretrial detainees typically spend their time in local jails, the quality of which not only varies widely, but which also are typically "more hostile and punitive" than prisons.[18] In addition, pretrial detainees, even those arrested for minor offenses, are usually subject to the same conditions as sentenced inmates, including being subjected to strip searches.[19]

Although the Supreme Court held in *Salerno* that detention is "regulation" and not "punishment," given how many defendants experience jail, it is difficult to see that distinction as anything other than a semantic one.[20] As the Vera Institute of Justice (Vera) reported in 2015 in *Incarceration's Front Door*, "even a brief stay in jail can be destructive to individuals, their families, and entire communities."[21] Jails are often overcrowded, with poor physical and mental health care.[22] For example, Vera reported that "83% of jail inmates with mental illness did not receive mental health care after admission."[23]

Jails also have fewer educational and vocational opportunities than prisons. A 2003 report by the Bureau of Justice Statistics highlighted that just 14.1 percent of jail inmates had participated in an educational program, compared to over 50 percent of state and federal inmates.[24] The same report noted that just 7 percent of jails reported having a vocational training program, compared to 94 percent of federal prisons and 56 percent of state prisons.[25] Many jails have higher death rates than the national average, and the suicide rate in jails is three times the rate in prisons.[26]

Two news stories highlight the high death rate in local jails. First, an investigation of North Carolina jails found that between 2012 and 2016, 151 inmates died in jail or in a hospital shortly after leaving jail. An investigation by the state Department of Health and Human Services found supervision violations in 51 of the deaths; many of those who died suffered from mental illness and/or drug addiction.[27] Second, a 2015 *Houston Chronicle* article about the Harris County, Texas, bail system (the subject of a federal lawsuit discussed in chapter 2) reported that 55 inmates had died in the county jail since 2009 while awaiting trial.[28] One of those inmates was Tung Nguyen, an eighty-three-year-old man, who was charged with aggravated assault for allegedly threatening his wife of sixty years with a knife. His bail was set at $40,000, which Nguyen was unable to make. Nguyen suffered from both mental illness and heart disease and eventually was found incompetent to stand trial. However, he was not released because his defense attorney and the prosecutor could not agree on a placement. He remained in jail for months, with frequent visits to the hospital to treat his pneumonia. After being rushed to the hospital in respiratory distress, he died three and a half months after his initial arrest.

In many jails, inmates are at risk of violence from staff and other inmates. For example, a 2012 report by the Citizen's Commission on Jail Violence in Los Angeles, California, described "a persistent pattern of unreasonable force" against inmates by sheriff's deputies.[29] The commission was convened after the Federal Bureau of Investigation launched an inquiry into numerous reports of violence.[30] Similarly, a 2015 report by the US Department of Justice (DOJ) on the jail on Rikers Island that housed adolescents aged sixteen to eighteen found the following:

> [A]dolescent inmates at Rikers are not adequately protected from harm, including serious physical harm from the rampant use of unnecessary and excessive force by DOC staff. In addition, adolescent inmates are not adequately protected from harm caused by violence inflicted by other inmates, including inmate-on-inmate fights. Indeed, we find that a deep-seated culture of violence is pervasive throughout the adolescent facilities at Rikers, and DOC staff routinely utilize force not as a last resort, but instead as a means to control the adolescent population and punish disorderly or disrespectful behavior. Moreover, DOC relies far too heavily on punitive segregation as a disciplinary measure, placing adolescent inmates—many of whom are mentally ill—in what amounts to solitary confinement at an alarming rate and for excessive periods of time.[31]

Although the report was limited to the adolescent jail, the DOJ noted that the investigation found that similar issues might be present in the other jails in the complex.[32]

Kalief Browder, whose story was introduced in chapter 1, is a particularly harrowing example of an inmate held in that same complex. Initially detained because he could not afford the $3,000 bail set in his case, Browder was ultimately denied bail and spent three years in the Rikers Island jail awaiting trial. During his time there, Browder was reportedly assaulted numerous times, by both officers and inmates, and spent nearly two years in solitary confinement.[33] While in solitary, Browder was unable to attend school; according to his brother, he lost a lot of weight because he was unable to supplement the meager rations he received with snacks bought at the commissary. Almost two years into his detention, he attempted suicide twice, first by hanging, and then, after being returned to solitary confinement just a few days later, by slitting his wrists.[34] Eventually Browder was released after prosecutors dismissed the charges against him, but just six months later, he attempted suicide once more.[35] Six months after that, he succeeded in killing himself.[36]

Although Browder's story is extreme, even those who spend relatively short periods of time in detention can suffer serious consequences. Sandra Bland, whose traffic stop in 2015 made headlines, was unable to post the $500 bail set in her case and three days after her arrest was found dead in her cell, an apparent suicide.[37] In his 2015 article in the *New York Times*, "The Bail Trap," Nick Pinto described the violence experienced by another detainee, Tyrone Tomlin, who was arrested in November 2014 and charged with possession of drug paraphernalia.[38] The item in question was a plastic straw, which Tomlin had obtained from a store to drink a can of soda, which he had just purchased. Although offered a plea deal, which would have required him to serve thirty days in jail, Tomlin declined. He knew that once the straw was tested, "it would show that he was telling the truth. In the meantime, there was no way he was pleading guilty to anything."[39] Although he was granted bail, it was set at $1,500, which Tomlin was unable to pay. As a result he too ended up in Rikers Island, where he was attacked by a group of men after he refused to get off the phone; he was "punched, kicked, and stomped," resulting in "his face [being] monstrously misshapen, his left eye swollen shut."[40] To make matters worse, days *before* this beating the district attorney had received the report showing the results of the testing of the straw, which, as Tomlin had predicted, came back negative. However, it wasn't until two weeks later that this evidence was presented in court and Tomlin was released.[41]

Given the trauma experienced by Bland, Browder, Tomlin, and others, it is not surprising that many defendants will do anything they can to get out of jail as soon as possible. For some, as discussed in chapter 2, this involves borrowing money or hiring a bail bond agent to pay bail. For others, as discussed in the next section, this involves pleading guilty, sometimes to a crime they did not commit, and suffering the consequences of having a criminal conviction.

## IMPACT OF PRETRIAL DETENTION ON CASE OUTCOMES

Scholars have been studying the impact of pretrial detention on case outcomes for more than fifty years and, not surprisingly, have generally found that it affects defendants negatively. In 1963 a study conducted by the then Vera Foundation in New York City found that defendants who were detained pretrial were more likely to be both convicted and sentenced to incarceration.[42] Almost fifty years later, the New York Criminal Justice Agency (NYCJA), which provides pretrial services to the City of New York, in a summary of research it conducted during the 2000s presented similar findings (discussed in more detail throughout this section), concluding that "pretrial detention had an adverse effect on every case outcome that was examined."[43] Controlling for factors such as offense type, charge severity, and criminal history, detained defendants were "more likely to be convicted, less likely to have their charges reduced and more likely to be sentenced to jail or prison" than those released.[44] The most recent studies have been even more rigorous; many were quasi-experimental, taking advantage of natural experiments such as random judge assignment.[45] As described in detail in the following subsections, overall these studies also found significant negative effects on case outcomes for defendants who are detained pretrial.

### Impact on Conviction and Guilty Pleas

In November 2000 Erma Faye Stewart, a thirty-year-old single mother of two, was arrested as part of a drug sweep in Hearne, Texas. The sweep was based solely on the word of a confidential informant.[46] Stewart spent four weeks in jail, unable to pay her bond, which was set at $70,000. Eventually, with no one to look after her children and after her codefendant and cellmate, Regina Kelly, was able to post bail, she pleaded guilty and was released an hour later.[47] As a result of her plea deal, she was sentenced to ten years of probation and $1,800 in fines. Ultimately, in March 2001, it became clear that the informant had lied to the prosecution, and all charges were dropped against Kelly and the other defendants who had gone to trial. Stewart, however, was out of luck; she was unable to withdraw her guilty plea, despite being innocent.[48]

Stewart's experience is not uncommon; numerous studies show that defendants who are assessed money bail and therefore are detained pretrial are more likely to be convicted and more likely to plead guilty than those who obtain release.[49] Three recent rigorous quasi-experimental studies are illustrative. In the first, a study of pretrial processes in Philadelphia, economist and law professor Megan Stevenson examined over 330,000 cases, both felonies and misdemeanors, that originated between 2006 and 2013.[50] She found that being detained pretrial led to a 13 percent increase in the likelihood of conviction, "mostly by increasing the likelihood that defendants, who otherwise would have been acquitted or had their charges dropped, plead guilty."[51] In their study of pretrial detention in Harris County, Texas, Paul Heaton (an economist and law professor) and colleagues examined more than 380,000 misdemeanor cases filed between 2008 and 2013. Accounting for differences such as offense seriousness and criminal history between released and detained defendants, they found that defendants held in pretrial detention were 25 percent more likely to plead guilty than similarly situated defendants who were released pretrial.[52]

Similarly, economist Will Dobbie, along with two law professor colleagues, conducted a study of over 400,000 defendants charged between 2006 and 2014 in Philadelphia County, Pennsylvania, and Miami-Dade County, Florida. They found that defendants released pretrial were 10.8 percent less likely to plead guilty than those who were detained pretrial.[53] The benefits of pretrial release were greater for defendants with no recent criminal history. The authors also found that those released pretrial got better plea deals than those detained pretrial; people released were more likely to be convicted of a lesser charge and were charged with fewer total offenses.[54] Similar results have been found outside of the United States. For example, in a study of 1,800 cases in Toronto in the early 1990s, criminologists Gail Kellough and Scot Wortley found that the odds of pleading guilty were two and a half times greater for detained defendants than for released ones.[55]

These findings are not surprising. Given the deprivation of liberty and the conditions of confinement experienced by pretrial detainees, "detention itself creates enough pressure to increase guilty pleas."[56] And indeed, it may incentivize *early* pleading, as plea bargaining is the quickest way to secure release for defendants who are unable to make bail. Interviews with defendants conducted by Kellough and Wortley support this, although it is important to note that in Canada, judges are not required to take into account time spent in pretrial custody when determining sentence length, so the pressure to plead is heightened. One defendant noted, "I will plead to a lesser charge to get it over with. If I was [sic] out on bail I would fight the charge all the way."[57] Another defendant pointed to "the overcrowding ... not enough beds ... rats and mice.... [E]ventually you will have some run-ins and the only way to avoid it is to plead and get it over with quickly and get transferred."[58]

More recently, criminologists Elsa Euvrard and Chloe Leclerc interviewed twenty-three convicted individuals in Montreal, Canada, about their guilty pleas.[59] They found that for most defendants (nineteen of twenty-three), pretrial detention exerted pressure to plead guilty. Some felt that custody was coercive. For example, one defendant claimed, "I pleaded guilty to something I did not do to get out. If you plead guilty, you get out immediately. Well, I wanted to get out! I was fed up, I wanted to get out."[60] Other defendants characterized the pressure of detention as an inducement rather than coercion. For example, one defendant stated, "When you have an end date, it's better than when you don't and you live in uncertainty."[61] Euvrard and Leclerc argued that being in custody is one of the factors that makes getting a favorable deal more difficult. They cited one defense attorney, who explained, "If someone is detained, we are in a weaker negotiating position."[62] Dobbie and colleagues also highlighted this consequence of pretrial detention, noting that increases in guilty pleas were "driven by changes in a defendant's bargaining position."[63]

Although these qualitative studies of how the conditions in jails pressure pretrial detainees to plead guilty were performed on Canadian samples, the same situation occurs in the United States. A 2017 multicounty study of California pretrial detainees conducted by Human Rights Watch concluded that many pretrial detainees plead guilty not because they have committed any criminal offense, but rather to escape harsh jail conditions:[64]

> Carlos Garcia's case is a classic example of an individual remaining in jail because he cannot afford bail, and entering a guilty plea to get out of jail. Carlos told Human Rights Watch that on September 9, 2010, his parents were attending a meeting of public housing tenants. Carlos stopped by to give his father a set of keys. A Housing Authority police officer stopped him, telling him the meeting was closed to the public. Carlos argued. The argument escalated. According to several witnesses, several officers grabbed Carlos, threw him down, and piled on him, cutting his lip and hurting his back.

The officers arrested Carlos, booked him at the station jail, accused him of "resisting arrest," and set a $10,000 bail according to the schedule. No one in his family had the money to pay. Carlos told Human Rights Watch that he sat in jail in pain from the beating. He said he looked around the cell and recognized people from his neighborhood who might be dangerous to him. So he sat with his back against the wall, staying awake all night.

The next morning, Carlos went to the San Fernando courthouse. He was not sure if there were witnesses that would testify to his innocence, but he knew if he was out, he could talk to people at the meeting and be better placed to defend himself against the charges. He also knew he would have to wait at least 30 days before he could go to trial—30 days of poor food, crowded jail cells, stress from other prisoners, and not taking his father to his dialysis appointments. He would lose his job, and miss taking his daughter to school.

The prosecutor offered him time served. Pick up trash on the side of the freeway for 15 days on his weekends. Take some anger management classes. Pay some money. Three years of probation. Get out of jail. Carlos took the deal.[65]

## Impact on Sentencing

For those who do plead guilty (or the comparatively small group who are convicted at trial), pretrial detention also affects both the likelihood of being sentenced to jail or prison (rather than receiving an alternative sentence such as probation or a fine) and the length of sentence imposed.[66] Most studies that have examined this issue have found that defendants who are detained pretrial have worse outcomes at sentencing than those granted pretrial release. For example, two studies of sentencing decisions in various Florida counties in the 1990s found that defendants who were detained pretrial were between four and ten times more likely to receive an incarceration sentence than those released before trial, and that those detained pretrial tended to receive longer sentences.[67] A study of pretrial detention decisions in New Jersey in 2004 found no relationship between pretrial detention and incarceration, but did find that pretrial detention resulted in longer incarceration sentences.[68] The NYCJA's review of bail research in New York found that the number of days spent in pretrial detention had a statistically significant effect on sentence length, particularly among felony cases.[69]

More recent studies are mixed, although most find a negative impact on sentencing outcomes. Noted pretrial justice researchers Christopher Lowenkamp, Marie VanNostrand, and Alexander Holsinger analyzed more than 153,000 cases from Kentucky that occurred in 2009 and 2010. After using multivariate statistics to control for a range of relevant factors, they reported that pretrial detainees were "4.44 times more likely to be sentenced to jail and 3.32 times more likely to be sentenced to prison" than defendants who were released from pretrial custody.[70] Further, they found that among those sentenced to incarceration, the jail sentence was 2.78 times longer for defendants who were detained for the entire pretrial period, and the prison sentence was 2.36 times longer.

Megan Stevenson found that pretrial detention in Philadelphia led to a 42 percent increase in the length of the incarceration sentence.[71] In addition, she found that defendants who were detained were liable for an additional $129 in nonbail court fees, 42 percent more than released defendants.[72]

Paul Heaton and colleagues similarly found that defendants detained pretrial in Harris County, Texas, were 43 percent more likely to be sentenced to jail.[73] They also reported that for those sentenced to jail, on average, their sentence was nine days longer than and more than twice as long as the sentences of those released pretrial. Further, they found that first-time defendants were more affected, with detention having twice the effect than on those with prior criminal history.[74]

On the other hand, Will Dobbie and colleagues found small differences in incarceration rates and sentence lengths between released and detained defendants, but these differences were not statistically significant. They explained that this is likely because many of the offenses in their sample resulted in minimal prison time, and that detained individuals usually pleaded guilty to time served.[75]

Federal defendants who are detained also face harsher sentences than those who are released on supervision. In a 2014 study, researchers examined federal cases that closed in 2010–2011 and found that pretrial detention both increased the likelihood of receiving a prison sentence and resulted in longer prison sentences.[76] In a 2017 paper, Stephanie Holmes-Didwania, a lawyer and economist, found similar results, showing that pretrial release reduced an individual's sentence length by about 67 percent.[77] She also reported that released defendants were more likely to receive shorter sentences than recommended by the US Sentencing Guidelines.[78]

There are several possible explanations for these case outcomes. First, release allows defendants to behave responsibly, demonstrate good behavior, and build a case for mitigation.[79] As Heaton and colleagues pointed out, these patterns "are consistent with an environment in which released defendants are able to engage in prophylactic measures—maintaining a clean record, engaging in substance abuse treatment or anger management, or providing restitution—that lead to charges being dismissed and encourage more lenient treatment," while those detained "have essentially accumulated credits toward a final sentence of jail as a result of their detention and are therefore more likely to accede to and receive sentences of imprisonment."[80]

Second, because defendants held in pretrial detention spend less time with their attorneys than those who are released, some scholars have suggested that pretrial detention can hinder defendants' ability to contribute to their defense.[81] Even the US Supreme Court has acknowledged that a detained defendant is "hindered in his ability to gather evidence, contact witnesses, or otherwise prepare his defense."[82] It is certainly logistically more difficult for attorneys to meet with clients who are detained, as New York attorney Rebecca Boucher explained in an article she wrote for the website The Marshall Project.[83] Boucher noted that if she wanted to meet her client at the jail, she would have to take an entire day off work, which might mean "neglecting the rest of [her] caseload," and so, like other attorneys, she requested that her client be brought to court when she needed to meet with her. However, because of the difficulties involved in contacting the New York City

Department of Correction, the rules put in place to request a visit, and inefficiencies at the court, this was not as simple as it sounds. She described how after finally arranging for her client to be brought to court, Boucher made it to the visiting room only to find that her client had already gone back to jail.[84]

Finally, defendants who are detained pretrial may fare worse at trial because of how they appear in court in comparison to defendants granted pretrial release, who can appear in court better groomed and well-dressed.[85] The US Supreme Court has long recognized that the manner in which defendants are dressed in court can affect juror perceptions of guilt. In *Estelle v. Williams* (1976), the defendant had been convicted of murder.[86] He appealed on the basis that his trial was impermissibly tainted because he was forced to appear in court wearing the inmate jumpsuit worn by jail inmates in the jurisdiction in question in the case. In reversing his conviction, the Court ruled that it violates due process to compel a defendant "to go to trial in prison or jail clothing because of the possible impairment of the presumption so basic to the adversary system."[87] In addition, the Court noted that there are equal protection concerns as well: "Similarly troubling is the fact that compelling the accused to stand trial in jail garb operates usually against only those who cannot post bail prior to trial. Persons who can secure release are not subjected to this condition. To impose the condition on one category of defendants, over objection, would be repugnant to the concept of equal justice embodied in the Fourteenth Amendment."[88]

Although *Williams* was concerned with the psychological impact of court attire on jurors, the same logic may apply to judges. Indeed, in a classic study from 1980, judges were asked to rate the attractiveness of previous defendants who had appeared before them.[89] The researcher then correlated those assessments with both case outcomes and the severity of punishment, revealing that more attractive defendants received fewer guilty verdicts and more lenient sentences. These cognitive biases might underlie the conventional wisdom among psychologists and lawyers alike that physical appearance and style of dress both impact how judges and jurors alike perceive a criminal defendant.[90] "The clothing defendants wear, the jewelry they display, the way they style their hair, can sometimes mean the difference between doing time and dodging jail."[91] Interestingly, this perception is relied upon by bail bond agents in their efforts to persuade defendants' family and friends to post bail, emphasizing that a defendant "might look 'more guilty' appearing in court in an orange jumpsuit rather than their own clothes."[92]

## IMPACT ON INCOME, EMPLOYMENT, AND FAMILIES

There is little doubt that pretrial detention wreaks havoc with the personal and professional lives of those who are detained. Indeed, the Open Society Foundations highlighted that "around the world, excessive pretrial detention prods people toward poverty. It pushes working class people toward unemployment, uncertainty, and the edge of poverty. It tips those on the edge of privation into poverty and plunges the already poor into even worse destitution. It limits the development of whole communities, wastes human potential, and misdirects State resources."[93]

Tyrone Tomlin would likely agree with this conclusion. As a result of his inability to make bail, he lost three weeks of income.[94] The consequences for Erma Faye Stewart were even more severe. Stewart was profiled in a 2004 report on the PBS news documentary show *Frontline*. That episode described Stewart's situation three years after her guilty plea:

> Three years after she pleaded guilty in order to go home and take care of her children, she is destitute. Because of the plea, she is not eligible for food stamps for herself or federal grant money for education. She can't vote until two years after she completes her 10-year probation. And she has been evicted from her public housing for not paying rent. Her children sleep in various homes and she spends her nights outside the housing project, waiting for the morning when she can go to work as a cook—a job that pays $5.25 an hour. She owes a $1,000 fine, court costs and late probation fees which she

has been pressured to pay. "They see it like, as long as I have a job, I can pay them," says Erma Faye. "I already told them, I'm having a hard time, buying my son medicine. I have to have his medicine for his asthma. They don't really care about that. All they want is, you know, the money."[95]

Erma Faye Stewart was able to retain custody of her children; others are not so lucky. In 2014 Adriana, a victim of domestic violence, was living at a shelter and left her young daughter with a friend while she went to get diapers. When she returned, she was arrested and charged with child endangerment. Despite having no criminal history, her bail was set at $1,500. Unable to pay this amount, Adriana spent two weeks on Rikers Island. She was eventually released, but while she was in jail, her daughter was placed in foster care. Five months after her arrest, she was still fighting to regain custody of her daughter.[96]

Pretrial detention may also negatively affect defendants' income and employment. In their study of cases in Philadelphia and Miami-Dade Counties, Dobbie and colleagues found that initially released defendants have significantly higher employment and formal sector employment than those who were detained pending trial.[97] Released defendants were 11.3 percent more likely to have employment two years after their bail hearing. And three to four years after their hearing, released defendants were 9.4 percent more likely to be employed in the formal labor sector than those who were held in pretrial detention.[98] In addition, released defendants, on average, had annual earnings $948 higher, were more likely to file a tax return, and were more likely to benefit from unemployment insurance or the earned income tax credit. The authors concluded that these long-term negative outcomes can be attributed to the increased likelihood of being convicted among those who are detained pretrial. What this means is that the negative employment consequences of having a criminal conviction, which is more likely if a defendant is detained pretrial, explain these worse employment outcomes.[99]

In addition to the diminished employment prospects suffered by people detained pretrial, pretrial detention may compound existing financial hardships by limiting eligibility for public benefits and child support and by compromising stable housing due to loss of wages and inability to pay rent.[100] Vera reported that jail stays can cause a suspension or termination of public assistance such as food stamps or Medicaid, which in some cases can take years to be reinstated, and highlights "the serious consequences for the large number of people leaving jail who have debt, little to no income from work, and may also have a chronic illness—an end result that is particularly disproportionate when people are accused of non-serious offenses, such as a traffic or ordinance violation."[101]

Even for defendants who are able to obtain pretrial release and their families, there can be financial repercussions. As explained in chapter 2, most defendants obtain release by paying a portion of the bond amount to a bail bond agency; this money, which is nonrefundable, is typically not paid by the defendant themselves, but instead by a family member, and is money that many can ill afford to pay.[102] A 2016 report by the Maryland Office of the Public Defender estimated that between 2011 and 2015, people in that state "were charged more than $256 million in non-refundable corporate bail bond premiums."[103] But bond premiums are not always paid all at once, and payment plans can result in years of interest and debt collection fees, even in cases in which the defendant showed up for all court dates, in which the defendant was acquitted, or in which charges were dropped.[104] And as we discuss next, the financial impacts of the US money bail system fall overwhelmingly on the poor and minorities.

## DISPARATE IMPACT ON RACIAL AND ETHNIC MINORITIES AND THE POOR

Racial and ethnic minorities are overrepresented in US jails. Although national data on the racial and ethnic breakdown of pretrial detainees are unavailable, minorities are overrepresented in the overall jail population. Blacks and Hispanics account for approximately 30 percent of the US population, yet they represent 50 percent of its jail population.[105] Further, as discussed in chapter 2, most studies find that racial and ethnic minorities are significantly more likely to be detained pretrial than White defendants.[106] Thus, the adverse consequences previously described disproportionately impact racial and ethnic minorities.[107] Since most people who are detained pretrial are there because they cannot afford to pay their bail, the negative consequences of pretrial detention fall heaviest on the economically disadvantaged. Given the relationship between race and poverty, many minority defendants, particularly Black men, are doubly disadvantaged.[108] In addition, the predatory practices of commercial bail companies described in chapter 2 "are often concentrated in the poorest communities and are disproportionately paid by Black people."[109] In Maryland, for example, on aggregate Black defendants accounted for more than two-thirds of all charged bail premiums.[110]

Intuitively, it makes sense that because the United States relies so heavily on money bail poorer defendants would be at a disadvantage. According to the Prison Policy Imitative, "the median bail bond amount in this country represents eight months of income for the typical detained defendant."[111] Indeed, there is a direct relationship between the amount of bail set and the likelihood of release. The Bureau of Justice Statistics found that when the bail amount was under $500, 70 percent of defendants were released. But the higher bail was set, the less likely it was defendants would get out of jail. Just 10 percent of defendants were released when the bail was set at $100,000 or more.[112] A more recent study of pretrial release in New Orleans found that when bail was set at $10,000 or less, almost three-quarters of defendants were able to pay the amount, and it took an average of seven days to pay it. However, less than half of those whose bail was set at between $24,000 and $99,000 were able to pay, and it took an average of twenty-four days for them to post it.[113]

However, because most studies of pretrial decision making rely on official court data, which typically lack information about the socioeconomic status of defendants, there has been little research on the issue. Recently, however, a few studies have used the median income in a defendant's zip code of residence as a proxy for income. Unsurprisingly, these studies reported that defendants from poorer neighborhoods are more likely to be detained. For example, Megan Stevenson found that defendants from low-income neighborhoods were 17 percent more likely to be detained than those from wealthier neighborhoods.[114] Similarly, Heaton and colleagues found that defendants from poorer zip codes were substantially more likely to be detained than those from the wealthiest zip codes; approximately 30 percent of defendants from the wealthiest zip codes were detained, compared to 60–70 percent from the poorest zip codes.[115] Although Stevenson found that some of the difference in detention rates was explained by the seriousness of the charge, Heaton and colleagues found that the difference was not explained by the seriousness of the offense, criminal history, or factors related to public safety.[116]

## THE COSTS OF PRETRIAL DETENTION

In addition to producing hardships for individual defendants and their families, pretrial detention contributes to the costs and inefficiency of the justice system. According to the Pretrial Justice Institute, pretrial detention costs taxpayers $38 million per day, or $14 billion per year— an amount that could support the employment of 250,000 elementary schoolteachers, the provision of free or reduced-cost lunch for thirty-one million children, or the provision of shelter and services for the country's 50,000 homeless veterans and homelessness prevention services for the 1.4 million veterans who are at risk of becoming homeless.[117] Further, the costs of pretrial detention far exceed the costs of alternatives to incarceration, including pretrial supervision. For example, in the federal system, it costs only $7.24 per day to keep a defendant under pretrial supervision, whereas it costs $73.03 per day to detain a pretrial defendant in jail.[118]

The primary justifications for denying defendants pretrial release are, first, to ensure that they appear at court hearings, and second, to protect public safety. There is little evidence that pretrial detention accomplishes the latter goal. First, while pretrial detention does inca-pacitate defendants pretrial, thus reducing crime in the short term, down the line it actually can increase crime, which causes additional costs to the criminal justice system and society. For example, econo-mist Arpit Gupta and colleagues found that assigning money bail, which increased the likelihood of pretrial detention, increased the like-lihood of future criminal behavior between 6 and 9 percent.[119] Simi-larly, Heaton and colleagues found that "although detention reduces defendant's criminal activity in the short term through incapacitation, by eighteen months post-hearing, detention is associated with a 30% increase in new felony charges and a 20% increase in new misdemeanor charges."[120] However, they did not find any long-term impact on public safety; specifically, they could identify no impact on either rearrests or new convictions within two years after the bail hearing.

It is difficult to argue that pretrial detention does not serve the goal of ensuring court appearance; it does. Pretrial detainees almost always appear in court, whereas it is undisputed that some defendants granted pretrial release do not. But there are fewer in the latter group than most people think. Dobbie and colleagues, for example, found that released defendants were 15.6 percent more likely to fail to appear in court than those in pretrial detention.[121] We think, however, that there are better ways to facilitate appearance in court than to deprive people of their liberty, especially in light of the high costs of doing so to both the accused and society as a whole. Put differently, the costs of these non-appearances are outweighed by the benefits of release. In their cost-benefit analysis, Dobbie and colleagues balanced the costs of a criminal conviction for the labor market with the costs of failures to appear and estimated that pretrial release provides a total net benefit per defendant of between $55,143 and $99,124.[122]

It is increasingly common for researchers and policy makers to focus on cost savings in criminal justice. In part in response to the fiscal crisis in corrections, which began in the mid-2000s, states began to look at ways to cut costs in their criminal justice systems.[123] Projects such as the Council of State Governments' Justice Reinvestment initiative funded (and continue to fund) states to reduce spending by instituting reforms that do not negatively impact public safety.[124] As law professor Hadar Aviram argued, the discourse of cost savings and financial prudence, which she called "humonetarianism," has dominated public conversations about corrections since 2008 and has facilitated bipartisan reform in a way that would not otherwise have been possible.[125]

Cost-benefit analysis (CBA) is a key tool in these efforts, particularly when it comes to examining the effectiveness of individual programs. The Vera Institute of Justice defined cost-benefit analysis as "an economic tool that compares an investment's costs and benefits in the long run. The hallmark of CBA is that costs and benefits are expressed in monetary terms so that they can be directly compared. Because the investment's effects are expressed in dollars, CBA enables decision makers to compare policies and programs that have different purposes and outcomes."[126] Rigorous CBA has five key elements: assessing the impacts of the investment, measuring the cost of the investment, measuring the costs and benefits of the investment's impact, comparing the costs and benefits, and testing the reliability of the results.[127] Traditionally a tool of economists, CBA is an increasingly important component of criminal justice policy. As researcher John Roman wrote in 2013, "Funders at all levels increasingly see themselves as investors and are concerned not only with outcomes but also with costs and benefits. They ask whether the investment of additional resources is worth the added costs—and whether they will see those benefits down the road in their budgets."[128]

As Roman noted, good CBA is "tricky."[129] In addition to the difficulty of quantifying participant outcomes such as recidivism, drug use, and employment into dollars, CBA must take account of alternative explanations for results. The best CBA considers a broad range of benefits and focuses less on return on investment and more on the impact of the intervention on clients, victims, and society. [130] Much CBA is done as part of impact evaluations of individual programs or other interventions;

given the differences in individual pretrial justice systems, it would appear difficult to conduct a CBA of pretrial detention nationwide.

Despite this drawback, law professor Shima Baradaran-Baughman attempted to do just that. In a 2017 article, she concluded that "judges can release significantly more defendants without increased economic or social costs."[131] She suggested that "fine-tuning detention decisions through cost-benefit analysis" could lead to saving $78 billion. Although her research was not peer reviewed, Baradaran did a good job of articulating the various costs of pretrial detention for both detainees and society and of explaining the costs of pretrial release, including the risks posed by defendants and the costs of any crimes they commit during their release.[132] Despite some of the limitations of her study, she was right to conclude that the cost of pretrial detention is an important consideration for policy makers.[133]

## CONCLUSION

The litany of negative impacts of pretrial detention is concerning. We need to remember that detained individuals have not yet been convicted of the offense with which they are charged, and many will ultimately not be convicted of anything. Yet they endure weeks, months, and sometimes years of detention, time that they cannot get back. And even if defendants are able to obtain release, they are likely to have relied on a for-profit bail bond company, with they or their families paying financial premiums that they will never get back. Compounding this, as discussed in the last two chapters, is the fact that the decision to impose pretrial detention is not always based on factors that predict the risk of a defendant either committing a new crime while awaiting trial or failing to appear at scheduled court hearings. Thus many people are being unnecessarily detained, driving significant growth in jail populations at a time when state prison populations are on the decline.

Until recently, criticisms of the US system of pretrial justice have resulted in little change. However, as we describe in chapters 2 and 3, there are signs of progress. Reforms have been enacted in numerous states and local jurisdictions around the country, including the elimination of money bail in a few places. And when changes are made, the impact can be significant. For example, after a report was issued criticizing the failure of courts in two Kentucky counties to set nonfinancial bonds, one judge changed his practices, and the population of the local jail dropped.[134] However, to date changes have been piecemeal, and pretrial detention remains the norm in the United States, particularly for the poor. With that reality in mind, we turn to our recommendations for systemic reform.

# CHAPTER FIVE

# The Path Forward

The Pretrial Justice Institute's website has a page entitled "The Solution" on which it lists eight recommendations for addressing the multi-faceted nature of the extensive problems that plague pretrial release and detention decision making in the criminal courts of the United States.[1] Although the website does not detail the rationale underlying each of the recommendations, the Pretrial Justice Institute draws upon recommendations made by a range of work by advocacy groups, including the American Bar Association, the American Council of Chief Defenders, the Constitution Project, the National Association of Criminal Defense Lawyers, and the National Institute of Corrections, as well as the work of numerous scholars.[2] These are the recommendations:

- Increased use of citation in lieu of arrest
- Elimination of bond schedules
- Screening of criminal cases by an experienced prosecutor
- Presence of defense counsel at initial appearance
- Use of pretrial risk assessment
- Expanded use of pretrial supervision and monitoring
- Availability of detention with due process
- Collection and analysis of performance measures

Of course we have already addressed several of these recommendations in detail and so will not rehash those points here. Suffice it to say that it should be clear that we fully support the elimination of bond schedules, for the reasons discussed in chapter 2. And it should also be clear from chapter 3 that we have serious concerns about the fairness of pretrial risk assessments, especially because there is reason to suspect that APRAIs perpetuate racial, ethnic, and socioeconomic injustice in pretrial release decisions. More research is needed to independently establish the validity and reliability of APRAIs. In addition, if reliable, properly validated pretrial risk assessments are utilized, they cannot be used mechanistically. They need to be interpreted as one of several important pieces of data when pretrial release decisions are made. Further, as we explained in chapter 2, although we believe that there are some forms of pretrial supervision that can be effective in decreasing the rates of failure to appear, we believe that there is not yet enough evidence to support widespread implementation of pretrial supervision and monitoring. Finally, we have already recommended in chapter 2 that commercial bail be eliminated. With that brief recap complete, we conclude this book with critiques of the other recommendations and offer some additional suggestions of our own.

## CITATION IN LIEU OF ARREST

When police officers have probable cause to make arrests for certain types of offenses, the laws of nearly all US states vest officers with the discretion to either take the suspect into custody or issue a citation instead of making a formal arrest.[3] A *citation* (known as a *summons* in some states) is a charging document that orders the person to whom it is issued to appear in court to answer the charge(s) specified in the citation.[4] In most US jurisdictions, the issuance of a citation preempts the necessity of taking a suspect into custody (usually in handcuffs), transporting the arrested person to a police station or intake facility, booking the suspect (which typically entails photographing, fingerprinting, and searching the suspect), and then detaining the arrestee until such time as a probable cause determination can be made before a neutral judicial officer (which can range from a few minutes to up to forty-eight hours).[5]

According to a major study conducted by the International Association of Chiefs of Police (IACP) in 2016 of a nationally representative sample of thirteen hundred law enforcement agencies in the United States, the practice is now so widespread that roughly 87 percent of agencies report using the citation in lieu of arrest process.[6] However, the process is only used in roughly one-third of all incidents—most commonly for theft, disorderly conduct, trespassing, driving on a suspended license, and simple possession of marijuana—in spite of the fact that the process saves much time, taking on average between 15 and 35 minutes, compared to 86 to 127 minutes to process an arrest.[7]

In addition to increasing officer efficiency, the process offers a host of other potential benefits, including

- enhanced community-police relations, largely as a function of sparing offenders the hardships associated with an arrest for minor offenses;[8]
- increased officer and public safety, primarily by reducing the "hands-on" requirements of making a custodial arrest;[9]
- reduced criminal justice system costs via reduced bookings and bail proceedings[10] (indeed, one study estimated the annual cost savings in Florida to be $44–$139 million);[11]
- reductions in jail overcrowding as a function of reducing unnecessary pretrial detentions;[12] and
- diminished burdens on low-level offenders, who avoid arrest records (which can negatively affect housing, employment, and loan opportunities), potential pretrial detention (including the potential need to post bail), financial burdens, and even unintended criminogenic influences—especially for young, first-time offenders.[13]

## The Law of Citation in Lieu of Arrest

In roughly half of US states, the law creates a presumption in favor of law enforcement officers issuing a citation for certain traffic and misdemeanor offenses, such as those that do not carry any period of incarceration as a potential penalty for the offense or, alternatively, those that carry a maximum period of incarceration of a certain number of days (e.g., fewer than 60, 90, or 120 days).[14] In other states, there is no presumption; rather, law enforcement officers are vested with the discretion to issue a citation for most traffic or misdemeanor offenses if they believe that certain conditions are satisfied.[15] For example, the following the approach is set forth in Wyoming law:

(a) A citation may issue as a charging document for any misdemeanor which the issuing officer has probable cause to believe was committed by the person to whom the citation was issued.

(b) A person may be released if, after investigation, it appears that the person:

(i) Does not present a danger to himself or others;

(ii) Will not injure or destroy the property of others;

(iii) Will appear for future court proceedings; and

(iv) Is willing to accept the citation, thereby promising to appear in court at the time and on the date specified in the citation.[16]

A handful of states, such as Alaska, Louisiana, Minnesota, and Oregon, even permit officers to issue citations in lieu of arrest for select nonviolent felonies.[17] Alaska made this change as part of its recent package of bail reform legislation.[18]

Citations in lieu of arrest are generally not permitted

if the suspect "does not furnish satisfactory evidence of identity";[19]

if the suspect is being charged with a domestic violence offense, driving while impaired, or vehicular homicide;[20]

if the officer reasonably believes that the suspect poses a danger to
  himself or herself or others;[21] or

if the suspect has outstanding warrants or refuses to sign the
  citation and agree to appear in court to answer the charges.[22]

### *Few Limits on Officers' Discretion to Arrest*

According to the National Conference of State Legislatures, citations
in lieu of arrest can help "to reduce jail populations and provide local
cost savings" while diverting "lower risk offenders from detention, [and]
reserving limited space and resources for more dangerous offenders."[23]
In addition, in light of the presumption of innocence and its relationship
to the principle of pretrial release under the least restrictive conditions,
the President's Task Force on 21st Century Policing and numerous advocacy organizations—including the American Bar Association and the
IACP—urge the use of citations instead of formal arrests for "non-violent
offenses when the individual's identity is confirmed and no reasonable
cause exists to suggest the individual may be a risk to the community
or to miss court dates."[24] Yet as previously mentioned, law enforcement
officers are granted broad discretion to issue a citation in lieu of arrest.
Unfortunately, that discretion is not always exercised wisely. And perhaps worse, the US Constitution offers little protection from the abuse of
such discretion, as illustrated by the leading case in this area of the law,
*Atwater v. City of Lago Vista*.[25]

In March 1997 Gail Atwater was driving her two small children in the
town of Lago Vista, Texas. Atwater was not wearing a seatbelt. It also
appeared to a police officer that her child was not wearing a seatbelt,
although it turned out that he was. Because the officer recognized Atwater from a previous encounter during which he had given her a verbal
warning for not wearing a seatbelt, he arrested Atwater for the seatbelt
offense, as well as for driving without carrying her driver's license and
proof of insurance.[26] The officer booked Atwater and detained her for
an hour until she was taken before a magistrate and released on bond.

Atwater eventually paid a $50 fine for the seatbelt violations, and the other charges were dismissed.[27]

Atwater subsequently filed a civil rights lawsuit against the City of Lago Vista, arguing that an arrest for a minor traffic offense punishable by a fine violated her rights under the Fourth Amendment to be free from unreasonable searches and seizures. The case made its way to the US Supreme Court, which in 2001 rejected Atwater's claims. A majority of five justices held that if "an officer has probable cause to believe that an individual has committed even a very minor criminal offense in his presence, he may, without violating the Fourth Amendment, arrest the offender."[28]

Four dissenting justices believed that Atwater's arrest was unreasonable and therefore violated the Fourth Amendment.[29] The dissenting justices were particularly concerned about both the consequences of arrests that are disproportionate to the offense and the "unfettered discretion" that some states vest in law enforcement officers:

> Such unbounded discretion carries with it grave potential for abuse. The majority takes comfort in the lack of evidence of an epidemic of unnecessary minor-offense arrests. But the relatively small number of published cases dealing with such arrests proves little and should provide little solace. Indeed, as the recent debate over racial profiling demonstrates all too clearly, a relatively minor traffic infraction may often serve as an excuse for stopping and harassing an individual. After today, the arsenal available to any officer extends to a full arrest and the searches permissible concomitant to that arrest. An officer's subjective motivations for making a traffic stop are not relevant considerations in determining the reasonableness of the stop.... But it is precisely because these motivations are beyond our purview that we must vigilantly ensure that officers' post-stop actions—which are properly within our reach—comport with the Fourth Amendment's guarantee of reasonableness.[30]

Legal scholars have widely criticized the decision in *Atwater*.[31] As constitutional law scholar Akhil Reed Amar asked, "Why jail a resident who was no flight risk, given that the underlying infraction itself could not be punished with jail time?"[32] Some scholars suggest that enforcement officers may opt to make an arrest rather than issue a citation, depending on whether the officer wants to search either the suspect or, if the person was driving, the motorist's vehicle.[33] This logic derives from the fact that law enforcement officers are empowered to conduct searches incident to lawful arrests, but pursuant to the US Supreme Court's decision in *Knowles v. Iowa*, officers may not conduct searches of persons or belongings when issuing a citation.[34]

The motivation to arrest in order to conduct a lawful search may be particularly important in criminal cases in which a defendant seeks to invoke the exclusionary rule to suppress evidence at trial, in light of *Virginia v. Moore*.[35] That case involved an illegal arrest for a traffic offense that was barred under Virginia state law, which mandates that a citation be issued in lieu of arrest for most traffic and low-level misdemeanor offenses.[36]After conducting a search incident to that arrest, police discovered the defendant was in illegal possession of a controlled substance. In spite of the fact that valid searches incident to arrest must usually be premised on the arrest being lawful, the US Supreme Court ruled that the illegality of the arrest under state law was of no consequence for exclusionary rule purposes so long as the arrest was supported by probable cause.

### Unknown and Unintended Consequences

The 2016 IACP report cited several "concerns and challenges" associated with citation in lieu of arrest.[37] First, there is insufficient data to know whether failure to appear rates are substantially higher for persons who are issued citations rather than being arrested and granted pretrial release. Indeed, there is a remarkable dearth of research on failure to appear rates that separates defendants based on whether they were cited or arrested. One study in 1995 reported significantly higher failure to appear rates for offenders in Charlotte, North Carolina, who were issued citations (23.2 percent) compared to those formally arrested (3.9 percent).[38] But that study was conducted roughly twenty-five years ago, before many courts began using telephone calls, postcards, and text messaging to remind people of their court dates.[39]

Second, IACP argued that law enforcement officers need "accurate, easily accessible data" to assist them in the field making the decision about whether to issue a citation or make a formal arrest.[40] Certainly such information is very important to guide officers in the exercise of discretionary decision making. But as we explain in the next subsection, we think police having less discretion is the better path forward in order to reduce racial and ethnic disparities. Rather than allowing discretionary citation in lieu of arrest, issuing a citation should be *required* for nearly all traffic and misdemeanor offenses other than for those people for whom an arrest warrant is outstanding and a small class of other offenders, explained in more detail later in this chapter.[41]

Third, some law enforcement officers view citations to be inferior to arrest because the former do not allow for the gathering of information during the arrest booking process that can in turn be used to solve both existing and future crimes, such as fingerprints.[42] There is no doubt that reducing arrests will result in the loss of some evidence for crimes. But as IACP suggested, this concern could be mitigated by "more complete data collection and tracking of citations."[43] Law professor Rachel Harmon has suggested the use of alternative methods to alleviate the concern about gathering evidence, "including *Terry* stops and frisks, consent searches, searches pursuant to the automobile exception to the warrant requirement, exigency searches, searches pursuant to a warrant, and noncustodial interviews."[44] To be sure, even if all of these approaches were used, they are not ideal substitutes for arrest. Still, when combined with better data collection and tracking of citations, these methods can help law enforcement officers gather evidence while reducing not only the impact of unnecessary arrests for low-level offenses, but also the associated strains that formal arrests place on pretrial justice officials and defendants alike.[45]

Another reason that some law enforcement personnel feel citations are inferior to arrests is that unlike formal arrests, citations are not recorded in criminal history databases.[46] However, this might actually be a positive outcome. Unlike in most countries, in the United States criminal records are easily accessible, and that can make it very difficult to for people with criminal arrest records, even if they have never been convicted of any offense, to qualify for housing and public benefits and to find employment.[47] Thus the "eternal criminal record" likely exacerbates the negative consequences of pretrial detention described in chapter 4.

Fourth, some people have expressed concerns about net widening. Net widening is a theoretical position that posits that as a sanction becomes less punitive, it will be applied to more people.[48] Applying the theory to citation in lieu of arrest suggests that officers may issue citations in situations where they previously would have done nothing, resulting in an overall net increase in the number of people interacting with the criminal justice system. But as IACP acknowledged, there is very little research demonstrating that citation in lieu of arrest is, in fact, widening the justice system's net.[49] One study from 1980 conducted in Omaha, Nebraska, found some evidence of net widening for larceny and simple assaults, although methodological limitations may account for these findings.[50] A research study of citation in lieu of arrest in Florida found little support for the net-widening hypothesis and concluded that the practice actually served its intended purpose of diversion from formal criminal justice involvement.[51]

Fifth, laws and policies that result in increased use of citations in lieu of arrest can create a problem in which police actions serve as moneymaking ventures.[52] The practices in Ferguson, Missouri, serve as a stark example of how such a situation, to paraphrase the editors of the *Harvard Law Review*, may be aptly described as policing for profit. The final report issued by the US Department of Justice (USDOJ) after investigating the Ferguson, Missouri, Police Department highlighted how citations can be abused in such a manner.[53] The USDOJ determined that numerous factors contributed to this problem in Ferguson, not the least of which was that officers' annual performance evaluations and promotion decisions depended on their "'productivity,' meaning the number of citations issued."[54] This in turn contributed to police officers viewing their constituents as "sources of revenue."[55] The President's Task Force on 21st Century Policing specifically recommended that law enforcement agencies need to refrain from measuring productivity by evaluating the number of investigative stops, citations issued, or arrests made "for reasons not directly related to improving public safety, such as generating revenue."[56] We concur wholeheartedly and urge that such metrics be abandoned. But the situation in Ferguson went beyond misplaced productivity measures for police officers; the judiciary also played an important role in exploiting vulnerable members of the community.

The municipal court in Ferguson failed to protect its citizens' rights. Court personnel were complicit in a scheme that compelled "the payment of fines and fees that advance[d] the City's financial interests."[57] As a result, not only did the fines and fees collected by the municipal court routinely account for between 12.3 and 23.3 percent of Ferguson's general fund revenue, but the amount of revenue collected each year also grew steadily—sometimes by as much as 30 percent annually.[58] Unsurprisingly, the burden of these unscrupulous revenue-generating practices fell disproportionately on African Americans, many of whom were living in poverty and as a result were unable to pay the high fines and punitive fees, which were assessed without regard to citizens' ability to pay.[59] The USDOJ issued numerous suggestions for remedying such abuses in Ferguson, including

implementing a robust system of true community policing;[60]

reforming stop, search, citation, and arrest practices to focus on public safety needs;[61]

increasing officer supervision and accountability practices;[62]

reducing bias and its effects on police behavior;[63]

improving officer training;[64] and

reforming municipal court practices to increase transparency, honor defendants' constitutional rights, implement systems for fine reductions, and provide alternatives to monetary payments for resolving municipal charges.[65]

We recognize that our endorsement of increasing citations in lieu of arrests runs the risk of providing financial incentives for overpolicing.[66] Nonetheless, we feel strongly that if the types of procedural safeguards recommended by the USDOJ in its Ferguson report are systematically implemented, the multiplicity of benefits associated with citations in lieu of arrests will outweigh the potential drawbacks—especially if fine reductions and alternatives to monetary payments are established so as not to compound the plight of the poor by leading them into a spiral of debt and associated consequences, some of which could be further offending.[67]

### *Potential Solutions*

There appear to be multiple benefits to expanding the use of citations in lieu of arrests with few corresponding drawbacks, provided that laws and administrative policies minimize discretionary decision making and thereby reduce potential racial and ethnic disparities between those who are cited and those who are arrested. Research suggests, for example, that racial and ethnic minorities are far more likely to be arrested than Whites, who are more likely to receive a citation in lieu of arrest.[68] IACP recommended that to avoid both explicit and implicit biases in the issuance of citations, police departments need to have clear policies that guide the exercise of officer discretion.[69] Although we concur wholeheartedly with the need for law enforcement agencies to have clear policies that curtail the exercise of police discretion in biased ways for all aspects of policing, that is not enough.

Nearly a half century of research has examined a wide range of issues related to police officers' discretionary decision making during citizen encounters, including whether to stop and frisk someone, issue a traffic ticket, make an arrest, use different levels of force, use canines, engage in pursuits, and activate body-worn cameras, just to name a few situations.[70] This body of literature emphasizes that clear policies are insufficient. Administrative policies must be supported by other effective practices, including careful recruitment of officers (both screening-in good candidates and screening-out poor ones), effective training (both in the academy and ongoing throughout officers' careers), meaningful supervision of officers with corresponding accountability for their actions, and external oversight.[71]

With regard to the control of police officer discretion as it relates to citation in lieu of arrest, however, additional steps can be taken to reduce racial and ethnic disparities. Specifically, two changes in the law can help to achieve such ends while simultaneously reducing the incidence of pretrial injustice by stemming the flow of low-level offenders into the criminal justice system.

## OVERTURN *ATWATER*

The Supreme Court majority in *Atwater* got it wrong. The decision should be overturned for the reasons set forth in the dissenting opinion, not the least of which is that all arrests—because they are seizures of people—are supposed to be "reasonable" to satisfy the command of the Fourth Amendment. Even the justices in the *Atwater* majority suggested that the officer's decision to arrest Ms. Atwater failed to meet this threshold when they wrote the following:

> If we were to derive a rule exclusively to address the uncontested facts of this case, Atwater might well prevail. She was a known and established resident of Lago Vista with no place to hide and no incentive to flee, and common sense says she would almost certainly have buckled up as a condition of driving off with a citation. In her case, the physical incidents of arrest were merely gratuitous humiliations imposed by a police officer who was (at best) exercising extremely poor judgment. Atwater's claim to live free of pointless indignity and confinement clearly outweighs anything the City can raise against it specific to her case.[72]

Nonetheless, the majority seemingly felt the need to establish a bright-line rule, rather than allow for case-by-case determinations of discretionary decisions. Of course *Atwater* offered such a rule, namely that "the Fourth Amendment generally forbids warrantless arrests for minor crimes not accompanied by violence or some demonstrable threat of it (whether 'minor crime' be defined as a fine-only traffic offense, a fine-only offense more generally, or a misdemeanor)."[73] The majority rejected that approach ostensibly because line officers may not know the penalties for many offenses.[74] Frankly, we think that reason fails to give sufficient credit to law enforcement personnel. Still, although it may be the prerogative of the justices to eschew one bright-line rule in favor of another, there is no escaping the Fourth Amendment's command of reasonableness.

In the 1967 case *Camara v. Municipal Court*, the US Supreme Court instructed that determinations of reasonableness require examination of the governmental interests asserted to justify intrusion on citizens' privacy interests. Unfortunately there can be no ready test for determining reasonableness other than by balancing the need to search against the invasion that the search entails."[75] Yet the majority in *Atwater* did not meaningfully examine the reasonableness of arresting someone for such a minor infraction of law, especially when the issuance of a citation can promote the safety issues underlying the offense in question.

The dissent in *Atwater* stated, "Giving police officers constitutional carte blanche to effect an arrest whenever there is probable cause to believe a fine-only misdemeanor has been committed is irreconcilable with the Fourth Amendment's command that seizures be 'reasonable.'"[76] Accordingly, the dissenting judges argued that when there is probable cause to believe that a minor offense—namely one publishable only by a fine—has been committed, there should be a constitutional presumption in favor of issuing a citation unless the law enforcement officer involved with the situation is "able to point to specific and articulable facts which, taken together with rational inferences from those facts, reasonably warrant [the additional] intrusion of a full custodial arrest."[77]

As a matter of Fourth Amendment jurisprudence, full custodial arrests should be "deemed presumptively unreasonable" when the offense is punishable only by a fine.[78] This is the approach that the Montana Supreme Court took when it rejected *Atwater* on state constitutional law grounds, holding in *State v. Bauer* that "it is unreasonable for a police officer to effect an arrest and detention for a non-jailable offense when there are no circumstances to justify an immediate arrest."[79] That case involved the arrest of a minor for being in possession of alcohol. A New Mexico case involving that same offense reasoned that the *Atwater* majority's analysis was flawed and instead adopted the dissenting justices' approach.[80] Notably, law enforcement officers in these states are entrusted to know which offenses are and are not punishable by a potential term of incarceration, undercutting one of the key reasons the *Atwater* majority offered in support of its holding.[81]

Beyond minor offenses punishable only by a fine, the balancing test Justice O'Connor suggested in her *Atwater* dissent can and should also be applied to all nonviolent misdemeanor offenses, just as the Ohio Supreme Court held when it departed from *Atwater*'s holding, on state constitutional grounds, in a case involving the illegal possession of a controlled substance.[82]

We recognize that it may be somewhat simplistic to simply call for *Atwater* to be overruled. Nonetheless, we think it is important to add our voice to the myriad calls from others for this mistakenly decided case to be set aside. Still, given that it is unlikely the US Supreme Court will overrule the case, states can address this problem. State courts can follow the lead of the Ohio Supreme Court in refusing to follow *Atwater*'s holding on state constitutional law grounds.[83] And state legislatures can make changes prohibiting custodial arrests for select classes of offenses, as detailed in the next subsection.

### STATE LEGISLATIVE CHANGES

Independent of the aforementioned change in constitutional law concerning the use of a balancing test to justify custodial arrests over the issuance of citations, changes in statutory law should also occur. Specifically, state arrest laws should be amended to limit when law enforcement officers are permitted to make custodial arrests.

Even before the *Atwater* decision, several states had enacted limitations on the general power to arrest for select traffic offenses and nonviolent misdemeanors.[84] To curb the unnecessary flow of arrestees into pretrial criminal justice processes that involve release, bail, or detention decisions made by judicial officers, all states should enact mandatory "citation in lieu of arrest" laws that require law enforcement offers to issue a citation for certain classes of offenses.

At the present time, only a few states have any type of mandatory citation in lieu of arrest laws.[85] Tennessee's statute appears in the appendix.[86] A review of that provision reveals, however, that it is limited to (1) traffic offenses other than those in which an accident caused serious bodily harm or death and (2) misdemeanors, other than driving while impaired. And although the statute does not mention domestic violence per se, it does specify that officers are prohibited from issuing a citation when there "is a reasonable likelihood" that an offense "would continue or resume, or that persons or property would be endangered by the arrested person."[87]

Alaska's statute is specifically designed to divert people from jail and requires that when an individual is stopped for committing an "infraction or a violation," an officer *shall* issue a citation except in limited circumstances, including where the individual has previously failed to appear or violated conditions of release.[88]

Other states should adopt laws similar to Alaska's and Tennessee's approaches concerning citation in lieu of arrest.

Some scholars have advocated for citation in lieu of arrest for most felony offenses. Law professor Rachel Harmon, for example, has explained that only about 5 percent of criminal cases involve violent felony offenses.[89] Excluding this comparatively small number of violent felonies, Professor Harmon argued that the citation in lieu of arrest would be appropriate in many of the remaining 95 percent of criminal cases. The empirical data summarized in chapter 3 concerning low failure to appear rates for felony defendants granted pretrial release supports such an approach to using citation in lieu of arrest for both nonviolent misdemeanors and felonies. Professor Harmon also pointed out that although citations in lieu of arrest in select felony cases "may seem radical, states already widely permit judges to issue summonses instead of arrest warrants for felony defendants, which have the same effect of commanding them to court rather than compelling their presence."[90]

Although Professor Harmon's points have merit, we think it is premature to make systemic changes in the law to facilitate citation in lieu of arrest for all nonviolent offenders, including those for whom there is probable cause to believe they have committed a nonviolent felony. As previously stated, more research is needed to evaluate differences in failure to appear rates between people issued citations and those who are formally arrested. Such research should include different types of offenses and be conducted in jurisdictions that utilize modern systems of technology to remind offenders of upcoming court dates. If differences in failure to appear rates turn out to be low, then it would seem wise to extend citation in lieu of arrest laws to nonviolent felonies as well. Until such time as research demonstrates the true costs and benefits associated with citations in lieu of arrest, however, limiting legal changes to traffic offenses and nonviolent misdemeanors would be an excellent start.

That being said, the US Supreme Court ruled in *Virginia v. Moore* that "warrantless arrests for crimes committed in the presence of an arresting officer are [always] reasonable under the Constitution," even if state law prohibits such arrests.[91] The decisions in *Atwater* and *Moore* might lead some to conclude that there is little benefit in legislatures changing state laws mandating citation in lieu of arrest because violations of those state laws would not trigger Fourth Amendment protections. But such a conclusion is unwarranted, for at least two reasons. First, the decisions in both *Atwater* and *Moore* concerned arrests for traffic offenses designated as criminal misdemeanors under applicable state law. In contrast, when state law defines traffic offenses as civil violations or infractions, several courts have held that *Atwater* and *Moore* do not apply.[92] Admittedly this approach would only have a real impact in cases involving noncriminal traffic offenses, but as previously mentioned, state courts could follow the lead of courts in Minnesota, Montana, Ohio, and New Mexico by ruling that their state constitutions provide more protections from warrantless arrests than the Fourth Amendment provides according to the decisions in *Atwater* and *Moore*.[93]

The second important reason that statutory reform should occur even if state courts do not depart from *Atwater* and *Moore* is that police departments can and should create formal policies curtailing formal arrest when state laws mandate the use of citations. If officers violate these laws and policies, proper supervision and accountability measures in police departments can curtail officers' discretionary decision making in ways that facilitate compliance even if evidence will not be suppressed under the exclusionary role or its state law counterparts.[94]

## SCREENING OF CRIMINAL CASES BY AN EXPERIENCED PROSECUTOR

It's difficult to imagine anyone taking issue with the recommendation that all jurisdictions ensure that "an experienced prosecutor conduct screening of criminal cases before the initial court appearance."[95] Such early screening allows prosecutors to determine whether formal charges should be filed, whether a case is eligible for referral to diversion programs (including specialized, problem-solving courts), whether the case is suitable for deferred prosecution, or even if the arrestee should be released without any charges being filed against him or her.[96] As detailed in the next subsection, when this recommendation is put into practice along with other discretion-controlling policies, not only can the strain on the pretrial justice system be reduced by stemming the flow of low-level offenders into the system, but racial disparities also can be reduced.

### The Milwaukee Experiment

When John Chisholm became the district attorney for Milwaukee County, Wisconsin, in 2007, he was concerned that although African Americans comprise only 6 percent of the population in Wisconsin, they account for 37 percent of the state's prison population.[97] He therefore invited researchers from the Vera Institute for Justice to review records in the prosecutor's office and interview staff employed there. They found a disturbing pattern of racial disparities in charging decisions. Prosecutors declined to move forward with possession of marijuana or drug paraphernalia cases in 41 percent of cases involving White arrestees, but in only 27 percent with Black arrestees.[98] In cases involving resisting or obstructing a police officer, 77 percent of charged defendants were Black, and most were already in custody (80 percent Black vs. 66 percent White).[99] And regarding domestic violence offenses, cases were 16 percent less likely to be charged if they involved Black victims compared to White victims—and when cases involved allegations of domestic violence by Black offenders against White victims, the chances of formal charges being filed were 34 percent higher than in cases involving White offenders and White victims.[100]

The data tell only part of the story:

> During a meeting to review declination rates, a finding that minorities were less likely to be prosecuted for property offenses was initially presented as evidence that there was no racial bias in how such cases were handled. Extensive discussions among managers within the office, however, yielded several other plausible and less comforting conclusions. Perhaps there were fewer cases with minority defendants because minority victims were reluctant to step forward, law enforcement was less willing to treat such crimes against minorities seriously, or prosecutors were less inclined to appropriately value the property rights of minority victims who are often demographically similar to their victimizers.[101]

The results of the Vera study caused Chisholm to revise the way in which his office did business. He emphasized that prosecutors should reduce crime in the communities they serve while simultaneously reducing mass incarceration and increasing racial justice. To achieve such goals, he established new charging instructions and retrained prosecutors.[102] Importantly, he structured charging decisions so that they would be made by more experienced prosecutors who were trained to think about their jobs through the lens of public health— keeping people and communities healthy: "[Chisholm] and his team started asking themselves in every instance why they were bringing that case. 'In those that were seen as minor, it was the least experienced people who were deciding whether to bring them. And these people saw that we had generally brought those cases in the past, so they went ahead with them again. But we started to ask, "Why are we charging these people with crimes at all?"'"[103]

In addition to increasing declinations of prosecutions, Chisholm instituted an early intervention program that increased the use of diversion programs and deferred prosecutions prior to an arrestee's formal arraignment in court.[104] As a result of these changes, prosecutions for possession of marijuana and drug paraphernalia decreased precipitously; indeed, the overall number of misdemeanor prosecutions has decreased by more than 42 percent.[105] Racial disparities in charging decisions for select crimes, such as burglary, have all but disappeared.[106] And the "number of African-American residents of Milwaukee County sent to state prison on drug charges has been cut in half since 2006."[107] That is not to say, however, that racial disparities have been eliminated. Indeed, violent crime disproportionately affects poor areas of the county where high concentrations of racial minorities live. Indeed, homicides and gun-related aggravated assaults in Milwaukee almost all involve Black perpetrators and victims.[108]

Of course the Milwaukee County Prosecutor's Office is relatively large and therefore has the luxury of assigning more seasoned attorneys to screen cases and make charging decisions, as is common in even larger prosecutors' offices. But limited resources in any jurisdiction might impact whether an experienced prosecutor is available to conduct initial screenings.[109] In addition, without the types of office-wide polices

Chisolm put in place in his county, there are reasons to question whether having an experienced prosecutor making such judgments by himself or herself would stem the tide of unnecessary criminal prosecutions and reduce the myriad burdens the pretrial justice system faces, especially as a result of the high volume of low-level offenses that clog the lower criminal courts.

## A Typology of Case Screening

The preliminary screening of a criminal case at intake typically involves a prosecutor's evaluation of four domains. First, a *legal sufficiency review* involves the examination of police reports to determine whether they contain sufficient factual details to establish the statutory elements of the crimes alleged. If any element is missing, the prosecutor can either decline to file charges or request that law enforcement personnel conduct additional investigations, which might reveal proof of the missing element(s).[110]

Second, prosecutors consider *system efficiency*. This component of case screening typically involves determinations of whether a case might be referred to a division program or otherwise be resolved efficiently through some quick disposition, such as an early plea bargain.[111]

Third, prosecutors evaluate the likelihood of offender rehabilitation. In some jurisdictions this involves little more than a cursory review of the arrestee's criminal record. First offenders are presumed to be amenable to rehabilitation, whereas repeat offenders are not.[112] In other jurisdictions, however, this review can take an "essentially humanitarian" approach in which the specific offenses alleged, and the accused's particular life circumstances, can be weighed.[113] Such an approach invites the extensive use of prosecutorial discretion, which may vary not only by specific office policies, but also in the particular attitudes of individual prosecutors.[114]

Finally, case screening involves a review of the evidence for *trial sufficiency*. This process includes an evaluation of the likelihood that a case could be proven beyond a reasonable doubt at trial.[115] This highly discretionary evaluation process not only examines the constitutionality of police actions in the case (especially for the possibility of key evidence being suppressed), but also involves an assessment of the strength of the evidence itself, including the availability of physical evidence and the credibility of potential witnesses—including the victim and the law enforcement officers involved in the case.[116]

## The Role of Discretion

The charging decisions that prosecutors make are governed by a panoply of laws, ranging from local rules of criminal procedure to the provisions of the US Constitution. There are also sometimes formal policies in prosecutors' offices that constrain the exercise of an individual prosecutor's discretion, such as mandatory deferred prosecution for certain offenses, mandatory prosecution of driving under the influence in cases in which defendants tested above a particular blood-alcohol concentration, and office-wide expectations of prison sentences for certain types of offenses.[117] These rules are fairly rare, largely because "it is difficult to write a policy for screening each case due to the variation in the factors of cases," which can lead to written policies' creating "more problems than [they] would solve."[118] But even when rules exist, they rarely provide prosecutors with meaningful guidance on how to exercise the nearly unfettered discretion they exercise with regard to filing criminal charges. According to the US Supreme Court, "So long as the prosecutor has probable cause to believe that the accused committed an offense defined by statute, the decision whether or not to prosecute, and what charge to file or bring before a grand jury generally rests entirely in his discretion."[119]

Prosecutorial decision making is a complex process that depends on a wide variety of legal and extralegal factors.[120] Partially in an attempt to guide the exercise of prosecutorial discretion, the American Bar Association promulgated formal *Criminal Justice Standards for the Prosecution Function*, which specified the following:

The primary duty of the prosecutor is to seek justice within the bounds of the law, not merely to convict. The prosecutor serves the public interest and should act with integrity and balanced judgment to increase public safety both by pursuing appropriate criminal charges of appropriate severity, and by exercising discretion to not pursue criminal charges in appropriate circumstances. The prosecutor should seek to protect the innocent and convict the guilty, consider the interests of victims and witnesses, and respect the constitutional and legal rights of all persons, including suspects and defendants.[121]

But as scholars have repeatedly pointed out, a guiding philosophy of "doing justice" does not operationalize the concept in any meaningful way.[122] Thus, some prosecutors equate justice as "fairness" in terms of consistency of processes and outcomes.[123] Often, however, case processing and outcomes may be adversely affected by problems associated with resources, such as high caseloads, understaffing of both attorneys and support personnel, and even a lack of judicial resources (courtroom space, judge, clerks, etc.) needed to adjudicate cases.[124] But even when resources are not a serious issue, the goal of consistency of process and outcomes may be difficult to achieve in light of changes that occur to internal policies designed to constrain broad discretionary decision making by individual prosecutors.

As evidenced by the example of John Chisholm in Milwaukee County, Wisconsin, prosecutorial intake and charging policies tend to be "top-down in nature—created, transmitted, and enforced by the chief prosecutor."[125] When the person in that role changes, the policies governing case screening may also change. The following example was documented in a 1981 study of different prosecutors' offices that detailed what occurred after the election of a new district attorney: "His predecessor, whom he had defeated at the polls, operated the office under a strict set of charging standards very similar to a Trial Sufficiency policy. Cases were not prosecuted unless a conviction was almost certain. As one senior deputy described it, 'the policy imposed an incredibly high standard for filing. The test was "Can you win this case at trial?" It was a cautious, conservative approach.' Under the new administration, the question was no longer 'Can you win this case?' but rather 'Can this case survive motions?'"[126]

Another ubiquitous constraint prosecutors face is the need for efficiency—both in their own offices and in the courts.[127] All prosecutors learn "that they have to dismiss, plead down, or otherwise ... get rid of cases."[128] This is especially important if prosecutors are to maintain effective relationships with judges, defense attorneys, law enforcement officers, and other members of the courtroom workgroup.[129] Oddly, though, declinations to prosecute many low-level offense are rare in comparison to those for more serious crimes, which in turn suggests that prosecutorial discretion is underutilized during the charging process as a means of promoting systemic efficiency.[130] In a provocative article published in 2010, law professor Josh Bowers argued that this state of affairs should change. Specifically, he argued that charging decisions can—and should—involve the exercise of prosecutorial discretion to avoid charging people who are "insufficiently blameworthy," even though they may technically be guilty of committing some low-level crimes, such as public order offenses.[131]

As with the other, more traditional criteria underlying charging decisions, prosecutors are certainly empowered to make normative decisions about whether someone should be prosecuted. But the exercise of what Bowers refers to as *equitable discretion* arguably involves even broader levels of discretionary decision making than are involved in evaluating the legal sufficiency, system efficiency, and likelihood of success at trial that any particular case may present. Indeed, seasoning justice with mercy may invite the use of arbitrary or even invidious reasons to support charging decisions.[132] But even if such decision making could be constrained to valid, moral reasons for declining to charge an offender, Professor Bowers recognized that there are systemic barriers to increasing declinations on equitable discretions grounds: "First, prosecuting petty cases is an effective way to net a high rate and absolute number of convictions—figures that serve as particularly salient measures of prosecutorial performance. Second, prosecuting petty cases offers low-stress opportunities for new assistants to gain prosecutorial experience (and, notably, these new assistants are the very prosecutors who are most deferential to supervisory authority and are therefore least likely to buck policy by exercising case-specific equitable discretion in the rare case where the need for such discretion is readily apparent pre-charge)."[133]

Bowers's solution to the aforementioned challenges is to involve laypersons in charging decisions for low-level offenses. He is not the first person to suggest that nonprosecutors could participate in the charging process. Law professor Alafair S. Burke, for example, has recommended using advisory review committees as a check on police-prosecutor "tunnel vision," thereby reducing wrongful convictions.[134] Law professor Daniel S. Medwed has endorsed this proposal, arguing that including laypersons in screening decisions "would inject an important element of transparency and public accountability."[135] While additional layers of review before charges are filed would likely serve these ends, implementing such an approach would require "large structural reforms"—something that would be very difficult to achieve "in our cash-strapped, overwhelmed criminal justice system.[136] Professor Medwed, therefore, has recommended that charging review committees be limited to the cases in which the risk of wrongful convictions is most pronounced.[137] Of course his proposal was aimed at ways of reducing wrongful convictions, not the broader screening concerns Professor Bowers raised. But we think a middle ground offers some promise.

Just as civil review boards have grown to become important external checks on the operation of police departments, a civil review committee could periodically review charging decisions by prosecutorial intake units.[138] It would be unwise, from both a cost and workload perspective, to have such a committee review all charging decisions. But a committee could certainly review a random sample of cases on a regular basis (e.g., monthly, bimonthly, or quarterly) to provide a commonsense check on prosecutorial decision making with regard to charging. The feedback such committees provide could help prosecutors not only to identify potential tunnel vision in serious cases, but also to learn when community members feel the exercise of discretion can appropriately temper contemporary overcriminalization. As prosecutors learn the latter, presumably more and more minor cases—especially those related to order maintenance—would be screened out on the basis of equitable discretion, thereby reducing the number of people formally brought into the criminal justice system.

## PRESENCE OF DEFENSE COUNSEL AT INITIAL APPEARANCE

The Sixth Amendment to the US Constitution states that "in all criminal prosecutions, the accused shall ... have the Assistance of Counsel for his defence." In spite of what may appear to be the plain meaning of this language, for much of the history of the United States, the Sixth Amendment was not interpreted in a manner consistent with its text. And sadly, the right to counsel remains an unfulfilled promise for many criminal defendants today, especially in pretrial proceedings and misdemeanor prosecutions.

### *Origins of the Right to Counsel*

For much of the history of English common law, counsel was prohibited from appearing in court on behalf of any felony criminal defendant.[139] As a result, defendants facing potentially serious criminal penalties needed to defend themselves in court, largely without the assistance of counsel unless, in the discretion of the presiding judge, an exception was granted. Such exceptions were rare, for two reasons.

First, only wealthy defendants could afford to hire counsel; most defendants were without the financial means to do so.[140] Second, there was distrust of the bar. People feared that allowing a legally trained advocate to speak on behalf of a criminally accused person would allow courtrooms to "descend into a theater for avaricious counsel to actively mislead the court for financial and reputation gain."[141] In addition, people feared that the assistance of counsel would prove to be "an impediment to efficient and successful prosecution and punishment."[142]

Even when judges permitted counsel to appear with felony defendants, their role was largely limited to questions of law; in contrast, the accused was expected to address questions of fact. Put differently, criminal defendants had to speak on their own behalf to demonstrate their innocence. In theory, this was a truth-seeking measure, but a "terrified, inarticulate, or mentally less adroit prisoner was rarely able to offer the court any information beyond pleading for mercy, whether they had committed the offence or not."[143]

The first major exception to the general rule barring counsel in felony cases came in the Treason Act of 1696, which guaranteed the right to counsel for those facing capital treason charges.[144] But again, because charges of treason were typically brought against members of elite socioeconomic classes, this law primarily provided wealthy people with political influence the ability to hire counsel to represent them in high-profile political cases.[145]

By the 1730s English judges had grown markedly less averse to granting ordinary criminal defendants the benefits of having a legally trained advocate represent them.[146] Still, the decision to permit representation by counsel continued to be vested in the discretion of the trial court judge. And even when the court permitted counsel, lawyers continued to play a limited role, addressing only questions of law and cross-examining witnesses; "they could neither discuss facts nor address the jury in argument or present a defense."[147]

Parliament eventually enacted a statutory right to counsel in 1836, but that was forty-five years after the Bill of Rights was ratified in the United States.[148] The inclusion of the right to counsel in the Sixth Amendment appears to have been motivated in large part by the concerns of the framers of the Constitution about the limited role counsel had played in criminal trials in England, especially in trials for treason, which were often politically motivated to suppress free speech advocating for political reforms.[149] But even with such motivation, from the time of its adoption and for well over a century and a half, the Sixth Amendment was interpreted only as barring judges from preventing defendants from hiring attorneys to represent them in court.[150] In other words, the framers "did not intend to afford those charged with crimes and affirmative right to counsel, but rather the right to retrain counsel at their own expense."[151] Even today, a criminal defendant has a nearly unqualified right to be represented by his own privately retained attorney.[152] But the original interpretation of the Sixth Amendment's right to counsel has changed significantly as it concerns the appointment of counsel for those who cannot afford to hire their own defense attorneys. Unfortunately, however, the changes have not been sufficient to safeguard the rights of criminal defendants, especially in the earliest stages of criminal prosecutions.

### The Evolution of the Sixth Amendment Right to Counsel

In 1932 the US Supreme Court decided *Powell v. Alabama*.[153] Narrowly confining its ruling to the facts of the case, the Court held that a defendant facing a capital sentence had to be provided counsel at governmental expense if the accused was "incapable adequately of making his own defense because of ignorance, feeblemindedness, illiteracy or the like."[154] Importantly, the Court did not rely on the Sixth Amendment. Rather, its rationale rested on the Fourteenth Amendment guarantee of due process.

Five years later the Court squarely decided its first major Sixth Amendment case, holding in *Johnson v. Zerbst* that the federal government had to provide appointed counsel to all federal felony defendants who were unable to afford hiring privately retained counsel.[155] The Court reasoned:

> Even the intelligent and educated layman has small and sometimes no skill in the science of law. If charged with crime, he is incapable, generally, of determining for himself whether the indictment is good or bad. He is unfamiliar with the rules of evidence. Left without the aid of counsel, he may

be put on trial without a proper charge, and convicted upon incompetent evidence, or evidence irrelevant to the issue or otherwise inadmissible. He lacks both the skill and knowledge adequately to prepare his defence, even though he have a perfect one. He requires the guiding hand of counsel at every step in the proceedings against him.[156]

Four years later, however, the Court declined to extend its Sixth Amendment holding in *Johnson v. Zerbst* so that it applied to the states. In *Betts v. Brady*, the Court held that a right to appointed counsel was not essential to a fair trial process and therefore that the Fourteenth Amendment's Due Process Clause did not require states to appoint counsel for felony defendants in the same way that the federal government was required to do under *Johnson v. Zerbst*.[157] The Court reasoned that because resolution of the *Betts* case rested on the "simple issue" of judging the credibility of the defendant's alibi, and because the defendant was a man of "ordinary intelligence and ability," there was no deprivation of fundamental fairness.[158]

Under *Betts*, judges in state court felony trials had to decide whether the particular facts and circumstances of each case required the appointment of counsel to avoid fundamental unfairness. The approach yielded an outcome in which the exceptions swallowed the rule. In the twenty years following the *Betts* decision, the US Supreme Court decided more than thirty cases involving the Sixth Amendment right to counsel. In nearly all of these cases, the Court determined that the particular circumstances warranted the appointment of counsel to ensure that the defendants received a fundamentally fair trial. That state of affairs led the Court to overrule *Betts v. Brady* in the landmark 1963 decision in *Gideon v. Wainwright*.[159]

*Gideon* jettisoned a case-by-case approach to the Sixth Amendment and instead held that because the right to counsel is a fundamental right, the Fourteenth Amendment incorporated the Sixth Amendment such that its guarantee of the assistance of counsel applied to all state felony defendants.[160] The Court explained that "in our adversary system of criminal justice, any person haled into court, who is too poor to hire a lawyer, cannot be assured a fair trial unless counsel is provided for him."[161] The result in Gideon's trial and retrial attests to this reasoning. Clarence Gideon had been tried and convicted of robbery, but after his successful appeal to the Supreme Court, the court-appointed defense lawyer at Gideon's retrial was able to discredit the sole witness against Gideon, resulting in his acquittal.

In the 1972 case *Argersinger v. Hamelin*, the Court extended *Gideon's* holding to state misdemeanor prosecutions in which a defendant faces a potential jail sentence.[162] But in a retreat from the line of cases expanding access to counsel under the Sixth Amendment, the Court held in *Scott v. Illinois* that so long as an indigent defendant is not actually sentenced to a period of incarceration, then the state is not required to appoint counsel.[163]

Scholars have criticized the *Scott* decision for both its flawed logic and the outcomes it wrought.[164] But as law professor John D. King explained, the real impact of limiting *Argersinger's* reach did not become evident until the advent of "Broken Windows" policing and its associated effects on soaring misdemeanor prosecutions and increased collateral consequences for misdemeanor convictions—including deportation, sex offender registration, sentencing enhancements, and employment limitations.[165] Because calls to roll back collateral consequences have largely gone unheeded, Professor King called for *Scott v. Illinois* to be overruled and *Argersinger* to be extended such that the right to counsel would apply to *all* criminal cases.[166] We concur wholeheartedly. But the timing of the attachment of such a right matters significantly for those whose lack of financial means subject them to pretrial injustice.

## Attachment of the Right to Counsel and Pretrial Injustice

The right to counsel under the Sixth Amendment is not limited to trials. Rather, the Sixth Amendment "guarantees a defendant the right to have counsel present at all 'critical' stages of the criminal proceedings."[167] As early as *Powell v. Alabama*, the US Supreme Court framed the right to counsel around this notion of critical stages: "During perhaps the most critical period of the proceedings ... that is to say, from the time of their arraignment until the beginning of their trial, when consultation, thoroughgoing investigation and preparation [are] vitally important, the defendants ... [are] as much entitled to such aid [of counsel] during that period as at the trial itself."[168] As a result of this language, the critical stages test has long been operationalized to provide the right to effective assistance of counsel "once adversarial proceedings have commenced."[169] But the precise moment at which adversarial proceedings begin is not clear-cut.

The Court has explained that *critical stages* are those "where substantial rights of the accused may be affected," requiring the "guiding hand of counsel."[170] Thus, the Sixth Amendment right to counsel has been held to apply at

preliminary hearings,[171]

arraignments,[172]

postindictment interrogations,[173]

postindictment lineups,[174]

plea bargaining negotiations,[175]

trials,[176]

sentencing hearings,[177]

probation or parole revocation hearings (at least to some extent),[178] and

initial appeals that are taken as a matter of right.[179]

Whether the initial appearance before a judge, magistrate, or other judicial officer constitutes a critical stage of the prosecution, triggering the right to counsel under the Sixth Amendment, has proven to be a complex question.

The initial appearance is sometimes referred to as a "preliminary arraignment," an "arraignment on the complaint," a "*Gerstein* hearing," or a "probable cause hearing."[180] During this initial judicial proceeding, arrestees are typically informed of the charges against them. Moreover, as discussed in chapter 2, the conditions of initial pretrial release (e.g., recognizance, bail, or pretrial detention) are typically set at this proceeding.[181] In dicta in the *Gerstein* decision itself (which held that a probable cause hearing before a neutral judicial officer must generally be held within forty-eight hours of arrest), the Court stated that the probable cause hearing was not a critical stage at which defendants are entitled to the presence of counsel.[182] But initial appearances can be transformed into critical stages depending on what transpires during those proceedings.

In *Rothgery v. Gillespie County*, the US Supreme Court questionably asserted that it had at least twice before previously held that the Sixth Amendment right to counsel "applies at the first appearance before a judicial officer at which a defendant is told of the formal accusation against him and restrictions are imposed on his liberty."[183] Given that bail determinations are often made during initial appearances/probable cause hearings, the *Rothgery* decision implied that the aforementioned dicta in *Gerstein* was no longer good law. But that conclusion is not at all clear, for two reasons. First, the bail determination in *Rothgery* was not contested by the uncounseled defendant. Second, the *Rothgery* Court went to great lengths to distinguish between the technical attachment of the right to counsel at the initial appearance and the separate question of whether counsel must actually be present during that proceeding.[184] Under such an interpretation of the Sixth Amendment, counsel does not need to be present at the initial appearance, but rather must be appointed within a reasonable amount of time following the probable cause hearing to allow for adequate representation.

The concurring justices in *Rothgery* wrote that they joined the majority opinion only because they interpreted it as not holding that "a defendant is entitled to the assistance of appointed counsel as soon as his Sixth Amendment right attaches."[185] And in his dissent, Justice Thomas said that the Court had "never suggested that the accused's right to the assistance of counsel 'for his defence' entails a right to use counsel as a sword to contest pretrial detention."[186] In criticizing the morass that is the *Rothgery* decision, law professor Justin Marceau said, "Instead of capitalizing on an opportune moment to clarify that the right to appointed counsel applies to one's first opportunity to seek pretrial release, the Court went some distance in the opposite direction by clarifying that mere technical attachment and the requirement of appointment (and effective assistance) are not equivalent."[187]

In short, it is dreadfully unclear, as a matter of constitutional law, whether the Sixth Amendment requires the assistance of counsel for defendants during initial appearances if bail determinations are made at those proceeding. What is clear, however, is that prosecutors often offer binding plea deals at initial appearances when defendants are uncounseled. Indeed, during our own observations of misdemeanor proceedings in southern California, prosecutors routinely offered plea deals to defendants for whom counsel had not yet been appointed.

There is little doubt that representation by counsel matters. Indeed, the assistance of counsel is essential to serving the guarantees of due process and equal protection. A study in Baltimore, for example, evaluated an eighteen-month experiment in which lawyers provided representation to indigent arrestees accused of nonviolent crimes. Those who were represented by counsel were 2.5 times more likely to be released on their own recognizance (34 percent) than those who were unrepresented (13 percent).[188] For those for whom bail was ordered, counsel was successfully able to have the amount of bail set to something the accused could afford for 59 percent of clients, compared to only 14 percent of the unrepresented being successful at securing affordable bail for themselves.[189] Additional studies in other jurisdictions have reached similar conclusions, insofar as defendants represented by counsel obtain pretrial release sooner than their uncounseled counterparts, often for lower bail amounts and under less stringent conditions of pretrial release.[190]

According to the National Conference of State Legislatures, initial appearance procedures vary significantly from state to state, as do the procedures for appointment of counsel.[191] Some states require that defendants eligible for appointed counsel be provided an attorney in advance of any bail determination; most, however, do not.[192] Some states have even structured their processes in ways that were clearly designed to prevent defendants from having the assistance of counsel in early stages of the criminal justice process even though defendants are required to make decisions that they are ill-equipped to make. An example is the process in Colorado for misdemeanor offenses that was in effect until 2014.[193]

Colorado law required prosecutors to negotiate potential plea bargains with people accused of misdemeanor and traffic offenses *before* defendants had an opportunity to meet with counsel. In fact, the statute deferred the appointment of counsel "until after the prosecuting attorney has spoken with the defendant" about a potential disposition via a plea bargain:[194]

> There are strong incentives for defendants to accept a pre-counsel offer; indeed, by accepting an early, pre-counsel plea, a defendant may accrue sentencing or charge concessions from the prosecution. Moreover, and more significant, for defendants who are not released on bail, the consequences of refusing a pre-counsel plea offer are even more immediate: such a defendant faces the Hobson's choice of pleading guilty to a crime without the advice or assistance of counsel and thus obtaining one's immediate release from custody, or remaining in jail for several more days until a second appearance when counsel is appointed. That is to say, insisting on one's right to counsel in a misdemeanor case may come at a cost, both in terms of the ultimate sentence, and the length of the time they are subject to pre-trial detention. Even a defendant who is arrested for an offense for which jail is a most unlikely sentence could be held in jail for days while he is awaiting the appointment of counsel and the next round of plea negotiations if he is not released on bail at the initial appearance.[195]

Colorado amended its plea bargaining statute in 2014, but it still encourages the practice of early case disposition through plea offers in cases in which the charged offenses do not include a possible sentence of incarceration. In other words, states circumvent the spirit of the Sixth Amendment by plea bargaining with an uncounseled defendant when "the defendant is not eligible for appointment of counsel because the defendant is not indigent or the charged offense does not include a possible sentence of incarceration or because the defendant refuses appointment of counsel and has not retained counsel."[196]

The high courts of a handful of states have clearly held that bail proceedings are critical stages of criminal proceedings at which defendants must be provided with counsel.[197] This approach should be adopted nationwide—whether by state criminal procedure rules, by state statutes, or as a matter of Sixth Amendment constitutional law—because bail determinations are proceedings at which counsel helps the accused "in coping with legal problems or … meeting his adversary."[198] This need is underscored by the fact that during initial appearances (which, as explained in chapter 2, typically last only three to five minutes), more than two-thirds of misdemeanor defendants are not represented by counsel.[199]

Even worse than the sheer numbers of people who are unrepresented when an initial bail determination is made is the number of uncounseled people who enter binding pleas at that first judicial appearance. According to a 2009 national study, some judges pressure uncounseled defendants to enter guilty pleas, sometimes even using threats of high bail amounts or pretrial detention to encourage defendants to agree to immediate case dispositions.[200] Our own court observations bear this out. During an en masse initial appearance of roughly forty defendants, a Maricopa County, Arizona, justice of the peace offered roughly thirty driving under the influence arrestees the statutory minimum penalties for the offense (which were quickly summarized in a sentence or two) if they pled guilty on the spot. This "take it or leave it" offer from the bench was made to defendants who not only were unrepresented by counsel, but also were never even informed of any of their rights or the collateral consequences of a misdemeanor conviction. The only warning the justice of the peace provided was that if defendants passed up on this "one-time opportunity," they would face more severe penalties as their cases progressed through the system. Every eligible defendant in the courtroom accepted the offer by nodding and by remaining silent when the justice of the peace asked if anyone "wanted to take their chances with a trial." After a few seconds, the justice of the peace banged his gavel and thirty defendants were pronounced guilty.

Similarly, when felony defendants were offered plea deals during their initial appearances in Los Angeles County, many asked for more time to think over whether they wanted to accept the offer in exchange for admitting guilt. Each time that occurred, despite the fact that the defendants were represented by counsel, the judge told defendants that they had "today only offers." The judge specifically told defendants that if they did not accept the plea during the instant proceedings, the penalties they would face, including the length of incarceration, would undoubtedly increase.

Even in the absence of judicial coercion, however, between 70 and 80 percent of unrepresented misdemeanor defendants plead guilty or no contest during this first court appearance.[201] This situation gives rise to serious Sixth Amendment questions, especially in light of the decision in *Alabama v. Shelton*, in which the Supreme Court held that in the absence of a valid waiver, the right to counsel is violated when a defendant is sentenced to a suspended sentence without the assistance of counsel.[202] But the situation also implicates equal protection concerns in light of *Padilla v. Kentucky*'s holding that lawyers provide ineffective assistance of counsel when they fail to advise their clients about the collateral consequences of convictions, such as potential deportation.[203] Without counsel, though, unrepresented defendants are unlikely to know about either the direct or collateral consequences of a conviction.[204] Thus, those who can afford counsel can knowingly and intelligently enter binding pleas at initial appearances, whereas similarly situated defendants who cannot afford counsel enter such pleas ignorantly unless appointed counsel is provided to them *before* they enter pleas of guilty or no contest.[205]

The American Bar Association has long recommended that counsel be "provided to the accused as soon as feasible and, in any event, after custody begins, at appearance before a committing magistrate, or when formal charges are filed, whichever occurs earliest."[206] Dozens of other advocacy groups and scholars have similarly advocated that counsel be provided to all those who stand accused of criminal offenses at their first court appearance to ensure the assistance of counsel when pretrial release decisions are first made.[207] And as the Constitution Project pointed out, the cost saving realized through reductions in jail populations could provide the fiscal resources to provide counsel at initial pretrial release hearings.[208] The time has come for us to act on these calls and ensure that defendants are provided with the effective assistance of defense counsel at their initial appearances. And indeed, as we discuss in the next section, we would go further and recommend the provision of legal assistance at arrest.

### Providing Legal Assistance at Arrest

We know of no jurisdiction in the United States that automatically provides arrestees with legal assistance. However, in other countries, even poor countries, arrestees are routinely provided with legal advice and assistance. For example, England and Wales, a jurisdiction with one of the lowest rates of pretrial detention in the world, has long provided state-funded lawyers or paralegals (working under the supervision of a lawyer) to all suspects, regardless of means, at the local police station.[209] More recently, since 2005 Nigeria has provided lawyers known as duty-solicitors to suspects and detainees at police stations in four states. This initiative has "reduced the number of pretrial detainees by almost 20 percent and the duration of pretrial detention by 72 percent over a one year period."[210] Similar programs exist in Malawi, Ukraine, and Sierra Leone. In Sierra Leone the provision of paralegal assistance at police stations has led to significant achievements: "Over a one year period in 2011–2012, the paralegals provided assistance to 5,781 people in police stations. They succeeded in securing police bail in half of he cases. In addition, they succeeded in getting the charges dropped entirely in 28 percent of the cases, usually due to mistakes of identify, misunderstandings of facts, or lack of evidence."[211] The potential impact of providing legal assistance at local police stations in the United States is huge. It would provide all of the benefits previously discussed, but earlier in the process, thus avoiding even more justice system costs.

## AVAILABILITY OF DETENTION WITH DUE PROCESS

As explained in chapter 1, the Bail Reform Act of 1984 requires that defendants charged with certain federal felony offenses be denied pretrial release if a judicial officer is persuaded, by clear and convincing evidence, that "no condition or combination of conditions will reasonably assure the appearance of the person as required and the safety of any other person and the community."[212] Recall that in *United States v. Salerno*, the US Supreme Court upheld the constitutionality of the Bail Reform Act as it applied to preventative detention.[213] The Court acknowledged that detention prior to trial infringes on a significant constitutional protected liberty interest. But the Court reasoned that the governmental interest "in community safety can, in appropriate circumstances, outweigh an individual's liberty interest."[214] The Court rejected an Eighth Amendment challenge to the Bail Act, reasoning that pretrial detention is not punitive, but regulatory.[215] The Court also rejected a due process challenge to pretrial detention because of the procedural safeguards the act specifies must be honored before a judge denies a defendant pretrial release:

> Detainees have a right to counsel at the detention hearing.... They may testify in their own behalf, present information by proffer or otherwise, and cross-examine witnesses who appear at the hearing.... The judicial officer charged with the responsibility of determining the appropriateness of detention is guided by statutorily enumerated factors, which include the nature and the circumstances of the charges, the weight of the evidence, the history and characteristics of the putative offender, and the danger to the community.... The Government must prove its case by clear and

convincing evidence.... Finally, the judicial officer must include written findings of fact and a written statement of reasons for a decision to detain.... The Act's review provisions ... provide for immediate appellate review of the detention decision. We think these extensive safeguards suffice.[216]

As with the federal system, most states also provide for the pretrial detention of arrestees. In a handful of states, judges are required to deny pretrial release to defendants charged with capital crimes, such as treason or murder.[217] In most states, though, judges are vested with the discretion to order defendants charged with enumerated offenses, typically violent felonies, into pretrial detention.[218] Notably, some states have altered their laws to embrace the federal approach to pretrial detention for defendants deemed "dangerous" and, in doing so, have curtailed previously recognized rights to bail under state statutes.[219]

Few reasonable people would disagree that the most dangerous of presumed offenders should not remain at large pending trial. But the major problem with pretrial detention is that it does not concern such individuals. After all, fewer than 10 percent of all pretrial detainees are ordered remanded into custody.[220] Rather, the major problem with pretrial detention concerns judges who either unthinkingly set bail too high (often a problem associated with bail schedules, as explained in chapter 2) or who intentionally set bail to effect what law professor Lauryn Gouldin called *pretextual preventive detention*—setting bail so high as to make it unpayable as a means for managing judicial or public perceptions of a defendant's perceived dangerousness.[221] But as Professor Gouldin explained, such an approach to pretrial detention defies logic and, in most jurisdictions, violates law and public policy:

> This is the point in the pretrial detention system that seems to operate most illogically—and where judicial practice diverges most widely from statutory and constitutional requirements. Thirty-plus years after federal and state statutes were rewritten to fix this precise problem by permitting judges to order dangerous defendants to be detained, money bail is still used as a back-door means to manage dangerousness, even in cases where there is no serious risk of flight.

Properly calculated, money bail is set at the precise amount that will induce a released defendant to return to court (or, conversely, the amount of money that will dissuade a released defendant from fleeing the jurisdiction). Although there are real debates about how well bail serves this purpose, there is not much to debate about the purpose of bail. When priced to ensure detention on the basis of dangerousness, money bail violates both law and policy.

In many jurisdictions, statutes governing the setting of bail expressly state that the purpose of bail is to ensure appearance. Many jurisdictions also expressly condition the forfeiture of bail (i.e., the loss of bail money) on a failure to appear, not on the commission of a new offense. These provisions are consistent with a long history that makes clear that money bail is a tool for managing flight risk, not a legitimate means of managing danger.

Suggesting that bail—which is of questionable utility in managing flight risk, the very risk it was developed to manage—should be extended to manage public safety risk is also simply illogical. There is no evidence that threatening to withhold a bail payment if a person commits a crime while on pretrial release provides any marginal deterrence value over the existing blanket of criminal sanctions and penalties that a new crime would trigger. Viewed slightly differently, if a court views a defendant as being a high risk for committing a new crime on release, it does not seem appropriate to simply set a high price for release. Dangerous defendants do not become less dangerous by paying bail.[222]

It's all very well to say that preventative detention with adequate due process should be a part of the future of pretrial justice. We certainly concur with that recommendation. But this aspiration is a mirage—an abstraction that fails to account for the fact that the vast majority of pretrial detainees are not incarcerated because they were adjudicated to meet pretrial detention standards in an adversarial proceeding with a full panoply of due process protections. Rather, as previously explained, most defendants are granted bail during initial appearances that typically last three minutes—and often without the benefit of defense counsel. All too frequently, bail amounts are set unaffordably high during these assembly-line justice proceedings, either through inadvertence, routinized adherence to bail schedules, or purposeful actions designed to achieve pretextual preventative detention. To address the improper use of preventative detention, money bail should be eliminated, as discussed later in this chapter, just as it has been in several US jurisdictions, including in the District of Columbia since 1992.

## COLLECTION AND ANALYSIS OF PERFORMANCE MEASURES

At first blush, it may seem self-evident that jurisdictions need to collect and analyze performance measures in order to provide insight into the operations of their pretrial justice systems. But effectively implementing meaningful data collection and analysis programs involves time and money. As the Pretrial Justice Institute has acknowledged, data exist in different locations within a jurisdiction, including "state criminal history repositories, jails, police departments, sheriffs' offices, courts, and local pretrial services or probation departments."[223] Worse yet, the data storage systems in these locations may not be compatible with each other. For example, attempts to quantify the use of federal pretrial diversion, as well as outcomes for defendants granted diversion, have been stymied by at least two data collection issues. First, the Executive Office of the United States Attorney inconsistently enters data about diversion. And second, its US attorneys, who decide to whom diversion should be offered, and pretrial services officers, who supervise individuals on diversion programs, use different case management systems.[224] Jurisdictions must ensure that their data systems can interface with each other. And they must employ qualified research analysts to compile, clean, and analyze the data and then disseminate annual reports in ways that facilitate easy public access.

In 2011 the National Institute of Corrections published a white paper entitled *Measuring What Matters*, authored by members of its Pretrial Executives Network.[225] The document recommended that jurisdictions gather data related to all of the following outcomes:

- *Appearance rate*, which should be tracked for all defendant populations—those released on personal recognizance, financial conditions, and special conditions—for ordinance, misdemeanor, and felony offenses.

- *Safety rate*, which tracks reoffending as measured not only by rearrests, but also by whether new charges were filed by prosecutors. Technical violations need to be coded differently from ordinance, misdemeanor, and felony offenses. Moreover, the severity of the offense needs to be coded in a manner that differentiates property crimes, domestic/interpersonal violence offenses, driving under the influence, nonviolent drug offenses, and crimes of violence.

- *Concurrence rate*, the ratio of agreement between judicially imposed outcomes (e.g., release on recognizance, release on supervision, pretrial detention) for defendants statutorily eligible for pretrial release and the pretrial services classification of defendants' assessed level of risk for pretrial failure.

- *Success rate*, the percentage of defendants granted pretrial release who are revoked for technical violations, show up in court for all scheduled appearances, and are not charged with a new offense while on pretrial release.

- *Detainee length of stay*, an average of how long defendants eligible for pretrial release spend in pretrial detention.[226]

In addition, the document recommends gathering data on a variety of performance measures, including the percentage of people eligible for release who underwent pretrial services screening, the rate at which pretrial personnel follow their own risk assessment criteria when recommending pretrial release or detention, how often case managers respond in accordance with policies to defendants' noncompliance with court-ordered conditions of release, and the rate at which pretrial personnel are able to resolve outstanding bench warrants by encouraging self-surrender and by making arrests.[227] The National Institute of

Corrections also recommends that data be gathered on a number of mission-critical variables, such as caseload ratios, the time between a court order for supervision and the start of such supervision, the length of time clients spend under pretrial supervision, and the pretrial detention rate.[228]

In addition to the National Institute of Corrections's recommendations, we also encourage jurisdictions to follow the lead of select pretrial agencies by tracking referrals, enrollments, and compliance with substance abuse and mental health treatment plans; the number of people drug tested and the outcome of such screenings; the number of defendants who receive pretrial diversion; the number of diversion community service hours completed; and the amount of restitution paid to victims through diversion placements.[229]

## CONCLUSION

Bail reform is not simple. The Pretrial Justice Institute is correct to highlight the complexity of the problems with pretrial release, and as we have explained in this chapter—indeed throughout this book—some of their proposed solutions make sense. If we can divert individuals accused of committing low-level offenses from the formal criminal justice system, through citation in lieu of arrest and/or better screening of cases, that will go a long way toward reducing the number of people whose lives are devastated by pretrial detention.

There are also some important reforms that can be made to existing systems that rely on money bail. First, as we made clear in chapter 2, we believe that both bail schedules and commercial bail should be eliminated. However, if money bail is retained, it is important to ensure that defendants are guaranteed a determination of their ability to pay the money bail set. Harvard Law School's Criminal Justice Policy Program recommends procedures that should be included in that determination, such as notice to the defendant that bail determinations must be individualized, a presumption that defendants who are indigent are unable to pay money bail, a hearing on the record at which the defendant has the right to counsel, and the right to prompt review.[230] Including safeguards like these in pretrial release decision making would help ensure that where money bail is set, it is set no higher than necessary to incentivize appearance.[231]

That being said, as we explained in chapter 2, because there is no evidence that money bail effectively incentivizes court appearances or protects public safety, money bail should be abolished. There are simply no good arguments for retaining a system that fails to achieve either of its stated ends while it simultaneously punishes the poor. Instead, we cautiously recommend moving to a risk-based system of pretrial justice that utilizes PSAs. And like others, we point to the pretrial release system in the District of Columbia as a model. Its most recent data show that almost 90 percent of defendants in the District of Columbia remained in the community while awaiting their case resolution, without any revocation of their release. Similar percentages of defendants made all scheduled court appearances, and less than 10 percent of defendants were rearrested for a new crime while awaiting trial, most of these for nonviolent offenses.[232]

There are of course some caveats to this recommendation. As we argued in chapter 3, it is important that actuarial risk assessment tools be reliable tools that are properly validated. To be clear, most of the current pretrial risk assessment instruments fail to meet this criterion for being valid predictors of the two distinct types of pretrial risk (i.e., nonappearance and reoffending while on pretrial release). Moreover, with regard to the latter type of risk, reoffending of just any type should be insufficient. Rather, risk assessment should only target the likelihood of violent reoffending, since pretrial preventative detention is supposed to be limited to incapacitating those who are dangerous.[233] This line of inquiry should not be open-ended, either. Rather, as law professor Sandra Mayson suggested, predictions of violent recidivism risk in pretrial processes should be time-bounded, perhaps for a period of no more than six months.[234] But even honed instruments that validly predict pretrial risks as described would be insufficient. At a minimum, these tools must also be normed in ways that eliminate racial, ethnic, and socioeconomic disparities.[235] That's a tall order—one that may not even be achievable because pretrial risk assessment instruments use variables so statistically correlated with race, ethnicity, and low socioeconomic status that some critics rightfully refer to the variables in the tools as "proxies" for race, ethnicity, and poverty.[236] Even though some preliminary research suggests that algorithms might be developed using machine learning that can simultaneously serve the goals of public safety and social justice by reducing crime and racial disparities, it is far too soon to tell whether the machine learning can actually achieve such ends.[237] But even if such a goal proves to be unachievable, that does not mean that actuarial risk assessment should be jettisoned. In comparison to the purely subjective assessment of risk by judges, sophisticated actuarial methods that use diverse and large data sets and that are properly normed to reduce racial, ethnic, and socioeconomic disparities have the capacity to shed light on specific types of risk while countering both conscious and unconscious judicial biases.[238] To be sure, it is highly unlikely that bias can be completely eliminated. But it certainly can be minimized—not only through the use of better APRAIs, but also through better, more sophisticated decision making with regard to what "high risk" means and how to respond to it using the least-restrictive-means principle: "What if support, rather than jail, were the default response to risk? Risk, after all, is neither intrinsic nor immutable. It is possible to change the odds. A supportive, needs-oriented response to risk might help to change the odds for high-risk groups in the long term. In the short term, it would mitigate the immediate racial impact of prediction. If a high-risk classification meant greater access to social services and employment, a higher false-positive rate among [racial and ethnic minorities] would be less of a concern."[239]

Another important step forward would be for agencies and judges to ensure that conditions imposed on released defendants are limited to those that will increase the likelihood that they will appear at scheduled court dates. In particular, drug testing should be avoided, and electronic monitoring should only be used as a true alternative to detention for high-risk individuals who would otherwise be detained pretrial. Instead, we encourage agencies to use court date notification tools, which have been shown to be effective. In addition, it is important that any costs of pretrial supervision not be passed on to defendants, as to do so would defeat the purpose of eliminating money bail.

A recent reform effort in New York City presents some hope that providing *unconditional* assistance to defendants awaiting trial can be effective. In October 2018 Robert F. Kennedy Human Rights, an advocacy group, organized hundreds of volunteers to bail out 105 women and youth held in Rikers Island, at a cost of $1.2 million. Although detailed information about the released individuals, or how they were chosen, is unavailable, 92 percent were charged with a felony. Upon release, the defendants were connected to reentry experts and social workers to connect them with needed services. A report in the *New York Times* about the effort noted that "finding individuals a place to stay and providing them with a cellphone and a two-month unlimited Metro-Card proved to be some of the biggest factors in making sure the released could connect with their lawyers. They were sent text messages reminding them of their court dates."[240] Although there has not yet been a formal evaluation of the effort (and it is unclear whether one is underway), early results showed that the vast majority (eighty-eight of ninety) who had scheduled court appearances showed up for those appearances, and just four had been rearrested (all on prior allegations). There is a desperate need for more experiments like this one, particularly experiments that utilize random assignment and that will be rigorously evaluated. As evidenced by a recent request for proposals issued by the Laura and John Arnold Foundation, there finally appears to be funding to support such research.

There are also reforms that states could undertake based on successful practices abroad. We have already discussed the provision of legal assistance in police stations. In addition, in Belgium judges are not permitted to order an arrestee into pretrial preventative detention on charges for which the punishment is less than one year in prison.[241] Absent compelling public safety reasons that cannot be achieved with pretrial supervision, this should be the norm for all misdemeanor charges in the United States, at a minimum. And in light of the presumption of innocence, we can think of no principled reason why this should not also be the default practice for nonviolent felonies.

As of the writing of this book, we are unaware of any state acting on the full panoply of recommendations we outline here. The few jurisdictions that have undertaken bail reform have, in our opinion, missed the mark. For example, in August 2018 California legislatively abolished money bail in the state. The legislation contains several important features. On the positive side, the bill eliminates bail schedules, which as we argued in chapter 2 are likely unconstitutional. The bill also eliminates the commercial bail bonds industry, which as we also explained in chapter 2, is known for its corrupt and predatory practices.

On the other hand, the law imposes some burdensome conditions of pretrial release that can include "electronic monitoring, weekly check-ins, home detention, and drug testing" even though, as previously discussed, some of these measures are not effective in reducing pretrial risk.[242] The law also replaces money-based pretrial release with a risk-based system. And as its critics have pointed out, the legislation is problematic in how it relies on risk assessment tools and in the broad discretion it gives to judges to preventatively detain defendants.[243] While the state Judicial Council will maintain a list of approved tools, and a panel of experts will assess each county's tool and guidelines, SB 10 gives too much discretion to counties. They will be able to choose their own tools, which may or may not be properly validated to predict distinct types of pretrial risk by the time their use begins. And they will be able to use risk assessment instruments that fail to meet the commands of equal protection under law because they incorporate static metrics that are all but proxies for race, ethnicity, and socioeconomic status.

More worrying is the presumption against release (prior to court hearing) for a large number of defendants. While SB 10 requires many people assessed as low risk to be released on their own recognizance prior to arraignment, it prevents the PSA from releasing individuals charged with certain offenses (both felonies and misdemeanors) or who meet certain criteria, even if those individuals are assessed to be low risk. The new law also allows courts to establish rules limiting the pre-arraignment release of medium-risk defendants. While most of these defendants may be released by a judge at arraignment, SB 10 gives judges a considerable amount of discretion to detain defendants. Indeed, section 1320.20(a) of SB 10 includes a rebuttable presumption that defendants who are charged with a violent felony (regardless of assessed risk) and who are assessed to be high risk and meet certain conditions, including having a recent conviction for a serious felony, should be remanded into custody because "no condition or combination of conditions of pretrial supervision will reasonably assure public safety" in such cases. Thus, even though the new law purports to move from a system of money bail to a risk-based system, in certain circumstances it directs both PSAs and judges to ignore assessed risk. Further, judges tend to be risk averse, and thus concerns that judges will exercise their discretion to lock up more people prior to trial are well-founded.

Whether SB 10 will go into effect as intended is unclear. In addition to criticism from bail reform advocates, as noted in chapter 2 the law is being challenged by bail agents, a coalition of which collected enough signatures to put the law on the November 2020 ballot. Further, while SB 10 may moot some pending constitutional challenges,[244] both federal and state cases challenging existing law remain active. If it does go into effect, what impact it will have—whether it will make a difference to the thousands of people currently locked up awaiting trial simply because they are poor, or whether it will make an already bad system worse—will depend on the actions of counties and judges.

There is no doubt that our recommendation to establish and fund the operation of a high-functioning pretrial services system will be difficult for some jurisdictions to do. The District of Columbia Pretrial Services Agency has in part been so successful because it receives funding from the federal government.[245] Nonetheless, as we demonstrated in chapter 4, pretrial detention is a major contributor to mass incarceration, which currently costs states and counties billions of dollars. It was exactly these concerns that led Alaska to enact criminal justice reforms that included significant changes to that state's approach to pretrial justice. The Pew Charitable Trusts estimates that these reforms will reduce Alaska's prison population by 13 percent and save the state approximately $380 million.[246] It is too early tell what the impact will be of the Alaska reforms, as well as those in New Jersey, Maryland, and other jurisdictions described throughout this book. But the lessons from the District of Columbia are clear: "With alternative methods to manage risk, money can be virtually eliminated from the bail process without negatively affecting court appearance rates or public safety."[247] That would be a major step toward a system that does not punish people simply for being poor.

# APPENDIX: TENN. CODE ANN.
# § 40-7-118 (2018)

(b)

    (1) A peace officer who has arrested a person for the commission of a misdemeanor committed in the peace officer's presence, or who has taken custody of a person arrested by a private person for the commission of a misdemeanor, shall issue a citation to the arrested person to appear in court in lieu of the continued custody and the taking of the arrested person before a magistrate. If the peace officer is serving an arrest warrant or capias issued by a magistrate for the commission of a misdemeanor, it is in the discretion of the issuing magistrate whether the person is to be arrested and taken into custody or arrested and issued a citation in accordance with this section in lieu of continued custody. The warrant or capias shall specify the action to be taken by the serving peace officer who shall act accordingly.

    (2)

        (A) This subsection (b) does not apply to an arrest for the offense of driving under the influence of an intoxicant as prohibited by § 55-10-401, unless the offender was admitted to a hospital, or detained for medical treatment for a period of at least three (3) hours, for injuries received in a driving under the influence incident.

        (B) This subsection (b) does not apply to any misdemeanor offense for which § 55-10-207 or § 55-12-139 authorizes a traffic citation in lieu of arrest, continued custody and the taking of the arrested person before a magistrate.

(3) A peace officer may issue a citation to the arrested person to appear in court in lieu of the continued custody and the taking of the arrested person before a magistrate if a person is arrested for:

(A) The offense of theft which formerly constituted shoplifting, in violation of § 39-14-103;

(B) Issuance of bad checks, in violation of § 39-14-121;

(C) Use of a revoked or suspended driver license in violation of § 55-50-504, § 55-50-601 or § 55-50-602;

(D) Assault or battery as those offenses are defined by common law, if the officer believes there is a reasonable likelihood that persons would be endangered by the arrested person if a citation were issued in lieu of continued physical custody of the defendant; or

(E) Prostitution, in violation of § 39-13-513, if the arresting party has knowledge of past conduct of the defendant in prostitution or has reasonable cause to believe that the defendant will attempt to engage in prostitution activities within a reasonable period of time if not arrested.

(c) No citation shall be issued under this section if:

(1) The person arrested requires medical examination or medical care, or if the person is unable to care for the person's own safety;

(2) There is a reasonable likelihood that the offense would continue or resume, or that persons or property would be endangered by the arrested person;

(3) The person arrested cannot or will not offer satisfactory evidence of identification, including the providing of a field-administered fingerprint or thumbprint which a peace officer may require to be affixed to any citation;

(4) The prosecution of the offense for which the person was arrested, or of another offense, would thereby be jeopardized;

(5) A reasonable likelihood exists that the arrested person will fail to appear in court;

(6) The person demands to be taken immediately before a magistrate or refuses to sign the citation;

(7) The person arrested is so intoxicated that the person could be a danger to the person's own self or to others;

(8) There are one (1) or more outstanding arrest warrants for the person; or

(9) The person is subject to arrest pursuant to § 55-10-119 [vehicle accidents involving serious bodily injury or death].

(d) In issuing a citation, the officer shall:

   (1) Prepare a written order which shall include the name and address of the cited person, the offense charged and the time and place of appearance;

   (2) Have the offender sign the original and duplicate copy of the citation. The officer shall deliver one (1) copy to the offender and retain the other; and

   (3) Release the cited person from custody.

(e) By accepting the citation, the defendant agrees to appear at the arresting law enforcement agency prior to trial to be booked and processed. Failure to so appear is a Class A misdemeanor.

(f) If the person cited fails to appear in court on the date and time specified or fails to appear for booking and processing prior to the person's court date, the court shall issue a bench warrant for the person's arrest.

(g) Whenever a citation has been prepared, delivered and filed with a court as provided in this section, a duplicate copy of the citation constitutes a complaint to which the defendant shall answer. The duplicate copy shall be sworn to by the issuing officer before any person authorized by law to administer oaths.

(h) Nothing in this section shall be construed to affect a peace officer's authority to conduct a lawful search even though the citation is issued after arrest.

(i) Any person who intentionally, knowingly or willfully fails to appear in court on the date and time specified on the citation or who knowingly gives a false or assumed name or address commits a Class A misdemeanor, regardless of the disposition of the charge for which the person was originally arrested. Proof that the defendant failed to appear when required constitutes prima facie evidence that the failure to appear is willful.

(j) Whenever an officer makes a physical arrest for a misdemeanor and the officer determines that a citation cannot be issued because of one (1) of the eight (8) reasons enumerated in subsection (c), the officer shall note the reason for not issuing a citation on the arrest ticket. An officer who, on the basis of facts reasonably known or reasonably believed to exist, determines that a citation cannot be issued because of one (1) of the eight (8) reasons enumerated in subsection (c) shall not be subject to civil or criminal liability for false arrest, false imprisonment or unlawful detention.

(k)

    (1) Each citation issued pursuant to this section shall have printed on it in large, conspicuous block letters the following:
NOTICE: FAILURE TO APPEAR IN COURT ON THE DATE ASSIGNED BY THIS CITATION OR AT THE APPROPRIATE POLICE STATION FOR BOOKING AND PROCESSING WILL RESULT IN YOUR ARREST FOR A SEPARATE CRIMINAL OFFENSE WHICH IS PUNISHABLE BY A JAIL SENTENCE OF ELEVEN (11) MONTHS AND TWENTY-NINE (29) DAYS AND/ OR A FINE OF UP TO TWO THOUSAND FIVE HUNDRED DOLLARS ($2,500).

    (2) Each person receiving a citation under this section shall sign this citation indicating the knowledge of the notice listed in subdivision (k)(1). The signature of each person creates a presumption of knowledge of the notice and a presumption of intent to violate this section if the person should not appear as required by the citation.

    (3) Whenever there are changes in the citation form notice required by this subsection (k), a law enforcement agency may exhaust its existing supply of citation forms before implementing the new citation forms.

(l) This section shall govern all aspects of the issuance of citations in lieu of the continued custody of an arrested person, notwithstanding any provision of Rule 3.5 of the Tennessee Rules of Criminal Procedure to the contrary.

(m) In cases in which:

    (1) The public will not be endangered by the continued freedom of the suspected misdemeanant;

    (2) The law enforcement officer has reasonable proof of the identity of the suspected misdemeanant; and

    (3) There is no reason to believe the suspected misdemeanant will not appear as required by law,

the general assembly finds that the issuance of a citation in lieu of arrest of the suspected misdemeanant will result in cost savings and increased public safety by allowing the use of jail space for dangerous individuals and/or felons and by keeping officers on patrol. Accordingly, the general assembly encourages all law enforcement agencies to so utilize misdemeanor citations and to encourage their personnel to use those citations when reasonable and according to law.

# NOTES

## I. THE ORIGINS AND HISTORY OF BAIL IN THE COMMON LAW TRADITION

1. *Bail Legislation* (1964, p. 1).
2. *Bail Legislation* (1964, p. 3).
3. Devine (1991); see also Jacobson (2018).
4. Dolnick (2012, paras. 1–4).
5. Sernoffsky (2018, paras. 1–4).
6. *In re Humphrey* (2018).
7. Gonnerman (2014).
8. Sullivan (2010), as cited in Phillips (2012, p. 3).
9. Gonnerman (2014, para. 42).
10. Schwirtz & Winerip (2015, p. 4).
11. Gonnerman (2015, para. 2).
12. Jarecki, Blum, & Smerling (2015).
13. Jarecki et al. (2015).
14. Rabuy & Kopf (2016, p. 14, n. 11).
15. Pinto (2015, para. 8).
16. Phillips (2012, p. 116).
17. Pinto (2015, para. 9) ("locking people up"); Phillips (2012, p. 116) (inducing guilty pleas).
18. This section is adapted from Neubauer and Fradella's *America's Courts and the Criminal Justice System*, 13th edition, pp. 292–294. © 2019 South-Western, a part of Cengage, Inc. Reproduced by permission. www.cengage.com/permissions.

19. Pepin (2013, p. 3).

20. *Pelekai v. White* (1993); *Clark v. Hall* (2002).

21. *County of Riverside v. McLaughlin* (1991).

22. National Conference of State Legislatures (2016a).

23. Color of Change & American Civil Liberties Union (2017, p. 10).

24. Neubauer & Fradella (2019, p. 295).

25. Johnson (2015, p. 179); Neubauer & Fradella (2019, p. 295).

26. Color of Change & American Civil Liberties Union (2017).

27. Minton & Zeng (2015).

28. Reaves (2013, p. 15).

29. Reaves (2013).

30. Demuth (2003); Katz & Spohn (1995); Sacks, Sainato, & Ackerman (2015); Schnacke (2014).

31. See Milsom (1976).

32. Duker (1977, p. 35); see also Roth, Hoffner, & Michalowski (1997, p. 121).

33. See Ericksen & Horton (1992).

34. Abel (2010, p. 776); Duker (1977, pp. 35–36).

35. Duker (1977, p. 35, citing Downer [1972, p. 239]); Thorpe (1840, pp. 3–25).

36. *Wergild* is sometimes spelled *wergeld* or referred to simply as *wer.* Jeffrey (1957, p. 655).

37. Duker (1977, p. 35).

38. Duker (1977, p. 35); see also De Haas (1940, p. 14).

39. Duker (1977, pp. 41–42).

40. Duker, (1977, pp. 41–42, citing Pollock & Maitland [1898, p. 584]).

41. Duker (1977, p. 35, citing Thorpe [1840, pp. 199–201]).

42. Duker (1977, p. 35, citing Thorpe [1840, pp. 31–33]).

43. Duker, (1977, p. 35, citing Thorpe [1840, pp. 27–35]).

44. Duker, (1977, p. 35, citing Thorpe [1840, p. 163]).

45. Duker, (1977, p. 37).

46. Carbone (1983, p. 520).

47. Carbone (1983, p. 520).

48. See Pennington (1993).

49. Carbone (1983, citing Pollock & Maitland [1898, pp. 460–511]).

50. Pollock & Maitland (1898, pp. 460–511); Rosenblatt (2003, pp. 2137–2138).

51. Pollock & Maitland (1898, p. 138).

52. Simmons (2002, p. 5).

53. Rosenblatt (2003, pp. 2135–2138).

54. Baldwin (1961, pp. 613–614).

55. Duker (1977, pp. 42–43); McKehnie (1917).

56. Pollock & Maitland (1898, pp. 460–461).

57. Duker (1977, p. 44).

58. Carbone (1983, p. 522).

59. Pollock & Maitland (1898, p. 459).

60. Carbone (1983, p. 523); De Haas (1940, p. 65).

61. Carbone (1983, p. 523); De Haas (1940, p. 65).

62. 3 Edw., ch. 15 (1275).

63. Carbone (1983, p. 523).

64. Carbone (1983, p. 526).

65. See Duker (1977, pp. 51–56).

66. Carbone (1983, p. 527); Duker (1977, pp. 56–57).

67. 3 Hen. 7, ch. 3 (1486).

68. Carbone (1983, p. 528).

69. Kalhous & Meringolo (2012, p. 806).

70. 1 W. & M., ch. 2 (1689).

71. Carbone (1983, p. 528, n. 55); Duker (1977, pp. 61–66); Kalhous & Meringolo (2012, p. 806).

72. Carbone (1983, pp. 529–530, citing Brown [1964, p. 214]).

73. Carbone (1983, pp. 530–531, citing Whitmore [1889, p. 37]).

74. Carbone (1983, pp. 531–532, citing Keith [1917, p. 586]).

75. Hegreness (2013); National Conference of State Legislatures (2013a).

76. Hegreness (2013, pp. 923–924).

77. E.g., Ariz. Const. art. II, § 22; Cal. Const. art I, § 12; Or. Const. art I. § 14; Utah Const., art I, § 8.

78. Duker (1977, p. 86, citing *Ex parte Watkins* [1833], *Carlson v. Landon* [1952]).

79. *United States v. Steward* (1795).

80. *United States v. Feely* (1813).

81. See Duker (1977, p. 67); see also *Ewing v. United States* (1917).

82. *United States v. Feely* (1813, p. 1057); see also *Concord Cas. and Ser. Co. v. United States* (1934); *State v. Jakschitz* (1913); *State v. Seibert* (1932); *Western Surety Co. v. People* (1949); *Wallace v. State* (1952); *State v. Hinojosa* (1954); *Sawyer v. Barbour* (1956); *Central Casualty Co. v. State* (1961).

83. *Ex parte Milburn* (1835).

84. *Milburn* (1835, p. 710).

85. Duker (1977, p. 68); *United States v. Barber* (1891, p. 167); *Hudson v. Parker* (1895, p. 285) (presumption of innocence); Duker (1977, p. 68); *Adams v. Illinois* (1972); *Stack v. Boyle* (1951) (assisting counsel with defense).

86. See Duker (1977, p. 69, citing *Workman v. Cardwell* [1972]; *Reynolds v. United States* [1959]; *De Angelis v. South Carolina* [1971]) (keeps accused in pretrial detention); see also Duker (1977, p. 69, citing *United States v. Foster* [1948, p. 423], stating that "admission to bail is never a judicial license to continue the commission of crime") (assure appearance at trial).

87. *Bell v. Wolfish* (1979).

88. *Bell v. Wolfish* (1979, p. 533).

89. *People ex rel Shapiro v. Keeper of City Prisons* (1943).

90. *Shapiro* (1943, p. 500).

91. See, e.g., *United States v. Motlow* (1926) (implied by the text of the Eighth Amendment); *Carlson v. Landon* (1952).

92. *Carlson v. Landon* (1952, p. 545).

93. *Stack v. Boyle* (1951).

94. The Alien Registration Act (1940).

95. *Stack v. Boyle* (1951, p. 4).

96. *Stack v. Boyle* (1951, p. 4).

97. *Stack v. Boyle* (1951, p. 5, quoting Federal Rule of Criminal Procedure 46(c)).

98. *Stack v. Boyle* (1951, p. 7).

99. Duker (1977, p. 90).

100. Schnacke, Jones, & Brooker (2010, p. 3).

101. Carbone (1983, p. 546); Kalhous & Meringolo (2012, p. 807).

102. Carbone (1983, p. 552).

103. Foote (1954, pp. 1032–1033; 1966, p. 190).

104. Foote (1966, pp. 42–43, 79–82).

105. See Amar (1998, pp. 215–230); Neubauer & Fradella (2019, p. 24).

106. *Hunt v. Roth* (1981, p. 1155, n. 9); *Meechaicum v. Fountain* (1983, p. 791); *Pilkinton v. Circuit Court* (1963); *Sistrunk v. Lyons* (1981, p. 71).

107. Howe (2015, p. 1043).

108. *McDonald v. City of Chicago, Ill.* (2010, p. 765, n. 12).

109. *Schilb v. Kuebel* (1971, p. 365, internal citations omitted).

110. *Pilkinton v. Circuit Court* (1963) (Eighth Circuit decision); *Robinson v. California* (1962).

111. Howe (2015, pp. 1084).

112. Wiseman (2011, p. 26).

113. Howe (2015, pp. 1056–1058).

114. Howe (2015, pp. 1057).

115. Ares, Rankin & Sturz (1963); Vera Institute of Justice (1972).

116. Vera Institute of Justice (1972, p. 35).

117. *Bail Legislation* (1964, p. 5).

118. *Bail Legislation* (1964, p. 5).

119. Kastenmeier (1984, p. 21).

120. Kastenmeier (1984, p. 21); see also Kalhous & Meringolo (2012, p. 811).

121. Carbone (1983, p. 553).

122. 18 U.S.C. § 3146(b) (1969).

123. 18 U.S.C. § 3147(b) (1969).

124. Carbone (1983, p. 541); Kalhous & Meringolo (2012, pp. 811–812).

125. Kastenmeier (1984, pp. 10–11).

126. Kalhous & Meringolo (2012, p. 813).

127. See Kalhous & Meringolo (2012, p. 814).

128. E.g., Miller (1969) (conservative calls for stricter criteria). Kalhous & Meringolo (2012, p. 814, quoting Reagan Statement issued May 26, 1982).

129. Causey (2013–2014, p. 85).

130. 18 U.S.C. § 3142(e).

131. Carbone (1983, p. 559).

132. Causey (2013–2014, p. 86).

133. See Carbone (1983, pp. 540–543).

134. See, e.g., Angel, Green, Kaufman, & Van Loon (1971); Goldkamp (1983); Haapanen (1990); see generally Harcourt (2007).

135. Howe (2015, p. 1048).

136. *Wagenmann v. Adams* (1987).

137. *Wagenmann v. Adams* (1987, p. 213).

138. *United States v. McConnell* (1988).

139. Woodruff (2013, p. 244).

140. Reitz (2017).

141. Walmsley (2017).

142. Walmsley (2017).

143. Schönteich (2014, p. 17) (one-third of prisoners); Walmsley (2017, p. 2) (increased since 2000).

144. Walmsley (2017, p. 2) (three million people in pretrial detention); Schönteich (2014, p. 1) ("economically and politically marginalized").

145. Baradaran-Baughman (2018, p. 144); see also Schönteich (2014).

146. Open Society Foundations (2011, p. 15).

147. Baradaran-Baughman (2018, pp. 144–145).

## 2. PRETRIAL RELEASE DECISIONS AND OUTCOMES

1. Demuth & Steffensmeier (2004).
2. Demuth (2003).
3. Free (2001).
4. Pretrial Justice Institute (2010, p. 4).
5. Free (2001).
6. Ottone & Scott-Hayward (2018).
7. Ottone & Scott-Hayward (2018).
8. Demuth & Steffensmeier (2004).
9. Hegreness (2013, p. 966); see also, e.g., Wyo. Const. of 1889, art. I (Declaration of Rights), § 14: "All persons shall be bailable by sufficient sureties, except for capital offenses."
10. See, e.g., Pa. Const. of 1969, art. I § 14: "All prisoners shall be bailable by sufficient sureties, unless for capital offenses or for offenses for which the maximum sentence is life imprisonment or unless no condition of combination of conditions other than imprisonment will reasonably assure the safety of any person and the community when the proof is evident or presumption great."
11. Reaves (2013, p. 15).
12. Cal. Penal Code § 1320(a) (2018) (misdemeanor); Cal. Penal Code § 1320(b) (2018) (felony).
13. See, e.g., Cal. Penal Code § 978.5(a)(3) (2018).
14. See, e.g., Maine Rev. Stat. Ann. tit. 15, § 1026 (2013); see also Wiseman (2014).
15. American Bar Association (2007, Standard 10-1-A[a]).
16. Cohen & Reaves (2007, p. 2); Reaves (2013, p. 15).
17. Cohen & Reaves (2007, p. 3).
18. See, e.g., W. Va. Code § 62-1C-7 (2017) (bail forfeited); Cal. Penal Code § 978.5(a)(2) (bench warrant).
19. W. Va. Code § 62-1C-7(a) (2017); see also Cal. Penal Code § 1320.5 (2018).
20. W. Va. Code § 62-1C-7(b) (2017) (felony); W. Va. Code § 62-1C-7(c) (2017) (misdemeanor).
21. Cohen & Reaves (2007, p. 3).
22. Scott-Hayward & Ottone (2018).
23. Neubauer & Fradella (2019, pp. 286–288).
24. Neubauer & Fradella (2019, pp. 286–288).
25. Cal. Const. art. 1, §§ 12, 28 (state constitution); Cal. Penal Code §§ 1270, 1275 (2018) (state penal code); Cal. R. Ct. 4.105 (rules of court).

26. CAL. PENAL CODE § 1270 (2018).

27. CAL. PENAL CODE § 1269b(c) (2018).

28. AZ. REV. STAT. § 13-3967(A) (2017).

29. AZ. REV. STAT. § 13-3967(B) (2017).

30. D.C. CODE § 23–1321(b).

31. D.C. CODE § 23–1322(b)(2) (quotation); D.C. CODE § 23–1322(c) (in favor of detention).

32. D.C. CODE § 23–1322(e).

33. N.J. STAT. ANN. § 2A: 162-15.

34. N.J. STAT. ANN. § 2A: 162-17.

35. Scott-Hayward (2017, p. 62, quoting 18 U.S.C. § 3142[b]).

36. Scott-Hayward (2017, p. 63).

37. Oleson, VanNostrand, Lowenkamp, & Cadigan (2014, p. 14).

38. Smith & Madden (2011, pp. 14–15).

39. Ottone & Scott-Hayward (2018).

40. Ottone & Scott-Hayward (2018).

41. Ottone & Scott-Hayward (2018).

42. A. Rengifo (personal communication, May 22, 2018).

43. Court Watch NYC (2018).

44. Court Watch NYC (2018).

45. Ottone & Scott-Hayward (2018).

46. Ottone & Scott-Hayward (2018).

47. Beeley (1927/1966, cited in Thomas [1976, p. 13]).

48. Thomas (1976, pp. 14–15).

49. Goldkamp (1979, p. 157).

50. Phillips (2012, p. 57).

51. Phillips (2012, p. 57).

52. Ottone & Scott-Hayward (2018).

53. Ottone & Scott-Hayward (2018).

54. Ottone & Scott-Hayward (2018).

55. Steffensmeier, Ulmer, & Kramer (1998); Freiburger (2009).

56. Steffensmeier et al. (1998, p. 767).

57. Schlesinger (2005, p. 173).

58. Sacks, Sainato, & Ackerman (2015, p. 663).

59. Williams (2016).

60. Demuth & Steffensmeier (2004); Katz & Spohn (1995).

61. Demuth (2003); Demuth & Steffensmeier (2004).

62. Sacks et al. (2015, p. 675).

63. Sacks et al. (2015, p. 675).

64. Nagel (1983).

65. Katz & Spohn (1995).

66. Demuth & Steffensmeier (2004).

67. Sacks et al. (2015, p. 677).

68. Stevenson (2017, p. 4).

69. See, e.g., Albonetti (1987); Nagel (1983); Wooldredge (2012) (criminal history). See, e.g., Demuth (2003); Demuth & Steffensmeier (2004); Katz & Spohn (1995) (racial disparities).

70. Wooldredge (2012, p. 63).

71. Richey-Mann (1993).

72. Schlesinger (2005, p. 172).

73. Schlesinger (2005, p. 187).

74. Schlesinger (2005, p. 181).

75. Schlesinger (2005, pp. 187–188).

76. Arnold, Dobbie, & Yang (2018).

77. Arnold et al. (2018, p. 1889).

78. Arnold et al. (2018, p. 1929).

79. Heaton, Mayson, & Stevenson (2017); Stevenson (2017).

80. Thomas (1976, p. 211, citing CAL. PENAL CODE § 1269b [1970]) (bail schedules for misdemeanor); "Review of Selected 1973 California Legislation" (1974, p. 334) (felony bail schedules).

81. Thomas (1976, p. 211).

82. Superior Court of California (2018, p. 1).

83. ALA. R. CRIM. PROC. RULE 7.2(b).

84. CAL. PENAL CODE § 1269b (e) (2018); see also Superior Court of California (2018, p. 1).

85. CAL. PENAL CODE §§ 1269b(c), (g) (2018).

86. Pretrial Justice Institute (2010, pp. 3, 15).

87. Pretrial Justice Institute (2010, p. 8) (41 percent of counties that used bail schedules did so only before the initial appearance, while 7 percent used them at the initial appearance only).

88. GA. CODE ANN. § 17-6-1(f) (2017). (Georgia *allows* courts to establish bail schedules); CAL. PENAL CODE § 1269b(c) (2018) (California *requires* counties to establish bail schedules). Although SB 10, reform legislation enacted in California in 2018, eliminates bail schedules, at the time of writing it is unclear whether it will go into effect. Thanks to efforts by bail agents and their supporters, SB 10 will now appear on the November 2020 ballot (Ulloa, 2019).

89. Criminal Justice Policy Program (2016, p. 11).

90. *ODonnell v. Harris County* (2017).

91. *Jones v. City of Clanton* (2015).

92. *Jones v. City of Clanton* (2015).

93. Goldkamp (1985, p. 9, n. 31).

94. American Bar Association (2007, Standard § 10-5.3[e]).

95. Karnow (2008, pp. 14–16).

96. Goldkamp, Gottfredson, Jones, & Weiland (1995, p. 125).

97. Thomas (1976, p. 212).

98. The following sections analyzing the unconstitutionality of bail schedules are derived in large part from Scott-Hayward & Ottone (2018).

99. *Stack v. Boyle* (1951, p. 5, citing *United States v. Motlow* [1926]).

100. *United States v. Salerno* (1987, p. 741).

101. *Salerno* (1987, p. 742).

102. Wiseman (2011, pp. 24–26).

103. *Galen v. County of Los Angeles* (2006, p. 660).

104. *Galen* (2006, p. 661).

105. Wiseman (2011, pp. 26–27).

106. Wiseman (2011, p. 29).

107. Howe (2015, p. 1052).

108. Howe (2015, p. 1058).

109. *McDonald v. City of Chicago* (2010, p. 764).

110. *Fields v. Henry County* (2012, p. 184).

111. *Fields* (2012, p. 184).

112. Howe (2015, p. 1058).

113. Howe (2015, p. 1063).

114. *ODonnell v. Harris County* (2017); Ottone & Scott-Hayward (2018).

115. Brief for the United States as Amicus Curiae Supporting Neither Party in *Walker v. City of Calhoun* (2017, p. 20).

116. See generally Scott-Hayward & Ottone (2018, p. 176, n. 72).

117. *Griffin v. Illinois* (1956, pp. 18–19).

118. *Bearden v. Georgia* (1983, p. 672).

119. *Pugh v. Rainwater* (1978).

120. *Pugh v. Rainwater* (1978, p. 1057).

121. *ODonnell v. Harris County* (2017, p. 1059).

122. *ODonnell* (2017, p. 1062).

123. *ODonnell* (2018).

124. *ODonnell* (2018).

125. *ODonnell* (2017, p. 1059).

126. *ODonnell* (2018).

127. *In re Humphrey* (2018, p. 538).

128. *In re Humphrey* (2018, p. 526).

129. *In re Humphrey* (2018, pp. 539–540).

130. *In re Humphrey* (2018, p. 541).

131. Equal Justice Under Law (n.d.).

132. Superior Court of California (2014).

133. Cohen & Reaves (2007, p. 3).

134. Thomas (1976, p. 250).

135. Thomas (1976, p. xi).

136. Cohen & Reaves (2007, p. 2) (40 percent of defendants); Color of Change & American Civil Liberties Union, 2017, p. 10) (49 percent of releases).

137. Maruna, Dabney & Topali (2012, p. 328); Schnacke, Jones, & Brooker (2010, p. 7).

138. Schnacke et al. (2010, p. 7).

139. Schnacke et al. (2010, p. 7).

140. Neubauer & Fradella (2019, p. 295).

141. Johnson (2015, p. 179); Neubauer & Fradella (2019, p. 295).

142. State of New Jersey Commission of Investigation (2014); State of Utah Legislative Auditor General (2017).

143. Sullivan (2010).

144. National Conference of State Legislatures (2018).

145. Bauer (2014).

146. Thomas (1976, pp. 16–17).

147. Thomas (1976, p. 16, citing Freed & Wald [1964]).

148. Maruna et al. (2012, p. 328); see also Color of Change & American Civil Liberties Union (2017, p. 36).

149. California Department of Insurance (n.d.).

150. National Conference of State Legislatures (2013b).

151. E.g., Associated Press (2013); Bauer (2014); DuBos (2004); Fan (2018); Pierce (2016); Thomas (1976).

152. Color of Change & American Civil Liberties Union (2017, p. 36).

153. Thomas (1976, p. 7).

154. Billings (2016, p. 1355).

155. Page (2017).

156. Barto (2015, quoted in Page [2017]).

157. Blaylock (2017).

158. Page (2017).

159. Page (2017).

160. Page (2017).

161. Page (2017).

162. Color of Change & American Civil Liberties Union (2017, p. 33).

163. Baker, Vaughn, & Topalli (2008, p. 125).

164. Baker et al. (2008, p. 129).

165. Sullivan (2010).

166. Color of Change & American Civil Liberties Union (2017); Covert (2017); Neubauer & Fradella (2019, p. 295).

167. Color of Change & American Civil Liberties Union (2017, pp. 2, 6–7).

168. Color of Change & American Civil Liberties Union (2017, p. 7).

169. Color of Change & American Civil Liberties Union (2017, p. 24).

170. Page, Piehowski, & Soss (2019, p. 159).

171. Page et al. (2019, p. 164).

172. Page et al. (2019, p. 164).

173. Color of Change & American Civil Liberties Union (2017, pp. 40–43).

174. Maruna et al. (2012, pp. 327–328).

175. Color of Change & American Civil Liberties Union (2017, p. 40) ("to insulate and expand for-profit bail's role"); Gilbert & Schichor (2001) (minimization of the use of release on personal recognizance).

176. Color of Change & American Civil Liberties Union (2017, pp. 40–43).

177. Billings (2016, pp. 1338–1339).

178. N.J. Const. art. 1. §. 11.

179. Covert (2018).

180. Covert (2018).

181. Md. R. Ct., R. 4-216(b)(1)(A).

182. Md. R. Ct., R. 4-216(c)(1).

183. Dance (2018).

184. Simonson (2017, p. 600).

185. Bronx Freedom Fund (n.d.).

186. Massachusetts Bail Fund (n.d.).

187. Simonson (2017, p. 603).

188. Simonson (2017, p. 603).

189. Simonson (2017, p. 603).

190. Anderson, Buenaventura, & Heaton (in press).

191. Simonson (2017, p. 601).

192. National Bail Out (n.d.).

193. Pinto (2012).

194. Simonson (2017, p. 609).

195. Pinto (2012).

196. Pinto (2012).

197. Kastenmeier (1984, p. 21).

198. Schnacke et al. (2010, p. 12).

199. Pretrial Services Resources Center (1999, p. 4, n. 6); Schnacke et al. (2010, p. 12).

200. Pretrial Services Resources Center (1999, p. 4); Schnacke et al. (2010, p. 12).

201. Schnacke et al. (2010, p. 13).

202. Pretrial Justice Center for Courts (n.d., para. 1).

203. Hughes & Henkel (2015, p. 49).

204. Pretrial Justice Center for Courts (n.d., para. 2).

205. Clark & Henry (2003, pp. 41–42); Mamalian (2011, p. 26).

206. VanNostrand, Rose, & Weibrecht (2011, pp. 3–6); see also *United States v. Arzberger* (2008).

207. Cooprider (2014, p. 15).

208. Pretrial Justice Institute (2012, pp. 16–17).

209. See, e.g., Office of Probation and Pretrial Services (2003); Wolf (1997, p. 22).

210. For an analogous discussion of standard conditions of probation, see Doherty (2016, pp. 349–350).

211. Myers (2017, p. 678).

212. Mahoney, Beaudin, Carver, Ryan, & Hoffman (2001, p. 42).

213. Mahoney et al. (2001, p. 47).

214. Pretrial Justice Institute (2012, p. 17) ("verify the identity of the defendant through voice recognition"); Pretrial Justice Institute (2012, p. 22) (scanning).

215. Pretrial Justice Institute (2012, p. 17).

216. VanNostrand et al. (2011, p. 29).

217. Austin, Krisberg, & Litsky (1985); see also VanNostrand et al. (2011, p. 30).

218. Austin et al. (1985, pp. 531–532).

219. Goldkamp & White (2006, pp. 170–171).

220. Goldkamp & White (2006, p. 171).

221. VanNostrand et al. (2011, p. 30); see also Goldkamp & White (2006).

222. Bechtel, Holsinger, Lowenkamp, & Warren (2017, pp. 459–460).

223. Bechtel et al. (2017, p. 460).

224. Bechtel et al. (2017, pp. 460–461); see also Bornstein, Tomkins, Neeley, Herian, & Hamm (2013); Cooke et al. (2018); Schnacke et al. (2012).

225. Schnacke, Jones, & Wilderman (2012, p. 89).

226. Color of Change & American Civil Liberties Union (2017, p. 47).

227. Bechtel et al. (2017, p. 461); VanNostrand et al. (2011, p. 24); see also Gottfredson, Britt, & Goldkamp (1990); Goldkamp, Jones, Weiland, & Gottfredson (1990); Kapsch & Sweeny (1990); Toborg, Bellasai, Yezer, & Trost (1989); Visher (1992).

228. VanNostrand et al. (2011, p. 27); see also Lemke (2009); Maxfield & Baumer (1991).

229. Cadigan (1991, pp. 28–29).

230. Grommon, Rydberg, & Carter (2017, p. 498).

231. VanNostrand et al. (2011, p. 27); Wiseman (2014, pp. 1368–1371).

232. Pretrial Justice Institute (2012, p. 19); see also Brown, McCabe, & Wellford (2007, pp. 2–15).

233. Pretrial Justice Institute (2012, p. 19); see also Brown et al. (2007, pp. 2–33).

234. Alladina (2011, p. 144); Wiseman (2014, pp. 1372–1374); cf. Bales et al. (2010) (concluding the same for community supervision of convicted offenders in comparison to jail sentences).

235. Leone (2002). For an in-depth discussion of net widening, see McMahon (1990).

236. Nellis (1991, pp. 20, 23).

237. Hahn (2015, p. 16).

238. Hahn (2015, p. 16).

239. Hahn (2015, p. 19).

240. Hahn (2015, p. 19).

241. VanNostrand & Keebler (2009, pp. 6, 17).

242. VanNostrand (2011, p. 5).

243. Mamalian (2011, p. 13).

244. Wiseman (2014, p. 1375).

## 3. THE PROBLEMS WITH RISK-ASSESSMENT-BASED BAIL DETERMINATIONS

1. American Bar Association (2007); National Association of Pretrial Services Agencies (2004); Mahoney, Beaudin, Carver, Ryan, & Hoffman (2001) (NIJ).

2. Lowenkamp, Lemke, & Latessa (2008, p. 2); VanNostrand (2003, p. 3).

3. See "Bail Reform and Risk Assessment" (2018, p. 1130).

4. Schug & Fradella (2014, p. 480); see also, e.g., Macpherson (1997); Kemshall (1996).

5. Burgess (1928); see also Singh & Fazel (2010).

6. See, e.g., Heilbrun (2009); Otto & Douglas (2014); Singh & Fazel (2010).

7. Andrews, Bonta, & Wormith (2006); Schug & Fradella (2014).

8. Andrews et al. (2006); Schug & Fradella (2014).

9. Andrews et al. (2006); Schug & Fradella (2014).

10. Andrews et al. (2006); Campbell, French, & Gendreau (2009); Schug & Fradella (2014).

11. Schug & Fradella (2014, p. 478).

12. Campbell, French & Gendreau (2009, p. 568); Schug & Fradella (2014, p. 478).

13. Schug & Fradella (2014, p. 480); see also Grove, Zald, Lebow, Snitz, & Nelson (2000).

14. Campbell et al. (2009, p. 568); Schug & Fradella (2014, p. 478) ("were prone to error and bias"); Schug & Fradella (2014, p. 478) ("worse than that predicted by chance"). For a review, see Monahan (1981); see also Faust & Ziskin (1988); Monahan & Steadman (1994).

15. See Andrade, O'Neill, & Diener (2009, p. 11).

16. See Desmarais & Singh (2013, p. 5).

17. See Desmarais & Singh (2013, p. 5); Shapiro & Noe (2015, p. 1).

18. Desmarais & Singh (2013, p. 5).

19. Desmarais & Singh (2013, p. 5).

20. Shapiro & Noe (2015, p. 1).

21. Desmarais & Singh (2013, p. 6); Grove et al. (2000); Singh, Grann, & Fazel (2011).

22. Desmarais & Singh (2013, pp. 5–6); cf. Neller & Frederick (2013).

23. Desmarais & Singh (2013, p. 6).

24. Monahan et al. (2001).

25. Shapiro & Noe (2015, p. 3).

26. Heilbrun (2009); Fazel, Singh, Doll, & Grann (2012).

27. Schug & Fradella (2014, p. 481); see also Scherr (2003).

28. Schug & Fradella (2014, p. 481); see also Campbell et al. (2009, p. 568).

29. Hoffman & Beck (1974, 1976, 1980) (SFS); Nuffield (1989) (SIR); Harris, Rice, & Quinsey (1993) (VRAG).

30. Hoffman & Beck (1974, 1976, 1980); Hoffman (1983, 1994).

31. Bonta & Wormith (2007).

32. Hoffman (1983, 1994).

33. Nuffield (1989).

34. Nuffield (1989); Bonta, Harman, Hann, & Cormier (1996).

35. Nafekh & Motiuk (2002).

36. Harris, Rice, & Quinsey (1993).

37. See Grann, Belfrage, & Tengström (2000); Rice & Harris (1997).

38. Campbell et al. (2009, p. 568).

39. Campbell et al. (2009, p. 568).

40. Campbell et al. (2009, p. 568).

41. Byrne & Pattavina (2017, p. 244).

42. Schug & Fradella (2014, p. 408); see also Arrigo & Shipley (2001).

43. Schug & Fradella (2014, p. 408); see also Millon & Davis (1998).

44. Hare (2003).

45. Hare (2003).

46. See, e.g., Skeem, Polaschek, Patrick, & Lilienfeld (2011).

47. Schug & Fradella (2014, p. 410); Fulero (1995).

48. Schug & Fradella (2014, p. 421); see Hare, Clark, Grann, & Thornton (2000); Hemphill & Hare (2004); Salekin, Rogers, & Sewell (1996); Walters (2003).

49. Hemphill & Hare (2004); Salekin, Rogers, & Sewell (1996); Walters (2003).

50. Schug & Fradella (2014, p. 421) (internal citations omitted); see Douglas, Vincent, & Edens (2006); Grann, Långström, Tengström, & Kullgren (1999); Harris et al. (1993).

51. See Malterer, Lilienfeld, Neumann, & Newman (2010).

52. See Edens, Skeem, & Kennealy (2009) (questionable reliability); Theodorakis (2013, p. 50); see also Millon & Davis (1998) ("delicate, if not futile task").

53. Theodorakis (2013, p. 51); see also Anderson & Kiehl (2013); Boccardi (2013); Raine (1993).

54. Hare (1998).

55. E.g., Cooke, Forth, Newman, & Hare (1996) (psychopathy in other populations); Theodorakis (2013, p. 50); see also Edens et al. (2009) (females and adolescents).

56. Hare (1998).

57. See Edens (2001).

58. Byrne & Pattavina (2017, p. 244); Campbell et al. (2009, p. 568); Schug & Fradella (2014, p. 481).

59. Campbell et al. (2009, pp. 568–569); Singh et al. (2011).

60. Andrews & Bonta (1995) (LSI-R); Webster, Douglas, Eaves, & Hart (1997) (HCR-20); Loza, Neo, Shahinfar, & Loza-Fanous (2005) (SAQ); Wong & Gordon (2006) (VRS).

61. Lowenkamp, Lovins, & Latessa (2009).

62. Lowenkamp et al. (2009); Vose, Smith, & Cullen (2013) (predictive validity of recidivism); Vose, Smith, & Cullen (2013) (changes in recidivism risk).

63. Chenane, Brennan, Steiner, & Ellison (2015); Ostermann & Salerno (2016) (White and non-White persons); Holtfreter & Cupp (2007); Ostermann & Herrschaft (2013) (LSI-R does not completely account).

64. Austin (2006, pp. 60–63); Hess & Turner (2017, p. 94).

65. Webster et al. (1997); Douglas et al. (2014).

66. Douglas, Yeomans, & Boer (2005); Mills, Kroner, & Hemmati (2007).

67. Vojt, Thomson, & Marshall (2013).

68. Campbell et al. (2009, pp. 582–583). For a review, see Mitchell, Caudy, & MacKenzie (2013) (institutional and recidivist violence); Kubiak, Kim, Bybee, & Eshelman (2014) (certain populations of women).

69. Wong & Gordon (2006).

70. Wong & Gordon (2006); Wong, Olver, & Stockdale (2009).

71. E.g., Austin (2006); Duwe (2014).

72. See Hannah-Moffat (2013, p. 289).

73. Caudy, Durso, & Taxman (2013, p. 465); Hannah-Moffat (2013, p. 289).

74. Desmarais & Singh (2013, p. 5).

75. Byrne & Pattavina (2017, p. 246); Desmarais & Singh (2013, p. 5).

76. Latessa, Lemke, Makarios, Smith, & Lowenkamp (2010, p. 18).

77. Andrews et al. (2006, p. 7).

78. Byrne & Pattavina (2017, p. 246); Campbell et al. (2009).

79. Byrne & Pattavina (2017, p. 246); see Berk & Hyatt (2015); Hess & Turner (2017); Kubrin, Squires, & Stewart (2007).

80. National Council on Crime and Delinquency (2010) (CAIS); Latessa et al. (2010) (ORAS); Andrews, Bonta, & Wormith (2004) (LS/CMI); Northpointe Institute for Public Management (2012) (COMPAS).

81. National Council on Crime and Delinquency (2010) (CAIS); Baird, Heinz, & Bemus (1979) (WRN).

82. Casey et al. (2014, p. A-3).

83. Latessa et al. (2010).

84. Casey et al. (2014, p. A-53).

85. Girard & Wormith (2004) (LS/CMI); Andrews et al. (2012) (LSI-R).

86. Andrews, Dowden, & Rettinger (2001); Girard & Wormith (2004).

87. Andrews et al. (2006); Casey et al. (2014, p. A-3).

88. Casey et al. (2014, p. A-20); see also Northpointe Institute for Public Management (2012, p. 2).

89. Casey et al. (2014, p. A-23); see also Brennan, Dieterich, & Ehret (2009); Fass, Heilbrun, Dematteo, & Fretz (2008); Farabee, Zhang, Roberts, & Yang (2010); Lansing (2012).

90. Blomberg, Bales, Mann, Meldrum, & Nedelcc (2010).

91. Hanson & Thornton (2000); Hanson & Morton-Bourgon (2005).

92. Hanson & Morton-Bourgon (2009); Olver, Wong, Nicholaichuk, & Gordon (2007).

93. Clarke, Peterson-Badali, & Skilling (2017); Olver, Stockdale, & Wormith (2009).

94. Gouldin (2018, p. 683). Gouldin explains that these "low-cost nonappearances" include defendants

> who fail to appear for a range of different reasons, including: being unaware of or forgetting the date of the court appearance (which might reflect either ineffective notice by the court or poor calendar management by the defendant); illness or other unforeseen personal emergencies; external logistical challenges including employment conflicts, childcare issues, or lack of transportation; confusion or ignorance about the process or a general lack of capacity to navigate the process (this may reflect the complexity of the system and/or the defendant's cognitive limitations); fear of punishment relating to the pending charge; or lacking the funds to pay fines and fees that are owed at the courthouse (pp. 729–730).

95. For an in-depth discussion of the role of discretion in criminal justice decision making, see Gottfredson and & Gottfredson (1988).

96. See, e.g., *Walker v. City of Calhoun* (2017).

97. Hannah-Moffat (2013, pp. 290–291).

98. Pretrial Justice Institute (2015, p. 6); VanNostrand & Crime and Justice Institute (2007).

99. Blomberg et al. (2010).

100. Ares, Rankin & Sturz (1963); Vera Institute of Justice (1972).

101. Vera Institute of Justice (1972, p. 35).

102. Vera Institute of Justice (1972, p. 35).

103. Cadigan & Lowenkamp (2011); Goldkamp & Vîlcică (2009); Lowenkamp & Whetzel (2009); Winterfield, Coggeshall, & Harrell (2003).

104. Pretrial Justice Institute (2015, p. 4).

105. Pretrial Justice Institute (2015, pp. 4–5).

106. Summer & Willis (2010, p. 1); see also VanNostrand & Rose (2009).

107. Summer & Willis (2010, p. 1); see also Lowenkamp et al. (2008, pp. 2–3).

108. Summer & Willis (2010, p. 2); see also Lowenkamp et al. (2008, pp. 2–3).

109. Mamalian (2011, p. 9); Pretrial Justice Institute (2015, p. 3).

110. Bechtel, Holsinger, Lowenkamp, & Warren (2017) (residential stability); Cadigan & Lowenkamp (2011b); Goldkamp & Vîlcicā (2009); Lowenkamp & Whetzel (2009); Winterfield et al. (2003) (prediction of pretrial risk).

111. See, e.g., Flores, Travis, & Latessa (2003); Gottfredson & Moriarty (2006).

112. Winterfield et al. (2003, p. 1).

113. Winterfield et al. (2003, p. 33).

114. Summer & Willis (2010, p. 2); Winterfield et al. (2003, p. 33).

115. Kennedy, House, & Williams (2013, p. 30).

116. Kennedy et al. (2013, p. 30).

117. Pretrial Services Agency for the District of Columbia (n.d.).

118. VanNostrand (2003).

119. VanNostrand (2003, p. 4).

120. VanNostrand (2003, p. 6).

121. VanNostrand (2003, pp. 9–15).

122. VanNostrand & Rose (2009, p. 12).

123. Cooprider (2009).

124. Cooprider (2009, p. 15).

125. VanNostrand & Rose (2009, p. 12).

126. Rose (2016, slide 31).

127. Latessa et al. (2010).

128. Lowenkamp et al. (2008, p. 4).

129. Lowenkamp et al. (2008, p. 4).

130. Lowenkamp et al. (2008, p. 5).

131. Lowenkamp et al. (2008, p. 6).

132. Latessa, Smith, Lemke, Makarios, & Lowenkamp (2009, p. 21).

133. Northpointe Institute for Public Management (2012, p. 24).

134. For critiques of COMPAS on the dimensions of accuracy, bias, and transparency, see Angwin, Larson, Mattu, and Kirchner (2016); see also Stevenson & Mayson (2017, p. 13).

135. Blomberg et al. (2010).

136. Blomberg et al. (2010, p. 33).

137. Blomberg et al. (2010, p. 33).

138. Blomberg et al. (2010, p. 67).

139. Blomberg et al. (2010, pp. 90–91).

140. LJAF (2016a, p. 4).

141. Milgram, Holsinger, VanNostrand, & Alsdorf (2015, p. 220).

142. Milgram et al. (2015, p. 220).

143. Brauneis & Goodman (2018, p. 138).

144. Walsh (2017, p. 6, cited in Brauneis & Goodman [2018, p. 138, n. 134]); see also LJAF (2016b).

145. DeMichele et al. (2018).

146. DeMichele et al. (2018, p. 48).

147. DeMichele et al. (2018, p. 48).

148. DeMichele et al. (2018, pp. 48–49).

149. DeMichele et al. (2018, p. 49).

150. Gouldin (2018, pp. 729–735).

151. Mamalian (2011, p. 27); see also Pretrial Justice Institute (2009, p. 64).

152. Mamalian (2011, p. 27); see also Pretrial Justice Institute (2010, p. 10).

153. Mamalian (2011, p. 27); see also Pretrial Justice Institute (2009, pp. 65–66).

154. As the Center for Public Safety Initiatives has explained, "The issue with using only re-arrest data is that an offender is innocent until proven guilty, so it is not proven that he or she committed another crime" (Ruggero, Dougherty, & Klofas, 2015, p. 3).

155. Mamalian (2011, p. 27); see also Pretrial Justice Institute (2009, pp. 65–660.

156. See Cadigan (2009, p. 31).

157. Mamalian (2011, p. 26).

158. Mamalian (2011, p. 26); Clark & Henry (2003, pp. 41–42).

159. Mamalian (2011, p. 26).

160. Bureau of Justice Statistics (2010, p. 1).

161. Mamalian (2011, p. 28).

162. Mamalian (2011, p. 28).

163. VanBenschoten (2008).

164. Mamalian (2011, p. 32); Bhati (2010).

165. Bechtel et al. (2017, p. 452).

166. Bechtel et al. (2017, p. 454); see also Rice & Harris (2005); Desmarais & Singh (2013).

167. Bechtel et al. (2017, p. 459).

168. Bechtel et al. (2017, p. 447).

169. Silver & Miller (2002).

170. Hannah-Moffat (2012, p. 277); Simon (1988, p. 776).

171. Hannah-Moffat (2012, p. 278).

172. Baradaran & McIntyre (2012, p. 558).

173. Baradaran & McIntyre (2012, p. 558).

174. Baradaran & McIntyre (2012, p. 521); Foote (1954, p. 1035); Goldkamp (1980, p. 183).

175. Baradaran & McIntyre (2012, p. 521); see also Angel, Green, Kaufman, & Van Loon (1971, p. 311).

176. Angel et al. (1971, p. 308); Baradaran & McIntyre (2012, p. 527); Locke, Penn, Rock, Bunten, & Hare (1970, p. 2); Siddiqi (2009, p. 49); Wheeler & Wheeler (1981, p. 178) (between 8 and 16 percent); Pryor & Smith (1982, p. 2).

177. Angel et al. (1971, p. 308); Baradaran & McIntyre (2012, p. 527); Locke et al. (1970, p. 2); Siddiqi (2009, p. 49).

178. Baradaran & McIntyre (2012, p. 529).

179. Baradaran & McIntyre (2012, p. 528–529).

180. Baradaran & McIntyre (2012, p. 528).

181. Baradaran & McIntyre (2012, p. 521).

182. Foote (1954, p. 1036); Siddiqi (2009, p. 49).

183. Zimring & Hawkins (1986, p. 492).

184. Baradaran & McIntyre (2012, pp. 508–511).

185. Baradaran & McIntyre (2012, pp. 509–510).

186. Johnston (2003, p. 6).

187. See Mischel (1968).

188. Franklin (2013, para. 8).

189. Franklin (2013, para. 8).

190. Compare Angel et al. (1971, p. 313); Locke et al. (1970, pp. 40–41); Siddiqi (2009, p. 49).

191. Baradaran & McIntyre (2012, p. 530).

192. Baradaran & McIntyre (2012, p. 531).

193. See Guthrie, Rachlinski, & Wistrich (2001).

194. Wistrich, Rachlinski, & Guthrie (2015).

195. Gouldin (2016, p. 887); see also Sunstein (2002, p. 67).

196. Gouldin (2016, p. 887).

197. E.g., Alexander (2013, para. 7); Goldkamp & Vîlcică (2009, p. 149); Wiseman (2016, p. 5).

198. Wiseman (2016, p. 5).

199. Neubauer & Fradella (2019, p. 235) (retention votes); Wiseman (2016, p. 5); see also Goldkamp & Vîlcică (2009, p. 149).

200. Baradaran & McIntyre (2012, p. 558).

201. VanNostrand & Keebler (2009).

202. VanNostrand & Keebler (2009, pp. 5, 7, 15).

203. VanNostrand & Keebler (2009, p. 11).

204. VanNostrand & Keebler (2009, p. 5).

205. VanNostrand & Keebler (2009, p. 5).

206. VanNostrand & Keebler (2009, pp. 5, 13).

207. VanNostrand & Keebler (2009, p. 5).

208. Scott-Hayward (2011, p. 436) (probation or parole); VanNostrand & Keebler (2009, pp. 6, 17).

209. VanNostrand & Keebler (2009, pp. 6, 19).

210. Mamalian (2011, p. 13).

211. Thompson (2017).

212. Thompson (2017, p. 6).

213. Thompson (2017, p. 6); see Singh & Fazel (2010); Skeem & Lowenkamp (2016).

214. Whiteacre (2006).

215. Whiteacre (2006, p. 338).

216. Olver, Stockdale, & Wormith (2014, p. 160).

217. See Barrett (2014).

218. Angwin, Larson, Mattu, & Kirchner (2016).

219. Angwin et al. (2016, paras. 13–14); see also Larson, Mattum, Kirchner, & Angwin (2016).

220. Angwin et al. (2016, paras. 16–17); see also Larson et al. (2016).

221. Dieterich et al. (2016); Flores et al. (2016).

222. Flores et al. (2016, pp. 39–40).

223. Flores et al. (2016, p. 40).

224. Flores et al. (2016, p. 40).

225. Flores et al. (2016, p. 40).

226. Flores et al. (2016, p. 44).

227. As of the writing of this book, researchers Kristin Bechtel, Alexander Holsinger, Christopher Lowenkamp, and Madaline Warren had conducted the only meta-analysis on pretrial risk assessment instruments, which was published in 2017. The data from most prior research on APRAIs were so poor that only a few studies merited inclusion in their reanalyses. They concluded that "strong conclusions about the impact of pretrial release conditions cannot

be made as the quality of the pretrial research, overall, is weak at best" (p. 443).

228. Singh & Fazel (2010, p. 978); see also Edens & Campbell (2007); Guy, Edens, Anthony, & Douglas (2005); Olver et al. (2009); Schwalbe (2007); Skeem et al. (2004).

229. Singh & Fazel (2010, p. 978); see also Edens, Campbell, & Weir (2007); Gendreau, Goggin, & Little (1996); Leistico, Salekin, DeCoster, & Rogers (2008).

230. Thompson (2017).

231. Bechtel et al. (2017).

232. Starr (2015, p. 230).

233. Macartney, Bishaw, & Fontenot (2013); see also Institute for Research on Poverty (2016) (racial and ethnic minorities). See Starr (2014, 2015); van Eijk (2017).

234. Olusanya & Gau (2012, p. 160).

235. Starr (2015, p. 230); see also van Eijk (2017).

236. Starr (2015, p. 230).

237. Hamilton (2015, p. 262).

238. Durose, Copper & Snyder (2014); Frase, Roberts, Hester, & Mitchell (2015).

239. See Harcourt (2015, p. 240); see also Harcourt (2007, p. 3, 2008, pp. 270–271); see generally Van Cleve & Mayes (2015).

240. Harcourt (2007, 2015).

241. Skeem & Lowenkamp (2016, p. 700).

242. Skeem & Lowenkamp (2016, p. 700).

243. Skeem & Lowenkamp (2016, p. 700); see also Frase et al. (2015).

244. Skeem & Lowenkamp (2016, p. 700; italics in original).

245. Skeem & Lowenkamp (2016, p. 700).

246. "Bail Reform and Risk Assessment" (2018); Harcourt (2015).

247. "Bail Reform and Risk Assessment" (2018, p. 1133, citing Schuppe [2017]).

248. Corbett-Davies, Goel, & González-Bailón (2017, para. 1).

249. "Bail Reform and Risk Assessment" (2018, p. 1133).

250. Mayson (2018, p. 511); see also Berk, Sorenson, & Barnes (2016).

251. Kleinberg, Lakkaraju, Leskovec, Ludwig, & Mullainathan (2018, p. 241).

252. Kleinberg et al. (2018, p. 238).

253. Kleinberg et al. (2018, p. 238).

254. Arnold, Dobbie, & Yang (2018).

255. Mayson (in press, p. 3).

256. Mayson (in press, p. 3).

257. Berk, Heidari, Jabbari, Kearns, & Roth (2017, p. 1).

258. Spielkamp (2017, para. 10).

259. Corbett-Davies, Pierson, Feller, Goel, & Huq (2017, p. 8); see also Chouldechova (2017).

260. Spielkamp (2017, para.14).

261. Olusanya & Gau (2012); Van Cleve & Mayes (2015).

262. "Bail Reform and Risk Assessment" (2018, p. 1132).

263. Miller & Maloney (2013); Silver & Miller (2002); Stevenson (2019).

264. Clark & Henry (2003); Stevenson (2019).

265. Danner, VanNostrand, & Spruance, 2015.

266. Danner et al. (2015, p. 18).

267. "Bail Reform and Risk Assessment" (2018); Clark & Henry (2003); Pretrial Justice Institute (2009).

268. "Bail Reform and Risk Assessment" (2018, p. 1140); see Main (2016).

269. Stevenson (2019, p. 8); see also *ODonnell v. Harris County, Texas* (2017, p. 1092) (noting that hearing officers denied a personal bond in 56.3 percent of cases in which pretrial services personnel recommended release on an unsecured personal bond with standard conditions of supervision).

270. Starr (2015, p. 232).

271. Starr (2015, p. 232).

272. Oleson, VanBenschoten, Robinson, & Lowenkamp, 2011 (risk assessment instrument); Starr (2015, p. 232).

273. Berk & Hyatt (2015, p. 222).

274. See Menefee (2018).

275. See Mayson (in press, pp. 39–41).

276. "Bail Reform and Risk Assessment" (2018, p. 1134).

277. Pasquale (2015, p. 213).

## 4. THE IMPACT OF PRETRIAL DETENTION

1. Open Society Foundations (2011, p. 12) (three million people in pretrial detention); Zeng (2018, p. 4) (number has been growing).

2. Minton & Zeng (2015, p 1).

3. Zeng (2018, p. 4); see also Tafoya (2015).

4. Reaves (2013, p. 15).

5. Prison Policy Initiative (2016, p. 2).

6. Prison Policy Initiative (2016, p. i).

7. Prison Policy Initiative (2016, p. i).

8. Laisne, Wool, & Henrichson (2017, p. 5).

9. *Gerstein v. Pugh* (1975, p. 114).

10. Sykes (1958/2007); see also Irwin (1985).

11. Heaton, Mayson, & Stevenson (2017, p. 733).

12. Phillips (2012, p. 108 [eighteen days for a nonfelony], p. 110 [roughly half of all defendants]). Median detention lengths are five days for nonfelony cases and seven days for felony cases.

13. Blackwell & Cunningham (2004, p. 59).

14. Rosenberg (2015).

15. Kovaleski (2017).

16. Nikambule (2018).

17. 18 U.S.C. § 3585(b) (credit for the time they spend detained pretrial); US Department of Justice (2015, p. 60) (noting that the Ferguson municipal credit does not give credit for time served as a result of an arrest on a municipal warrant).

18. May, Applegate, Ruddell, & Wood (2014, p. 252).

19. *Florence v. Board of Chosen Freeholders* (2012).

20. *United States v. Salerno* (1987, pp. 747–748).

21. Subramanian, Delaney, Roberts, Fishman, & McGarry (2015, p. 2).

22. Vera Institute of Justice (2011).

23. Subramanian et al. (2015, p. 12).

24. Harlow (2003, p. 5).

25. Harlow (2003, p. 5).

26. Reilly & Liebelson (2016) (higher death rates); Mumola (2005).

27. Kane & Raynor (2017).

28. Pinkerton & Caruba (2015).

29. Citizens' Commission on Jail Violence (2012).

30. Stoltze (2012).

31. US Department of Justice (2014, p. 3).

32. US Department of Justice (2014, p. 3).

33. Gonnerman (2014, pp. 27, 30).

34. Gonnerman (2014, p. 30).

35. Gonnerman (2014, p. 32).

36. Schwirtz & Winerip (2015).

37. Associated Press (2016).

38. Pinto (2015, p. 40).

39. Pinto (2015, p. 40).

40. Pinto (2015, p. 42).
41. Pinto (2015, p. 43).
42. Ares, Rankin, & Sturz (1963).
43. Phillips (2012, p. 115).
44. Phillips (2012, p. 115).
45. See, e.g., Stevenson (2017).
46. Blume & Helm (2014, p. 174).
47. *Frontline* (2004).
48. *Frontline* (2004).
49. See, e.g., Gupta, Hansman, & Frenchman (2016).
50. Stevenson (2017).
51. Stevenson (2017, p. 26).
52. Heaton et al. (2017).
53. Dobbie, Goldin, & Yang (2018).
54. Dobbie et al. (2018, p. 234).
55. Kellough & Wortley (2002, p. 199).
56. Phillips (2012).
57. Kellough & Wortley (2002, p. 199).
58. Kellough & Wortley (2002, p. 200).
59. Euvrard & Leclerc (2017).
60. Euvrard & Leclerc (2017, p. 532).
61. Euvrard & Leclerc (2017, p. 534).
62. Euvrard & Leclerc (2017, p. 535).
63. Dobbie et al. (2018, p. 234).
64. Human Rights Watch (2017, pp. 51–64).
65. Human Rights Watch (2017, pp. 54–55).
66. Stevenson (2017).
67. Tartaro & Sedelmaier (2009, pp. 212, 215); Williams (2003, pp. 312–313).
68. Sacks & Ackerman (2014).
69. Phillips (2012, p. 120).
70. Lowenkamp, VanNostrand, & Holsinger (2013, p. 10).
71. Stevenson (2017, p. 18).
72. Stevenson (2017, p. 18).
73. Heaton et al. (2017, p. 717).
74. Heaton et al. (2017, p. 749).
75. Dobbie et al. (2018, p. 225).
76. Oleson, Lowenkamp, Wooldredge, VanNostrand, & Cadigan (2017).
77. Holmes-Didwania (2018, p. 30).

78. Holmes-Didwania (2018, p. 31).

79. Holmes-Didwania (2018); Phillips (2012, 118); Williams (2003).

80. Heaton et al. (2017, p. 747).

81. Allan, Allan, Giles, Drake, & Froyland (2005); Sacks, Sainato, & Ackerman (2015).

82. *Barker v. Wingo* (1972, p. 533).

83. Boucher (2017).

84. Boucher (2017).

85. Klein (1997, 14).

86. *Estelle v. Williams*, 425 U.S. 501 (1976).

87. *Williams* (1976, p. 504).

88. *Williams* (1976, pp. 505–506) (internal citations omitted).

89. Stewart (1980).

90. Hanson (2012).

91. Paul (1997, para. 1).

92. Page, Piehowski, & Soss (2019, p. 163).

93. Open Society Foundations (2011, p. 12).

94. Pinto (2015, p. 43).

95. *Frontline* (2004).

96. Pinto (2015, pp. 43–44).

97. Dobbie et al. (2018, p. 227).

98. Dobbie et al. (2018, p. 227).

99. Agan & Starr (2018) (negative employment consequences); Dobbie et al. (2018, p. 236).

100. Neal (2012, pp. 13–14).

101. Subramian et al. (2015, p. 17).

102. Page et al. (2019, p. 159).

103. Maryland Office of the Public Defender, Gupta, Swanson, & Frenchman (2016, p. 4).

104. Maryland Office of the Public Defender et al. (2016, p. 8).

105. Minton & Zeng (2015).

106. Demuth (2003); Demuth & Steffensmeier (2004); Katz & Spohn (1995).

107. Sacks et al. (2015).

108. Prison Policy Initiative (2016, p. 2).

109. Ofer (2017).

110. Maryland Office of the Public Defender et al. (2016, p. 4).

111. Prison Policy Initiative (2016, p. 2).

112. Cohen & Reaves (2007, p. 3).

113. Laisne et al. (2017, p. 9).
114. Stevenson (2017, p. 4).
115. Heaton et al. (2017, p. 737).
116. Heaton et al. (2017, p. 737).
117. Pretrial Justice Institute (2017, p. 2).
118. Administrative Office of the United States Courts (2013).
119. Gupta et al. (2016, p. 495).
120. Heaton et al. (2017, p. 718).
121. Dobbie et al. (2018, p. 226).
122. Dobbie et al. (2018, p. 237).
123. See generally Scott-Hayward (2009).
124. Council of State Governments Justice Center (2018).
125. Aviram (2015, p. 4).
126. Henrichson & Rinaldi (2014, pp. 5–6).
127. Henrichson & Rinaldi (2014, p. 6).
128. Roman (2013, p. 31).
129. Roman (2013, p. 31).
130. Roman (2013, p. 7).
131. Baradaran-Baughman (2017, p. 30).
132. Baradaran-Baughman (2017, pp. 5–9).
133. Baradaran-Baughman, (2017, p. 28).
134. Kleppinger (2018).

## 5. THE PATH FORWARD

1. Pretrial Justice Institute (2018).
2. American Bar Association (2007); American Council of Chief Defenders (2011); Constitution Project (2015); e.g., Colorado Criminal Defense Institute, & The Colorado State Public Defender (2015); National Association of Criminal Defense Lawyers (2012); National Institute of Corrections (2011); e.g., Danner, VanNostrand, & Spruance 2015); Herian & Bornstein (2010); Goldkamp & White (2006); Solomon (2013) (numerous scholars).
3. Davis (2005, p. 314).
4. According to the IACP (2016), the process of citation in lieu of arrest is also known as "summons in lieu of arrest, violation citation, cite and release, citation release, field release, field citation, and desk appearance tickets (DAT)" in different parts of the United States (p. 7).
5. See Ferdico, Fradella, & Totten (2015, pp. 271–274).

6. IACP (2016, pp. 9–10).

7. IACP (2016, p.14) (one-third of all incidents); IACP (2016, p. 13); see also "An Analysis of the Citation System" (1974); Davis (2005) (process an arrest).

8. IACP (2016, p. 18); see also Busher (1978, pp. 92–93).

9. IACP (2016, p. 18).

10. IACP (2016, pp. 18–19); see also Hirschel & Dean (1995, p. 10).

11. Florida Tax Watch (2011, p. 6).

12. IACP (2016, p. 19); see also Baumer & Adams (2006, pp. 400–401).

13. IACP (2016, p. 19); see also Gless (1980); Lowenkamp, VanNostrand, & Holsinger (2013); Monaghan & Bewley-Taylor (2013).

14. National Conference of State Legislatures (2017, para. 2); see also, e.g., CAL. PENAL CODE §§ 853.5, 853.6, & 818 (2018); MD. CODE ANN., CRIM. PROC. § 4-101 (2018); TEX. CODE CRIM. PROC. art. 14.06(b) (2017); W. VA. CODE § 62-1-5a (2017).

15. E.g., TEX. CODE CRIM. PROC. art. 14.06(b) (2017); W. VA. CODE § 62-1-5a (2017).

16. WYO. STAT. § 7-2-103 (2017).

17. ALASKA STAT. § 12.25.180(a) (2017); LA. CODE CRIM. PROC. art. 211(a)(1); MINN. CRIM. PROC. R. 6.01, subd. 2; OR. REV. STAT. § 133.055(1) (2017).

18. Covert (2018).

19. ALASKA STAT. § 12.25.180(a)(1) (2017).

20. E.g., OR. REV. STAT. § 133.055(2) (2017) (domestic violence offense); e.g., TENN. CODE ANN. §§ 55-10-207 & 55-10-203(a)(3) (2018) and VA. CODE §§ 19.2–74(A)(1) & 19.2–81(D) (2018) (driving while impaired); e.g., TENN. CODE ANN. §§ 55-10-207 & 55-10-203(a)(2) (2018) (vehicular homicide).

21. E.g., ALASKA STAT. § 12.25.180(a)(2) (2017); LA. CODE CRIM. PROC. art. 211(a)(1)(b).

22. E.g., HAW. REV. STAT. § 8-306(b)(2) (outstanding warrants); § 8-306(b) & (c)(8) (answer the charges).

23. National Conference of State Legislatures (2017, para. 6); see also Davis (2005); Hirschel & Dean (1995).

24. President's Task Force on 21st Century Policing (2015, p. 43) (Action Item 4.1.1); American Bar Association (2007, Standards for Criminal Justice, Standard 10-1.3); IACP (2016); Pretrial Justice Institute (2018) (quotation); see also American Bar Association (2007, Standards for Criminal Justice, Standard 10-1.3).

25. *Atwater v. City of Lago Vista* (2001).

26. *Atwater* (2001, p. 324).

27. *Atwater* (2001, p. 324).

28. *Atwater* (2001, p. 354).

29. *Atwater* (2001, pp. 361–373) (O'Connor, J., dissenting).

30. *Atwater* (2001, p. 372) (O'Connor, J., dissenting) (internal quotations and citations omitted).

31. Amar (2001); Frase (2002); Katz (2013).

32. Amar (2001, para. 4).

33. Katz (2013, pp. 1414, 1445–1450).

34. See Ferdico et al. (2015, pp. 276–297) (incident to lawful arrests); *Knowles v. Iowa* (1998).

35. *Virginia v. Moore* (2008).

36. VA. CODE ANN. § 19.2-74(A)(2) (2018).

37. IACP (2016, pp. 20–25).

38. Hirschel & Dean (1995, p. 8).

39. E.g., Bornstein, Tomkins, Neeley, Herian, & Hamm (2013); Cooke et al. (2018); Schnacke, Jones, & Wilderman (2012).

40. IACP (2016, pp. 20–21).

41. IACP (2016, p. 21).

42. IACP (2016, p. 21); see also Perbix (2013).

43. IACP (2016, p. 21).

44. Harmon (2016, p. 357).

45. IACP (2016, pp. 21).

46. IACP (2016, p. 21); see also Perbix (2013).

47. Jacobs (2015).

48. Leone (2002). For an in-depth discussion of net widening, see McMahon (1990).

49. IACP (2016, pp. 21–22).

50. Horney (1980, pp. 426–428).

51. Nadel, Pesta, Blomberg, Bales, & Greenwald (2018, pp. 303–306).

52. Policing and profit (2015, p. 1723).

53. US Department of Justice (2015, p. 2).

54. US Department of Justice (2015, pp. 3, 10–15).

55. US Department of Justice (2015, p. 2).

56. President's Task Force on 21st Century Policing (2015, p. 26, Recommendation 2.9).

57. US Department of Justice (2015, p. 3).

58. US Department of Justice (2015, pp. 3, 9–10).

59. US Department of Justice (2015, pp. 4–5, 52–54).

60. US Department of Justice (2015, p. 90).

61. US Department of Justice (2015, p. 91).

62. U.S. Department of Justice (2015, pp. 91–92, 95–96).

63. US Department of Justice (2015, p. 94).

64. US Department of Justice (2015, pp. 94–95).

65. US Department of Justice (2015, pp. 96–102).

66. See, e.g., Baicker & Jacobson (2007); Bibas (2012); Policing and profit (2015).

67. See, e.g., Rios (2011).

68. E.g., Brown & Frank (2005, p. 448). Even beyond the realm of citation in lieu of arrest, it is clear that when it comes to the decision to make a formal arrest, "race matters." Kochel, Wilson, & Mastrofski (2011, p. 498).

69. IACP (2016, p. 22).

70. See, e.g., Klockars, Ivkovich, Harver, & Haberfeld (2000); Skolnick & Fyfe (1993); Weisburd, Greenspan, Hamilton, Williams, & Bryant (2000); White & Fradella (2016, 2018).

71. For an in-depth discussion of these factors, see White & Fradella (2016, pp. 117–145).

72. *Atwater* (2001, pp. 346–347).

73. *Atwater* (2001, pp. 347–348).

74. *Atwater* (2001, pp. 348–349).

75. *Camara v. Municipal Court* (1967, pp. 536–537).

76. *Atwater* (2001, pp. 365–366) (O'Connor, J., dissenting).

77. *Atwater* (2001, p. 366) (O'Connor, J., dissenting).

78. Amar (2001, para. 8).

79. *State v. Bauer* (2001, p. 897); see also *State v. Rodarte* (2005).

80. *State v. Rodarte* (2005, p. 651); see also *State v. Askerooth* (2004).

81. *Atwater* (2001, pp. 348–349).

82. *State v. Brown* (2003).

83. *State v. Brown* (2003).

84. E.g., N.C. Gen. Stat. § 15A-401 (1999); R.I. Gen. Laws § 12-7-3 (2000); S.D. Codified Laws §23A-3-2 (1998).

85. E.g., Ohio Rev. Code § 2935.26 (2017).

86. Tenn. Code Ann. § 40-7-118 (2018).

87. Tenn. Code Ann. § 40-7-118(c)(2) (2018).

88. Alaska Stat. § 12.25.180(b) (2017).

89. Harmon (2016, pp. 348–356).

90. Harmon (2016, pp. 348).

91. *Virginia v. Moore* (2008, p. 178).

92. *Bostic v. Rodriguez* (2009); *Glasgow v. Beary* (2014); *Smith v. Kelly* (2012).

93. *State v. Askerooth* (2004); *State v. Bauer* (2001); *State v. Bayard* (2003); *State v. Bricker* (2006); *State v. Brown* (2003).

94. For a detailed discussion on how proper supervision of officers with corresponding accountability measures can facilitate officer compliance with laws and policies, see White & Fradella (2016).

95. Pretrial Justice Institute (2018).

96. See, e.g., Heyerly (2013).

97. Toobin (2015, para. 1).

98. Toobin (2015, para. 3); see also Vera Institute of Justice (2014, p. 17).

99. Toobin (2015, para. 3); see also Vera Institute of Justice (2014, p. 17).

100. Vera Institute of Justice (2014, p. 17).

101. McKenzie, Stemen, Coursen, & Farid (2009, p. 7).

102. Toobin (2015, para. 4); Vera Institute of Justice (2014, p. 17).

103. Toobin (2015, para. 16).

104. Toobin (2015, para. 25).

105. Toobin (2015, para. 44).

106. Toobin (2015, para. 44).

107. Toobin (2015, para. 44).

108. Toobin (2015, para. 45).

109. Wright & Miller (2002, p. 63).

110. Stemen & Frederick (2013, p. 69); see also Mellon, Jacoby, & Brewer (1981, pp. 60–62).

111. Stemen & Frederick (2013, p. 69); see also Mellon et al. (1981, pp. 62–65).

112. Mellon et al. (1981, pp. 65–66).

113. Mellon et al. (1981, pp. 65–66).

114. Mellon et al. (1981, pp. 65–66); Stemen & Frederick (2013, pp. 69–73).

115. Stemen & Frederick (2013, p. 59); see also Mellon et al. (1981, p. 52).

116. Miller & Wright (2008, p. 131) (evidence being suppressed); Stemen & Frederick (2013, p. 66) (involved in the case).

117. Stemen & Frederick (2013, pp. 27–28).

118. Stemen & Frederick (2013, p. 28).

119. Bordenkircher v. Hayes (1978, p. 364).

120. For a review, see Stemen & Frederick (2013).

121. American Bar Association (2015, Standard 3-1.2[b]).

122. E.g., Stemen & Frederick (2013, pp. 18–27).

123. Stemen & Frederick (2013, pp. 21–22).

124. Stemen & Frederick (2013, pp. 39–46).

125. Stemen & Frederick (2013, p. 71).

126. Mellon et al. (1981, pp. 68–69).

127. Stemen & Frederick (2013, pp. 49–53).

128. Stemen & Frederick (2013, p. 50).

129. Stemen & Frederick (2013, pp. 53–68); see also Neubauer & Fradella (2019, pp. 148–153, 189–191).

130. Bowers (2010, pp. 1715–1722).

131. Bowers (2010, p. 1657).

132. Bowers (2010, p. 1681).

133. Bowers (2010, pp. 1703–1704).

134. Burke (2006, pp. 1622–1624).

135. Medwed (2010, p. 2209).

136. Bibas (2011, p. 17).

137. Medwed (2010, p. 2210).

138. See Findley & Scott (2006).

139. Beaney (1955, pp. 8–12).

140. For a fascinating exploration of how wealth affected the criminal justice process in England, see Phillips (2013, pp. 35–36); see also Langbein (2003, pp. 273–277, 332).

141. Griffiths (2014, p. 36).

142. Tomkovicz (2002, pp. 6–7).

143. Griffiths (2014, p. 28); see also Langbein (2003, p. 48).

144. An Act for Regulateing of Tryals in Cases of Treason and Misprision of Treason, 1696, 7 & 8 Will. 3, c. 3, § 1 (Eng.). For a discussion about how the Treason Act laid the groundwork for the right to counsel in Great Britain and the United States, see Hashimoto (2014).

145. Hashimoto (2014, pp. 2005–2006).

146. Hashimoto (2014, p. 2006); Langbein (2003, pp. 307–313).

147. Hashimoto (2014, p. 2006); see also Beattie (1991, p. 221).

148. The Prisoners' Counsel Act of 1836, 6 & 7 Will. 4, ch.14 (1836); see also Beaney (1955, pp. 8–12).

149. Hashimoto (2014, pp. 2006–2007); Jonakait (1995, p. 109).

150. Tomkovicz (2002, pp. 20–21).

151. King (2013, p. 8).

152. *Chandler v. Fretag* (1954).

153. *Powell v. Alabama* (1932).

154. *Powell* (1932, p. 287).

155. *Johnson v. Zerbst* (1938).

156. *Zerbst* (1938, p. 463).

157. *Betts v. Brady* (1942, p. 473).

158. *Betts* (1942, pp. 473, 472).

159. *Gideon v. Wainwright* (1963).

160. *Gideon* (1963, pp. 353–345).

161. *Gideon* (1963, p. 344).

162. *Argersinger v. Hamlin* (1972, pp. 27–29).

163. *Scott v. Illinois* (1979, pp. 373–374).

164. E.g., Herman & Thompson (1979); King (2013).

165. King (2013, pp. 17–34).

166. King (2013, p. 49).

167. *Missouri v. Frye* (2012, p. 140).

168. *Powell* (1932, p. 57).

169. E.g., *Kirby v. Illinois* (1972, pp. 688–689); *Brewer v. Williams* (1977, p. 401).

170. *Mempa v. Rhay* (1967, p. 134).

171. *Coleman v. Alabama* (1970, p. 8).

172. *Hamilton v. Alabama* (1961, p. 53).

173. *Massiah v. United States* (1964, pp. 205, 207).

174. *United States v. Wade* (1967, pp. 219–220).

175. *Missouri v. Frye* (2012, p. 143–144).

176. *Gideon* (1963, pp. 353–345); *Argersinger* (1972, pp. 27–29).

177. *Mempa* (1967, p. 137).

178. *Mempa* (1967, p. 137); *Gagnon v. Scarpelli* (1973, pp. 781–782).

179. *Douglas v. California* (1963, pp. 353–358).

180. *Rothgery v. Gillespie County* (2008, p. 199); Neubauer & Fradella (2018, pp. 286–288).

181. *Rothgery* (2008, p. 199); Neubauer & Fradella (2018, pp. 286–288).

182. *Gerstein v. Pugh* (1975, p. 120; see also p. 126) (Stewart, J., concurring).

183. *Rothgery* (2008, p. 194).

184. *Rothgery* (2008, pp. 211–212).

185. *Rothgery* (2008, pp. 213–214) (Alito, J., concurring).

186. *Rothgery* (2008, p. 235) (Thomas, J., dissenting).

187. Marceau (2012, p. 1207).

188. Colbert, Paternoster, & Bushway (2002, pp. 1720, 1753).

189. Colbert et al. (2002, p. 1753).

190. Fazio et al. (1985, p. 210); cf. Williams (2017, p. 13) (reporting that although Florida defendants "with public defenders were more likely to be

denied bail and less likely to be released, they also benefited from lower bail amounts and non-financial release options").

191. National Conference of State Legislatures (2016b).

192. Bunin (2016, p. 23); see also The Constitution Project (2015, p. 16); *Rothgery* (2008, p. 205).

193. Co. Rev. Stat. § 16-7-301(1) (2011).

194. Co. Rev. Stat. § 16-7-301(4)(a) (2011) (repealed).

195. Marceau & Rudolph (2012, pp. 327–328).

196. Co. Rev. Stat. § 16-7-301(1) (2017).

197. Bunin (2016, p. 23); see also *DeWolfe v. Richmond* (2013); *Hurrell-Harring v. State* (2010, p. 223); *Gonzalez v. Comm'r of Correction* (2013, pp. 635–636); *State v. Fann* (1990, p. 1026); *State v. Detter* (1979, p. 583).

198. *Rothgery* (2008, p. 212, n.16).

199. Smith & Madden (2011, p. 15).

200. Boruchowitz, Brink, & Dimino (2009, p. 8).

201. Boruchowitz et al. (2009, p. 8); Smith & Madden (2011, pp. 15, 23).

202. See Bright & Sanneh (2013) (Sixth Amendment questions); *Alabama v. Shelton* (2002, p. 662).

203. *Padilla v. Kentucky* (2010, pp. 367–369); see also *Lafler v. Cooper* (2012).

204. King (2013, pp. 23–36).

205. See Roberts (2011).

206. American Bar Association (1992, Standard 5-6.1).

207. E.g., Bunin (2016); Colbert et al. (2002); The Constitution Project (2015); King (2013); Marceau (2012); Marceau & Rudolph (2012); Pretrial Justice Institute (2018); Thompson (2016).

208. The Constitution Project (2015, pp. 40–41).

209. Schönteich (2014, pp. 155–156).

210. Schönteich (2014, p. 113).

211. Schönteich (2014, p. 156).

212. 18 U.S.C. § 3142(e).

213. *United States v. Salerno* (1987, p. 755).

214. *Salerno* (1987, p. 748).

215. *Salerno* (1987, p. 747).

216. *Salerno* (1987, pp. 751–752).

217. E.g. Mich. Comp. Laws Ann. § 765.5 (2017); Ohio Const. art. I, § 9.

218. E.g. Ariz. Rev. Stat. § 13-3961(B) (2017); Cal. Penal Code § 1275 (2017); Vt. Stat. tit. 13, § 7553 (2018); S.C. Code § 22-5-510 (2017).

219. E.g. GA. CODE ANN. § 17-6-1 (2017); MASS. GEN. LAWS ch. 276, § 58A (2017); N.H. REV. STAT. § 597:1-d (2017); see also Hegreness (2013, pp. 965–966).

220. Reaves (2013, p. 15).

221. Gouldin (2016, p. 862).

222. Gouldin (2016, pp. 863–864) (internal citations omitted).

223. Pretrial Justice Institute (2018).

224. Scott-Hayward (2017, p. 21, n. 101).

225. National Institute of Corrections (2011).

226. National Institute of Corrections (2011, pp. 3–4).

227. National Institute of Corrections (2011, p. 5).

228. National Institute of Corrections (2011, p. 7).

229. National Institute of Corrections (2011, pp. 13–15).

230. Criminal Justice Policy Program (2016, p. 11).

231. Criminal Justice Policy Program (2016, p. 11).

232. Pretrial Services Agency for the District of Columbia (n.d.).

233. Mayson (2018, p. 560).

234. Mayson (2018, pp. 560–563).

235. Huq (2019); see also Chander (2017).

236. Harcourt (2007, 2015); Starr (2015); van Eijk (2017).

237. See Kleinberg, Lakkaraju, Leskovec, Ludwig, & Mullainathan (2018).

238. Mayson (in press, p. 40); see also Banks & Ford (2009).

239. Mayson (in press, pp. 42–43).

240. Mays (2018).

241. Kalmthout, Knapen, & Morgenstern (2009).

242. Eckhouse (2018, para. 13).

243. Eckhouse (2018).

244. Ulloa (2019).

245. Criminal Justice Policy Program (2016, p. 15).

246. The Pew Charitable Trusts (2016, p. 1).

247. Criminal Justice Policy Program (2016, p. 15).

# REFERENCES

## PUBLICATIONS, WEB DOCUMENTS, AND CASE LAW

Abel, C.F. (2010). Restitution. In B.S. Fisher & S.P. Lab (Eds.), *Encyclopedia of victimology and crime prevention*. Thousand Oaks, CA: Sage. http://dx.doi .org/10.4135/9781412979993.n262

Adams v. Illinois, 405 U.S. 278 (1972).

Administrative Office of the United States Courts. (2013). *Supervision costs significantly less than incarceration in federal system*. Retrieved from www.uscourts .gov/news/2013/07/18/supervision-costs-significantly-less-incarceration-fed eral-system

Agan, A., & Starr, S. (2018). Ban the box, criminal records, and racial discrimination: A field experiment. *The Quarterly Journal of Economics*, *133*(1), 191–235. doi:10.1093/qje/qjx028

Alabama v. Shelton, 535 U.S. 654 (2002).

Albonetti, C. (1987). Prosecutorial discretion: The effects of uncertainty. *Law & Society Review*, *21*(2), 291–313. doi:10.2307/3053523

Alexander, K.L. (2013, February 9). 11 defendants on GPS monitoring charged with violent crimes in past year in DC. *Washington Post*. Retrieved from www .washingtonpost.com/local/11-defendants-on-gps-monitoring-charged-with -violent-crimes-in-past-year-in-dc/2013/02/09/9237be1e-6c8b-11e2-adao-5ca5 fa7ebe79_story.html?noredirect=on&utm_term=.188330f78642

Alladina, N. (2011). The use of electronic monitoring in the Alaska criminal justice system: A practical yet incomplete alternative to incarceration. *Alaska Law Review*, *28*, 125–160.

Allan, A., Allan, M.M., Giles, M., Drake, D., & Froyland, I. (2005). An observational study of bail decision-making. *Psychiatry, Psychology, and Law, 12*(2), 319–333. doi:10.1375/pplt.12.2.319

Amar, A.R. (1998). *The bill of rights: Creation and reconstruction.* New Haven, CT: Yale University Press.

Amar, A.R. (2001, April 29). The law: An unreasonable view of the 4th Amendment. *Los Angeles Times.* Retrieved from http://articles.latimes.com/2001/apr/29/opinion/op-57091

American Bar Association. (1992). *American Bar Association criminal justice standards on providing defense services* (3rd ed.). Washington, DC: Author.

American Bar Association. (2007). *American Bar Association criminal justice standards on pretrial release* (3rd ed.). Washington, DC: Author.

American Bar Association. (2015). *American Bar Association criminal justice standards for the prosecution function.* (4th ed.). Washington, DC: Author.

American Council of Chief Defenders. (2011). *Policy statement on fair and effective pretrial justice practices.* Retrieved from www.pretrial.org/download/policy-statements/ACCD%20Pretrial%20Release%20Policy%20Statement%20June%202011.pdf

An analysis of the citation system in Evanston, Illinois: Its value, constitutionality and viability. (1974). *Journal of Criminal Law & Criminology, 65*(1), 75–86. doi:10.2307/1142353

Anderson, J.M., Buenaventura, M., & Heaton, P.S. (2019). The effects of holistic defense on criminal justice outcomes. *Harvard Law Review, 132,* 819–893. Retrieved from https://harvardlawreview.org/wp-content/uploads/2019/01/819-893_Online.pdf

Anderson, N., & Kiehl, K.A. (2013). Functional imaging and psychopathy. In K.A. Kiehl & W.P. Sinnott-Armstrong (Eds.), *Handbook on psychopathy and law* (pp. 131–149). Oxford, UK: Oxford University Press.

Andrade, J.T., O'Neill, K., & Diener, R.B. (2009). Violence risk assessment and risk management: A historical overview and clinical application. In J.T. Andrade (Ed.), *Handbook of violence risk assessment and treatment: New approaches for mental health professionals* (pp. 3–39). New York, NY: Springer Publishing Company.

Andrews, D.A., & Bonta, J. (1995). *Level of Service Inventory–Revised.* Toronto, ON: Multi-Health Systems.

Andrews, D.A., Bonta, J., & Wormith, J.S. (2004). *The Level of Service/Case Management Inventory (LS/CMI).* Toronto, ON: Multi-Health Systems.

Andrews, D. A., Bonta, J., & Wormith, J. S. (2006). The recent past and near future of risk and/or needs assessment. *Crime & Delinquency, 52*(1), 7–27. doi:10.1177/0011128705281756

Andrews, D. A., Dowden, C., & Rettinger, L. J. (2001). Special populations within corrections. In J. A. Winterdyk (Ed.), *Corrections in Canada: Social reactions to crime* (pp. 170–212). Toronto, ON: Prentice Hall.

Andrews, D. A., Guzzo, L., Reynor, P., Rowe, R. C., Rettinger, L. J., Brews, A., & Wormith, J. S. (2012). Are the major risk/need factors predictive of both female and male reoffending? A test with the eight domains of the Level of Service/Case Management Inventory. *International Journal of Offender Therapy and Comparative Criminology, 56*(1), 113–133. doi:10.1177/0306624X10395716

Angel, A. R., Green, E. D., Kaufman, H. R., & Van Loon, E. E. (1971). Preventive detention: An empirical analysis. *Harvard Civil Rights and Civil Liberties Law Review, 6*, 300–396.

Angwin, J., Larson, J., Mattu, S., & Kirchner, L. (2016, May 23). Machine bias. ProPublica. Retrieved from www.propublica.org/article/machine-bias-risk -assessments-in-criminal-sentencing

Ares, C., Rankin, A., & Sturz, H. (1963). The Manhattan Bail Project: An interim report on the use of pretrial parole. *New York University Law Review, 38*, 67–92.

Argersinger v. Hamlin, 407 U.S. 25 (1972).

Arnold, D., Dobbie, W., & Yang, C. S. (2018). Racial bias in bail decisions. *The Quarterly Journal of Economics, 133*(4), 1885–1932. doi:10.1093/qje/qjy012

Arrigo, B. A., & Shipley, S. (2001). The confusion over psychopathy (I): Historical considerations. *International Journal of Offender Therapy and Comparative Criminology, 454*(3), 325–344. doi:10.1177/0306624X01453005

Associated Press (2013, May 17). Charges: Bondsman sought sex before posting bail. *Topeka Capital Journal.* Retrieved from www.cjonline.com/news/2013 -05-17/charges-bondsman-sought-sex-posting-bail

Associated Press (2016, March 2). Texas trooper indicted in Sandra Bland traffic stop and arrest is formally fired. *The Guardian.* Retrieved from www.the guardian.com/us-news/2016/mar/02/texas-trooper-fired-sandra-bland-death

Atwater v. City of Lago Vista, 532 U.S. 318 (2001).

Austin, J. (2006). How much risk can we take? The misuse of risk assessment in corrections. *Federal Probation, 70*(2), 58–63.

Austin, J., Krisberg, B., & Litsky, P. (1985). The effectiveness of supervised pretrial release. *Crime & Delinquency, 31*(4), 519–537. doi:10.1177/0011287850310004004

Aviram, H. (2015). *Cheap on crime: Recession-era politics and the transformation of American punishment*. Berkeley, CA: University of California Press.

Baicker, K., & Jacobson, M. (2007). Finders keepers: Forfeiture laws, policing incentives, and local budgets. *Journal of Public Economics, 91,* 2113–2136. doi:doi:10.1016/j.jpubeco.2007.03.009

*Bail legislation: Hearing before the Subcommittee on Constitutional Rights and Improvements in the Judicial Machinery,* Senate, 88th Cong. (August 4, 1964) (testimony of Attorney General Robert F. Kennedy). Retrieved from www.justice.gov/sites/default/files/ag/legacy/2011/01/20/08-04-1964.pdf

Bail reform and risk assessment: The cautionary tale of federal sentencing. (2018). *Harvard Law Review, 131,* 1125–1146.

Baird, C. S., Heinz, R. C., & Bemus, B. J. (1979). *The Wisconsin case classification /staff deployment project: A two-year follow-up report.* Madison, WI: Wisconsin Division of Corrections.

Baker, S. M., Vaughn, M. S., & Topalli, V. (2008). A review of the powers of bail bond agents and bounty hunters: Exploring legalities and illegalities of quasi-criminal justice officials. *Aggression and Violent Behavior, 13*(2), 124–130. doi:10.1016/j.avb.2008.02.003

Baldwin, J. W. (1961). The intellectual preparation for the canon of 1215 against ordeals. *Speculum, 36*(4), 613–636.

Bales, W., Mann, K., Blomberg, T., Gaes, G., Barrick, K., Dhungana, K., & McManus, B. (2010). *A quantitative and qualitative assessment of electronic monitoring.* Tallahassee, FL: Florida State University, Center for Criminology and Public Policy Research. Retrieved from www.ncjrs.gov/pdffiles1/nij /grants/230530.pdf

Banks, R. R., & Ford, R. T. (2009). (How) does unconscious bias matter? Law, politics, and racial inequality. *Emory Law Journal, 58*(5), 1053–1122.

Baradaran, S., & McIntyre, F. (2012). Predicting violence. *Texas Law Review, 90,* 497–570.

Baradaran-Baughman, S. (2017). Costs of pretrial detention. *Boston University Law Review, 97,* 1–30.

Baradaran-Baughman, S. (2018). *The bail book: A comprehensive look at bail in America's criminal justice system.* New York, NY: Cambridge University Press.

Barker v. Wingo, 407 U.S. 514 (1972).

Barrett, D. (2014, August 1). Holder cautions on risk of bias in big data use in criminal justice. *Wall Street Journal.* Retrieved from www.wsj.com/articles /u-s-attorney-general-cautions-on-risk-of-bias-in-big-data-use-in-criminal -justice-1406916606

Barto, D. (2015). *You arrested me for what? A bail bondsman's observations of Virginia's criminal justice system* [Self-published]. Available at Amazon.com.

Bauer, S. (2014). Inside the wild, shadowy, and highly lucrative bail industry. *Mother Jones.* Retrieved from www.motherjones.com/politics/2014/06/bail-bond-prison-industry/

Baumer, T., & Adams, K. (2006). Controlling a jail population by partially closing the front door: An evaluation of a summons in lieu of arrest policy. *The Prison Journal, 86*(3), 386–402. doi:10.1177/0032885506291036

Beaney, W.M. (1955). *The right to counsel in American courts.* Ann Arbor, MI: University of Michigan Press.

Bearden v. Georgia, 461 U.S. 660 (1983).

Beattie, J.M. (1991). Scales of justice: Defense counsel and the English criminal trial in the eighteenth and nineteenth centuries. *Law and History Review, 9*(2), 221–267. doi:10.2307/743649

Bechtel, K., Holsinger, A.M., Lowenkamp, C.T., & Warren, M.J. (2017). A meta-analytic review of pretrial research: Risk assessment, bond type, and interventions. *American Journal of Criminal Justice, 42*(2), 443–467. doi:10.1007/s12103-016-9367-1

Beeley, A.L. (1966). *The bail system in Chicago.* Chicago, IL: University of Chicago Press (Original work published 1927)

Bell v. Wolfish, 441 U.S. 520 (1979).

Berk, R.A., Heidari, H., Jabbari, S., Kearns, M., & Roth, A. (2017). Fairness in criminal justice risk assessments: The state of the art. Retrieved from arXiv:1703.09207v2 [stat.ML], https://arxiv.org/abs/1703.09207v2

Berk, R.A., & Hyatt, J. (2015). Machine learning forecasts of risks in criminal justice settings. *Federal Sentencing Reporter, 27*(4), 222–228. doi:10.1525/fsr.2015.27.4.222

Berk, R.A., Sorenson, S.B., & Barnes, G. (2016). Forecasting domestic violence: A machine learning approach to help inform arraignment decisions. *Journal of Empirical Legal Studies, 13*(1), 94–155. doi:10.1111/jels.12098

Betts v. Brady, 316 U.S. 455 (1942).

Bhati, A. (2010). *Reassessing risk assessment: Measuring latent risk in pretrial populations to predict crime.* [Working paper]. Gaithersburg, MD: Maxarth LLC.

Bibas, S. (2011). The pitfalls of professionalized prosecution: A response to Josh Bowers's "Legal guilt, normative innocence, and the equitable decision not to prosecute." *Columbia Law Review Sidebar, 111,* 14–17.

Bibas, S. (2012). *The machinery of criminal justice.* New York, NY: Oxford University Press.

Billings, T. (2016). Private interest, public sphere: Eliminating the use of commercial bail bondsmen in the criminal justice system. *Boston College Law Review, 57*, 1337–1365.

Blackwell, B. S., & Cunningham, C. D. (2004). Case studies in conservative and progressive legal orders: Taking the punishment out of the process: From substantive criminal justice through procedural justice to restorative justice. *Law and Contemporary Problems, 67*, 59–86.

Blaylock, D. (2017, June 1). I'm a bail bondsman who's tired of being demonized. The Marshall Project. Retrieved from www.themarshallproject.org/2017/06/01/i-m-a-bail-bondsman-who-s-tired-of-being-demonized

Blomberg, T., Bales, W., Mann, K., Meldrum, R., & Nedelec, J. (2010). *Validation of the COMPAS risk assessment classification instrument.* Tallahassee, FL: Florida State University Center for Criminology and Public Policy Research. Retrieved from http://criminology.fsu.edu/wp-content/uploads/Validation-of-the-COMPAS-Risk-Assessment-Classification-Instrument.pdf

Blume, J. H., & Helm, R. K. (2014). The unexonerated: Factually innocent defendants who plead guilty. *Cornell Law Review, 100*, 157–191.

Boccardi, M. (2013). Structural brain images and psychopathy. In K. A. Kiehl & W. P. Sinnott-Armstrong (Eds.), *Handbook on psychopathy and law* (pp. 150–160). Oxford, UK: Oxford University Press.

Bonta, J., Harman, W. G., Hann, R. G., & Cormier, R. B. (1996). The prediction of recidivism among federally sentenced offenders: A re-validation of the SIR scale. *Canadian Journal of Criminology, 38*, 61–79.

Bonta, J., & Wormith, S. J. (2007). Risk and need assessment. In G. McIvor & P. Raynor (Eds.), *Developments in social work with offenders* (pp. 131–152). London, UK: Jessica Kingsley Publishers.

Bordenkircher v. Hayes, 434 U.S. 357 (1978).

Bornstein, B. H., Tomkins, A. J., Neeley, E. M., Herian, M. N., & Hamm, J. A. (2013). Reducing courts' failure-to-appear rate by written reminders. *Psychology, Public Policy, and Law, 19*(1), 70–80. doi:10.1037/a0026293

Boruchowitz, R. C., Brink, M. N., & Dimino, M. (2009). *Minor crimes, massive waste: The terrible toll of America's broken misdemeanor courts.* Washington, DC: National Association of Criminal Defense Lawyers. Retrieved from www.nacdl.org/WorkArea/DownloadAsset.aspx?id=20808

Bostic v. Rodriguez, 667 F. Supp. 2d 591, 609 (E.D.N.C. 2009).

Boucher, R. (2017, July 28). Hell is trying to visit my jailed client. The Marshall Project. Retrieved from www.themarshallproject.org/2017/07/27/hell-is-trying-to-visit-my-jailed-client

Bowers, J. (2010). Legal guilt, normative innocence, and the equitable decision not to prosecute. *Columbia Law Review, 110,* 1655–1726.

Brauneis, R., & Goodman, E. P. (2018). Algorithmic transparency for the smart city. *Yale Journal of Law & Technology, 20,* 103–176.

Brennan, T., Dieterich, W., & Ehret, B. (2009). Evaluating the predictive validity of the COMPAS risk and needs assessment system. *Criminal Justice and Behavior, 36*(1), 2–40. doi:10.1177/0093854808326545

Brewer v. Williams, 430 U.S. 387 (1977).

Brief for the United States as amicus curiae supporting neither party in *Walker v. City of Calhoun,* No. 16-10521 (11th Cir. September 13, 2017). Retrieved from www.justice.gov/crt/case-document/walker-v-calhoun-brief-amicus

Bright, S. B., & Sanneh, S. M. (2013). Fifty years of defiance and resistance after *Gideon v. Wainwright. Yale Law Journal, 122,* 2150–2174.

Bronx Freedom Fund. (n.d.) The Bronx Freedom Fund. Retrieved from www.thebronxfreedomfund.org/

Brown, E. G. (1964). *British statutes in American law, 1776–1836.* Ann Arbor, MI: University of Michigan.

Brown, R. A., & Frank, J. (2005). Police-citizen encounters and field citations: Do encounter characteristics influence ticketing? *Policing: An International Journal of Police Strategies and Management, 28*(3), 435–454. doi:10.1108/13639510510614546

Brown, T. M. L., McCabe, S. A., & Wellford, C. (2007). *Global positioning system (GPS) technology for community supervision: Lessons learned.* Washington, DC: U.S. Department of Justice, National Institute of Justice. Retrieved from www.ncjrs.gov/pdffiles1/nij/grants/219376.pdf

Bunin, A. (2016). The constitutional right to counsel at bail hearings. *Criminal Justice, 31*(1), 23–26, 47.

Bureau of Justice Statistics. (2010, March). *Data advisory: State Court Process Statistics data limitations.* Washington, DC: Author. Retrieved from www.bjs.gov/content/pub/pdf/scpsdl_da.pdf

Burgess, E. W. (1928). Factors determining success or failure on parole. In A. A. Bruce, E. W. Burgess, & A. J. Harno (Eds.), *The workings of the indeterminate sentence law and the parole system in Illinois* (pp. 221–234). Springfield, IL: State Board of Parole.

Burke, A. S. (2006). Improving prosecutorial decision-making: Some lessons of cognitive science. *William and Mary Law Review, 47*(5), 1587–1633.

Busher, W. (1978). *Citation release: An alternative to pretrial detention: Concepts and guidelines.* Sacramento, CA: American Justice Institute. Retrieved from www.ncjrs.gov/pdffiles1/digitization/64883ncjrs.pdf

Byrne, J., & Pattavina, A. (2017). Next generation assessment technology. *Probation Journal, 64*(3), 242–255. doi:10.1177/0264550517720851

Cadigan, T. P. (1991). Electronic monitoring in federal pretrial release. *Federal Probation, 55*(1), 26–30.

Cadigan, T. P. (2009). Implementing evidence-based practices in federal pretrial services. *Federal Probation, 73*(2), 30–32.

Cadigan, T. P., & Lowenkamp, C. T. (2011). Implementing risk assessment in the federal pretrial services system. *Federal Probation, 75*(2), 30–34.

California Department of Insurance. (n.d.) *Bail agent.* Retrieved from www.insurance.ca.gov/0200-industry/0050-renew-license/0200-requirements/bail-agent.cfm

Camara v. Municipal Court, 387 U.S. 523 (1967).

Campbell, M. Ann, French, S., & Gendreau, P. (2009). The prediction of violence in adult offenders: A meta-analytic comparison of instruments and methods of assessment. *Criminal Justice and Behavior, 36*(6), 567–590.

Cape, E., & Smith, T. (2016), *The practice of pre-trial detention in England and Wales: Research report.* Bristol, UK: University of the West of England, Centre for Legal Research. Retrieved from www.fairtrials.org/wp-content/uploads/Country-Report-England-and-Wales-MASTER-Final-PRINT.pdf

Carbone, J. (1983). Seeing through the emperor's new clothes: Rediscovery of basic principles in the administration of bail. *Syracuse Law Review, 34,* 518–574.

Carlson v. Landon, 342 U.S. 524 (1952).

Casey, P. M., Elek, J. K., Warren, R. K., Cheesman, F., Kleiman, M., & Ostrom, B. (2014). *Offender risk & needs assessment instruments: A primer for courts.* Williamsburg, VA: National Center for State Courts. Retrieved from www.ncsc.org/~/media/microsites/files/csi/bja%20rna%20final%20report_combined%20files%208-22-14.ashx

Cassidy, M. (2018, August 29). Facing extinction, California bond firms decry bill ending cash bail, launch ballot drive. *San Francisco Chronicle.* Retrieved from www.sfchronicle.com/crime/article/Facing-death-of-industry-California-bail-agents-13192267.php

Caudy, M. S., Durso, J. M., & Taxman, F. S. (2013). How well do dynamic needs predict recidivism? Implications for risk assessment and risk reduction. *Journal of Criminal Justice, 41*(6), 458–466. doi:10.1016/j.jcrimjus.2013.08.004

Causey, A. (2013–2014). Reviving the carefully limited exception: From jail to GPS bail. *Faulkner Law Review, 5,* 59–114.

Central Casualty Co. v. State, 346 S. W. 2d 193 (Ark. 1961).

Chander, A. (2017). The racist algorithm. *Michigan Law Review, 115*(6), 1023–1045.

Chandler v. Fretag, 438 U.S. 3 (1954).

Chenane, J.L., Brennan, P.K., Steiner, B., & Ellison, J.M. (2015). Racial and ethnic differences in the predictive validity of the level of service inventory-revised among prison inmates. *Criminal Justice and Behavior, 42*(3), 286–303. doi:10.1177/0093854814548195

Chouldechova, A. (2017). Fair prediction with disparate impact: A study of bias in recidivism prediction instruments. *Big Data, 2,* 153–163. Retrieved from arXiv:1610.07524 [stat.AP], https://arxiv.org/abs/1610.07524

Citizens' Commission on Jail Violence. (2012). *Report of the citizens' commission on jail violence.* Los Angeles, CA: County of Los Angeles. Retrieved from http://ccjv.lacounty.gov/wp-content/uploads/2012/09/CCJV-Report.pdf

Clark v. Hall, 53 P.3d 416 (Okla. Ct. Crim. App. 2002).

Clark, J., & Henry, D.A. (2003). *Pretrial services programming at the start of the 21st century: A survey of pretrial services programs.* Washington, DC: U.S. Department of Justice, Bureau of Justice Assistance. Retrieved from www.ncjrs.gov/pdffiles1/bja/199773.pdf

Clarke, M.C., Peterson-Badali, M., & Skilling, T.A. (2017). The relationship between changes in dynamic risk factors and the predictive validity of risk assessments among youth offenders. *Criminal Justice and Behavior, 44*(10), 1340–1355. doi:10.1177/0093854817719915

Cleckley, H. (1941). *The mask of sanity.* London, UK: Henry Kimpton.

Cohen, T.H., & Reaves, B.A. (2007). *Pretrial release of felony defendants in state courts.* Washington, DC: U.S. Department of Justice, Bureau of Justice Statistics. Retrieved from www.bjs.gov/content/pub/pdf/prfdsc.pdf

Colbert, D.L., Paternoster, R., & Bushway, S. (2002). Do attorneys really matter? The empirical and legal case for the right of counsel at bail. *Cardozo Law Review, 23,* 1719–1793.

Coleman v. Alabama, 399 U.S. 1 (1970).

Color of Change & American Civil Liberties Union. (2017). *Selling off our freedom: How insurance corporations have taken over our bail system.* Retrieved from www.aclu.org/report/selling-our-freedom-how-insurance-corpora tions-have-taken-over-our-bail-system

Colorado Criminal Defense Institute & The Colorado State Public Defender. (2015). *Colorado bail book: A defense practitioner's guide to adult pretrial release.* Washington, DC: The National Association of Criminal Defense Lawyers. Retrieved from www.bja.gov/Publications/Colorado_Bail_Book_Pretrial _Release.pdf

Concord Cas. and Ser. Co. v. United States, 69 F.2d 78 (2d Cir. 1934).

Constitution Project, The. (2015). *Don't I need a lawyer? Pretrial justice and the right to counsel at first judicial bail hearing.* Washington, DC: The Constitution Project National Right to Counsel Committee. Retrieved from https://constitutionproject.org/wp-content/uploads/2015/03/RTC-DINAL_3.18.15.pdf

Cooke, B., Diop, B. Z., Fishbane, A., Hayes, J., Ouss, A., & Shah, A. (2018). *Using behavioral science to improve criminal justice outcomes: Preventing failures to appear in court.* Chicago, IL: University of Chicago Urban Labs Crime Lab & Ideas 42. Retrieved from http://urbanlabs.uchicago.edu/attachments/store/f0f92 10ecb1a295beoaf54cee2c7364564c570a857a33d758a162d6faafd/I42-954_NYC SummonsPaper_final.pdf

Cooke, D.J., Forth, A.E., Newman, J.P., & Hare, R.D. (Eds). (1996). *Issues in criminological and legal psychology no. 24: International perspectives on psychopathy.* Leicester, UK: British Psychological Society.

Cooprider, K. (2009). Pretrial risk assessment and case classification: A case study. *Federal Probation, 73*(1), 12–15.

Cooprider, K. (2014). A descriptive analysis of pretrial services at the single-jurisdictional level. *Federal Probation, 78*, 9–15.

Corbett-Davies, S., Goel, S., & González-Bailón, S. (2017). Even imperfect algorithms can improve the criminal justice system. *The New York Times.* Retrieved from www.nytimes.com/2017/12/20/upshot/algorithms-bail-criminal-justice -system.html

Corbett-Davies, S., Pierson, E., Feller, A., Goel, S., & Huq, A. (2017). Algorithmic decision making and the cost of fairness. *Proceedings of the 23rd ACM SIGKDD International Conference on Knowledge Discovery and Data Mining, 2017*, 797–806. Retrieved from arXiv:1701.08230 [cs.CY], https://arxiv.org /abs/1701.08230

Council of State Governments Justice Center. (2018). *Justice reinvestment: How states use data to design innovative strategies to reduce crime, recidivism, and costs.* Washington DC: The Council of State Governments. Retrieved from https://csgjusticecenter.org/wp-content/uploads/2018/05/May-2018 _JR_2Pager.pdf

County of Riverside v. McLaughlin, 500 U.S. 44 (1991).

Court Watch NYC. (2018, May 21). *Last week in court: May 7–May 14.* Retrieved from www.courtwatchnyc.org/

Covert, B. (2017, October 17). America is waking up to the injustice of cash bail. *The Nation.* Retrieved from www.thenation.com/article/america-is-waking -up-to-the-injustice-of-cash-bail/

Covert, B. (2018, January 10). This deep red state just ended cash bail. *The Appeal*. Retrieved from https://theappeal.org/alaska-ends-its-reliance-on-money-bail-ff1cc0e19730/

Criminal Justice Policy Program. (2016). *Moving beyond money: A primer on bail reform*. Cambridge, MA: Harvard Law School. Retrieved from http://cjpp.law.harvard.edu/assets/FINAL-Primer-on-Bail-Reform.pdf

Dance, S. (2018, January 16). Since bail reform, Maryland holding fewer people who can't afford bond, assembly panel told. *The Baltimore Sun*. Retrieved from www.baltimoresun.com/news/maryland/politics/bs-md-bail-reform-statistics-20180116-story.html

Danner, M.J.E., VanNostrand, M., & Spruance, L.M. (2015). *Risk-based pretrial release recommendation and supervision guidelines*. St Petersburg, FL: Luminosity, Inc. Retrieved from www.pretrial.org/download/research/Risk%20Based%20Pretrial%20Release%20Rec%20&%20Superv%20Guidelines%20-%20Danner,%20VanNostrand,%20&%20Spruance%202015.pdf

Davis, W. (2005). Should Georgia change its misdemeanor arrest laws to authorize issuing more field citations? *Georgia State University Law Review, 22*, 313–379.

De Angelis v. South Carolina, 330 F. Supp. 889 (D.S.C. 1971).

De Haas, E. (1940). *Antiquities of bail: Origin and historical development in criminal cases to the year 1275*. New York, NY: Columbia University Press.

DeMichele, M., Baumgartner, P., Wenger, M., Barrick, K., Comfort, M., & Misra, S. (2018). *The Public Safety Assessment: A re-validation and assessment of predictive utility and differential prediction by race and gender in Kentucky*. Retrieved from https://ssrn.com/abstract=3168452

Demuth, S. (2003). Racial and ethnic differences in pretrial release decisions and outcomes: A comparison of Hispanic, black, and white felony arrestees. *Criminology, 41*(3), 873–907. doi:10.1111/j.1745-9125.2003.tb01007.x

Demuth, S, & Steffensmeier, D. (2004). The impact of gender and race-ethnicity in the pretrial release process. *Social Problems, 51*(2), 222–242. doi:10.1525/sp.2004.51.2.222

Desmarais, S.L., & Singh, J.P. (2013). *Risk assessment instruments validated and implemented in correctional settings in the United States*. New York, NY: Council of State Governments Justice Center. Retrieved from https://csgjusticecenter.org/wp-content/uploads/2014/07/Risk-Assessment-Instruments-Validated-and-Implemented-in-Correctional-Settings-in-the-United-States.pdf

Devine, F.E. (1991). *Commercial bail bonding: A comparison of common law alternatives*. Santa Barbara, CA: Praeger.

DeWolfe v. Richmond, 76 A.3d 1019 (Md. 2013).

Dieterich, W. (2010). *Kent County Pretrial Services outcomes study: Developing and testing the COMPAS pretrial release risk scale.* Traverse City, MI: Northpointe.

Dieterich, W., Mendoza, C., & Brennan, T. (2016). *COMPAS risk scales: Demonstrating accuracy equity and predictive parity.* Traverse City, MI: Northpointe. Retrieved from http://go.volarisgroup.com/rs/430-MBX-989/images/ProPublica_Commentary_Final_070616.pdf

Dobbie, W., Goldin, J., & Yang, C.S. (2018). The effects of pretrial detention on conviction, future crime, and employment: Evidence from randomly assigned judges. *American Economic Review, 108*(2), 201–240. doi:10.1257/aer.20161503

Doherty, F. (2016). Obey all laws and be good: Probation and the meaning of recidivism. *Georgetown Law Journal, 104,* 291–354.

Dolnick, S. (2012, June 18). At penal unit, a volatile mix fuels a murder. *The New York Times.* Retrieved from www.nytimes.com/2012/06/19/nyregion/at-a-new-jersey-halfway-house-a-volatile-mix-fuels-a-murder.html

Douglas v. California, 372 U.S. 353 (1963).

Douglas, K.S., Hart, S.D., Webster, C.D., Belfrage, H., Guy, L.S., & Wilson, C.M. (2014). Historical-Clinical-Risk Management-20, version 3 (HCR-20$^{V3}$): Development and overview. *International Journal of Forensic Mental Health, 13,* 93–108. doi:10.1080/14999013.2014.906519

Douglas, K.S., Vincent, G.M., & Edens, J.F. (2006). Risk for criminal recidivism: The role of psychopathy. In C.J. Patrick (Ed.), *Handbook of psychopathy* (pp. 533–554). New York, NY: The Guilford Press.

Douglas, K.S., Yeomans, M., & Boer, D.P. (2005). Comparative validity analysis of multiple measures of violence risk in a sample of criminal offenders. *Criminal Justice and Behavior, 32*(5), 479–510. doi:10.1177/0093854805278411

Downer, L.J. (Ed.). (1972). *Leges Henrici Primi.* Oxford, UK: Clarendon Press.

Dubos, C. (2004). We all pay. *The Advocate: Gambit.* Retrieved from www.theadvocate.com/gambit/new_orleans/news/clancy_dubos/article_bb745ab7-80c1-5702-9487-924935913999.html

Duker, W.F. (1977). The right to bail: A historical inquiry. *Albany Law Review, 42,* 33–120.

Durose, M.R., Cooper, A.D., & Snyder, H.N. (2014). *Recidivism of prisoners released in 30 states in 2005: Patterns from 2005 to 2010.* Washington, DC: US Department of Justice, Bureau of Justice Statistics. Retrieved from www.bjs.gov/content/pub/pdf/rprts05p0510.pdf

Duwe, G. (2014). The development, validity, and reliability of the Minnesota Screening Tool Assessing Recidivism Risk (MnSTARR). *Criminal Justice Policy Review, 25*(5), 579–613. doi:10.1177/0887403413478821

Eckhouse, L. (2018, August 31). California abolished money bail. Here's why bail opponents aren't happy. *The Washington Post: Monkey Cage* [Web log post]. Retrieved from www.washingtonpost.com/news/monkey-cage /wp/2018/08/31/california-abolished-money-bail-heres-why-bail-opponents -arent-happy/?noredirect=on&utm_term=.647ae373be75

Edens, J.F. (2001). Misuses of the Hare Psychopathy Checklist-Revised in court: Two case examples. *Journal of Interpersonal Violence, 16*(10), 1082–1093. doi:10.1177/088626001016010007

Edens, J.F., & Campbell, J.S. (2007). Identifying youths at risk for institutional misconduct: A meta-analytic investigation of the Psychopathy Checklist measures. *Psychological Services, 4*(1), 13–27. doi:10.1037/1541-1559.4.1.13

Edens, J.F., Campbell, J.S., & Weir, J.M. (2007). Youth psychopathy and criminal recidivism: A meta-analysis of the Psychopathy Checklist measures. *Law and Human Behavior, 31*(1), 53–75. doi:10.1007/s10979-006-9019-y

Edens, J.F., Skeem, J.L., & Kennealy, P.J. (2009). The Psychopathy Checklist in the courtroom. In J.L. Skeem, K.S. Douglas, & S.O. Lilienfeld (Eds.), *Psychological science in the courtroom: Consensus and controversy* (pp. 175–201). New York, NY: The Guilford Press.

Equal Justice Under Law. (n.d.). *Ending American money bail.* Retrieved from https://equaljusticeunderlaw.org/money-bail-1

Ericksen, K.P., & Horton, H. (1992). Blood feuds: Cross-cultural variations in kin group vengeance. *Cross-Cultural Research, 26*(1-4), 57–85. doi:10.1177/106 939719202600103

Estelle v. Williams, 425 U.S. 501 (1976).

Euvrard, E., & Leclerc, C. (2017). Pre-trial detention and guilty pleas: Inducement or coercion? *Punishment & Society, 19*(5), 525–542. doi:10.1177/146247 4516670153

Ewing v. United States, 240 F. 241 (6th Cir. 1917).

*Ex parte* Milburn, 34 U.S. (9 Pet.) 704 (1835).

*Ex parte* Watkins, 32 U.S. (7 Pet.) 568 (1833).

Fan, T. (2018, July 13). Conspiracy theories, criminal investigations plentiful in NC bail bonds world. *WRAL.* Retrieved from www.wral.com/conspiracy -theories-criminal-investigations-plentiful-in-nc-bail-bonds-world/17333869/

Farabee, D., Zhang, S., Roberts, R.E.L., & Yang, J. (2010). *COMPAS validation study: Final report.* Los Angeles, CA: University of California Semel Institute for Neuroscience and Human Behavior. Retrieved from www.cdcr.ca.gov /adult_research_branch/Research_Documents/COMPAS_Final_report _08-11-10.pdf

Fass, T. L., Heilbrun, K., Dematteo, D., & Fretz, R. (2008). The LSI-R and the COMPAS: Validation data on two risk-needs tools. *Criminal Justice and Behavior, 35*(9), 1095–1108. doi:10.1177/0093854808320497

Faust, D., & Ziskin, J. (1988). The expert witness in psychology and psychiatry. *Science, 241*, 31–35.

Fazel, S., Singh, J. P., Doll, H., & Grann, M. (2012). The prediction of violence and antisocial behaviour: A systematic review and meta-analysis of the utility of risk assessment instruments in 73 samples involving 24,827 individuals. *British Medical Journal, 345*, e4692. doi:10.1136/bmj.e4692

Fazio, E. J., Wexler, S., Foster, T., Lowy, M. J., Sheppard, D., & Musso, J. A. (1985). *Early representation by defense counsel field test: Final evaluation report.* Washington, DC: US Department of Justice, National Institute of Justice. Retrieved from www.ncjrs.gov/pdffiles1/Digitization/97596NCJRS.pdf

Ferdico, J. N., Fradella, H. F., & Totten, C. D. (2015). *Criminal procedure for the criminal justice professional* (12th ed.). Boston, MA: Cengage.

Fields v. Henry County, 701 F.3d 180 (6th Cir. 2012).

Findley, K. A., & Scott, M. S. (2006). The multiple dimensions of tunnel vision in criminal cases. *Wisconsin Law Review, 2006*, 291–397.

Florence v. Board of Chosen Freeholders, 566 U.S. 318 (2012).

Flores, A. W., Bechtel, K., & Lowenkamp, C. T. (2016). False positives, false negatives, and false analyses: A rejoinder to "Machine bias: There's software used across the country to predict future criminals. and it's biased against blacks." *Federal Probation, 80*(2), 38–46.

Flores, A. W., Travis, L. F., III, & Latessa, E. J. (2003). *Case classification for juvenile corrections: An assessment of the Youth Level of Service Case Management Inventory (YLS/CMI).* Cincinnati, OH: University of Cincinnati, Center for Criminal Justice Research. Retrieved from www.uc.edu/content/dam/uc/ccjr/docs/reports/project_reports/NIJYLSI.pdf

Florida Tax Watch. (2011). *Research report: Expansion of civil citation programs statewide would save taxpayers tens of millions of dollars and improve public safety.* Tallahassee, FL: Center for Smart Justice. Retrieved from http://files.ctctcdn.com/b3c26bd1101/62215712-7f80-4638-9321-bce1a8322d6b.pdf

Foote, C. (1954). Compelling appearance in court: Administration of bail in Philadelphia. *University of Pennsylvania Law, 102*, 1031–1079.

Foote, C. (1966). *Studies on bail.* Philadelphia, PA: The University of Pennsylvania Law Review.

Franklin, K. (2013, January 3). "The best predictor of future behavior is … past behavior": Does the popular maxim hold water? *Psychology Today* [Web log post]. Retrieved from www.psychologytoday.com/us/blog/witness/201301 /the-best-predictor-future-behavior-is-past-behavior

Frase, R S. (2002). What were they thinking? Fourth amendment unreasonableness in *Atwater v. City of Lago Vista*. *Fordham Law Review, 71*, 329–421.

Frase, R.S., Roberts, J.R., Hester, R., & Mitchell, K.L. (2015). *Criminal history enhancements sourcebook*. Minneapolis, MN: Robina Institute of Criminal Law and Criminal Justice. Retrieved from https://robinainstitute.umn. edu/publications/criminal-history-enhancements-sourcebook

Free, M.D. (2001). Racial bias and the American criminal justice system: Race and presentencing revisited. *Critical Criminology, 10*(3), 195–223. doi:10.1023 /A:1015796321587

Freed, D.J., & Wald, P.M. (1964). *Bail in the United States, 1964*. Washington, DC: US Department of Justice & The Vera Foundation.

Freiburger, T.L. (2009). Race and the sentencing of drug offenders: An examination of the focal concerns perspective. *Southwest Journal of Criminal Justice, 6*(2), 163–177.

*Frontline*. (2004). The plea: Erma Faye Stewart and Regina Kelly. PBS [Television series]. Retrieved from www.pbs.org/wgbh/pages/frontline/shows /plea/four/stewart.html

Fulero, S.M. (1995). Review of the Hare Psychopathy Checklist-Revised. In J.C. Conoley & J.C. Impara (Eds.), *The twelfth mental measurements yearbook* (pp. 453–454). Lincoln, NE: Buros Institute of Mental Measurements.

Gagnon v. Scarpelli, 411 U.S. 778 (1973).

Galen v. County of Los Angeles, 477 F.3d 652 (9th Cir. 1987).

Gendreau, P., Goggin, C., & Little, T. (1996). *Predicting adult offender recidivism: What works?* (Cat. No. JS4-1/1996-7E). Ottawa, ON: Public Works and Government Services Canada.

Gerstein v. Pugh, 420 U.S. 103 (1975).

Gideon v. Wainwright, 372 U.S. 335 (1963).

Gilbert, M.J., & Schichor, D. (2001). *Privatization of criminal justice: Past, present, and future*. New York, NY: Routledge.

Girard, L., & Wormith, J.S. (2004). The predictive validity of the Level of Service Inventory-Ontario Revision on general and violent recidivism among various offender groups. *Criminal Justice and Behavior, 31*(2), 150–181. doi:10.1177/0093854803261335

Glasgow v. Beary, 2 F. Supp. 3d 419 (E.D.N.Y. 2014).

Gless, A.G. (1980). Arrest and citation: Definition and analysis. *Nebraska Law Review, 59*, 279–326.

Goldkamp, J. S. (1979). *Two classes of accused: A study of bail and detention in American justice.* Cambridge, MA: Ballinger.

Goldkamp, J. S. (1980). Philadelphia revisited: An examination of bail and detention two decades after Foote. *Crime & Delinquency, 26*(2), 179–192. doi:10.1177/0011128780026000204

Goldkamp, J. S. (1983). Questioning the practice of pretrial detention: Some empirical evidence from Philadelphia. *Journal of Criminal Law and Criminology, 74*(4), 1556–1588.

Goldkamp, J. S. (1985). Danger and detention: A second generation of bail reform. *Journal of Criminal Law and Criminology, 76*(1), 1–56. doi:10.2307/1143353

Goldkamp, John S. (2002). Bail. In J. Dressler (Ed.), *Encyclopedia of crime and justice* (2nd ed., pp. 93–101). New York, NY: Macmillan Reference.

Goldkamp, J. S., Gottfredson, M. R., Jones, P. R., & Weiland, D. (1995). *Personal liberty and community safety: Pretrial release in criminal court.* New York, NY: Plenum.

Goldkamp, J. S., Jones, P. R., Weiland, D., & Gottfredson, M. R. (1990). *Measuring the impact of drug testing at the pretrial release stage: Experimental findings from Prince George's County and Milwaukee County.* Philadelphia, PA: Crime and Justice Institute.

Goldkamp, J. S., & Vîlcicā, E. R. (2009). Judicial discretion and the unfinished agenda of American bail reform: Lessons from Philadelphia's evidence-based judicial strategy. In A. Sarat (Ed.), *Studies in law, politics, and society volume 47: New perspectives on crime and criminal justice* (pp. 115–157). Bingly, UK: Emerald Publishing.

Goldkamp, J. S., & White, M. D. (2006). Restoring accountability in pretrial release: The Philadelphia pretrial release supervision experiments. *Journal of Experimental Criminology, 2*(2), 143–181. doi:10.1007/s11292-006-9001-1

Gonnerman, J. (2014, October 6). Before the law. *The New Yorker.* Retrieved from www.newyorker.com/magazine/2014/10/06/before-the-law

Gonnerman, J. (2015, June 7). Kalief Browder, 1993–2015. *The New Yorker.* Retrieved from www.newyorker.com/news/news-desk/kalief-browder-1993-2015

Gonzalez v. Comm'r of Correction, 68 A.3d 624 (Conn.), *cert. denied*, 571 U.S. 1045 (2013).

Gottfredson, M. R., Britt, C. L., & Goldkamp, J. S. (1990). *Evaluation of Arizona pretrial services drug testing programs: Final report.* Washington, DC: US Department of Justice, National Institute of Justice.

Gottfredson, M. R., & Gottfredson, D. M. (1988). *Decision-making in criminal justice: Toward the rational exercise of discretion.* New York, NY: Plenum.

Gottfredson, S.D., & Moriarty, L.J. (2006), Statistical risk assessment: Old problems and new applications. *Crime and Delinquency*, 52(1), 178–200. doi:10.1177/0011128705281748

Gouldin, L.P. (2016). Disentangling flight risk from dangerousness. *Brigham Young University Law Review*, 2016, 837–898.

Gouldin, L.P. (2018). Defining flight risk. *University of Chicago Law Review*, 85, 677–742.

Grann, M., Belfrage, H., & Tengström, A. (2000). Actuarial assessment of risk for violence: Predictive validity of the VRAG and the historical part of the HCR-20. *Criminal Justice and Behavior*, 27(1), 97–114. doi:10.1177/0093854800 027001006

Grann, M., Långström, N., Tengström, A., & Kullgren, G. (1999). Psychopathy (PCL-R) predicts violent recidivism among criminal offenders with personality disorders in Sweden. *Law and Human Behavior*, 23(2), 205–217. doi:10.1023/A:1022372902241

Griffin v. Illinois, 351 U.S. 12 (1956).

Griffiths, C.C. (2014). The Prisoners' Counsel Act of 1836: Doctrine, advocacy, and the criminal trial. *Law, Crime, and History*, 2014(2), 28–47.

Grommon, E., Rydberg, J., & Carter, J.G. (2017). Does GPS supervision of intimate partner violence defendants reduce pretrial misconduct? Evidence from a quasi-experimental study. *Journal of Experimental Criminology*, 13(4), 483–504. doi:10.1007/s11292-017-9304-4

Grove, W.M., Zald, D.H., Lebow, B.S., Snitz, B.E., & Nelson, C. (2000). Clinical versus mechanical prediction: A meta-analysis. *Psychological Assessment*, 12(1), 19–30. doi:10.1037/1040-3590.12.1.19

Gupta, A., Hansman, C., & Frenchman, E. (2016). The heavy costs of high bail: Evidence from judge randomization. *Journal of Legal Studies*, 45(2), 471–505. doi:10.1086/688907

Guthrie, C., Rachlinski, J.J., & Wistrich, A.J. (2001). Inside the judicial mind. *Cornell Law Review*, 86, 777–830.

Guy, L.S., Edens, J.F., Anthony, C., & Douglas, K.S. (2005). Does psychopathy predict institutional misconduct among adults? A meta-analytic investigation. *Journal of Consulting and Clinical Psychology*, 73(6), 1056–1064. doi:10.1037/ 0022-006X.73.6.1056

Haapanen, R.A. (1990). *Selective incapacitation and the serious offender: A longitudinal study of criminal career patterns*. New York, NY: Springer.

Hahn, J.W. (2015). *An experiment in bail reform: Examining the impact of the Brooklyn supervised release program*. New York, NY: Center for Court Innovation.

Retrieved from www.courtinnovation.org/sites/default/files/documents/BK%20SRP_Research%20Report_FINAL.pdf

Hamilton v. Alabama, 368 U.S. 52 (1961).

Hamilton, M. (2015). Risk-needs assessment: Constitutional and ethical challenges. *American Criminal Law Review, 52*, 231–291.

Hannah-Moffat, K. (2013). Actuarial sentencing: An "unsettled" proposition. *Justice Quarterly, 30*(2), 270–296. doi:10.1080/07418825.2012.682603

Hanson, L. (2012, August 13). Hey, defendants: Wardrobe can be a factor in verdict. *The Virginian-Pilot*. Retrieved from https://pilotonline.com/news/local/crime/article_cce8832c-e861-5941-bcd7-fad3bedf2191.html

Hanson, R.K., & Morton-Bourgon, K.E. (2005). The characteristics of persistent sexual offenders: A meta-analysis of recidivism studies. *Journal of Consulting and Clinical Psychology, 73*(6), 1154–1163. doi:10.1037/0022-006X.73.6.1154

Hanson, R.K., & Morton-Bourgon, K.E. (2009). The accuracy of recidivism risk assessments for sexual offenders: A meta-analysis of 118 prediction studies. *Psychological Assessment, 21*(1), 1–21. doi:10.1037/a0014421

Hanson, R.K., & Thornton, D. (2000). Improving risk assessments for sex offenders: A comparison of three actuarial scales. *Law & Human Behavior, 24*(1), 119–136. doi:10.1023/A:1005482921333

Harcourt, B.E. (2007). *Against prediction: Profiling, policing, and punishing in an actuarial age*. Chicago, IL: University of Chicago Press.

Harcourt, B.E. (2008). A reader's companion to "against prediction": A reply to Ariela Gross, Yoram Margalioth, and Yoav Sapir on economic modeling, selective incapacitation, governmentality, and race. *Law and Social Inquiry, 33*(1), 265–283. doi:10.1111/j.1747-4469.2008.00102.x

Harcourt, B.E. (2015). Risk as a proxy for race: The dangers of risk assessment. *Federal Sentencing Reporter, 27*(4), 237–243. doi:10.1525/fsr.2015.27.4.237

Hare, R.D. (1998). The Hare PCL-R: Some issues concerning its use and misuse. *Legal and Criminological Psychology, 3*, 99–119. doi:10.1111/j.2044-8333.1998.tb00353.x

Hare, R.D. (2003). *The Hare Psychopathy Checklist–Revised (PCL-R): Second edition, technical manual*. Toronto, ON: Multi-Health Systems.

Hare, R.D., Clark, D., Grann, M., & Thornton, D. (2000). Psychopathy and the predictive validity of the PCL-R: An international perspective. *Behavioral Sciences and the Law, 8*(5), 623–645. doi:10.1002/1099-0798(200010)18:5{{lt}}623::AID-BSL409{{gt}}3.0.CO;2-W

Harlow, C.W. (2003). *Education and correctional populations*. Washington DC: US Department of Justice, Bureau of Justice Statistics: Retrieved from www.bjs.gov/content/pub/pdf/ecp.pdf

Harmon, R.A. (2016). Why arrest? *Michigan Law Review, 115*, 307–364.

Harris, G. T., Rice, M.E., & Quinsey, V.L. (1993). Violent recidivism of mentally disordered offenders: The development of a statistical prediction instrument. *Criminal Justice and Behavior, 20*(4), 315–335. doi:10.1177/009385489 3020004001

Hashimoto, E.J. (2014). An originalist argument for a Sixth Amendment right to competent counsel. *Iowa Law Review, 99*, 1999–2013.

Heaton, P.S., Mayson, S., & Stevenson, M. (2017). The downstream consequences of misdemeanor detention. *Stanford Law Review, 69*, 711–794.

Hegreness, M.J. (2013). America's fundamental and vanishing right to bail. *Arizona Law Review, 55*(4), 909–996.

Heilbrun, K. (2009). *Evaluation for risk of violence in adults.* New York, NY: Oxford University Press.

Hemphill, J.F., & Hare, R.D. (2004). Some misconceptions about the Hare PCL-R and risk assessment. *Criminal Justice and Behavior, 31*(2), 203–243. doi:10.1177/0093854803261326

Henrichson, C., & Rinaldi, J. (2014). *Cost-benefit analysis and justice policy toolkit.* New York, NY: Vera Institute of Justice. Retrieved from www.vera.org /publications/cost-benefit-analysis-and-justice-policy-toolkit

Herian, M.N., & Bornstein, B.H. (2010, September). Reducing failure to appear in Nebraska: A field study. *Nebraska Lawyer*, 11–14.

Herman, L., & Thompson, C.A. (1979). *Scott v. Illinois* and the right to counsel: A decision in search of a doctrine? *American Criminal Law Review, 17*, 71–117.

Hess, J., & Turner, S. (2017) Accuracy of risk assessment in corrections population management: what's the value added? In F. Taxman (Ed.), *Handbook on risk and need assessment: Theory and practice* (pp. 93–113). New York, NY: Routledge.

Heyerly, M. (2013). *Pretrial reform in Kentucky.* Frankfort, KY: Pretrial Services, Administrative Office of the Courts, Kentucky Court of Justice. Retrieved from www.pretrial.org/download/infostop/Pretrial%20Reform%20in%20 Kentucky%20Implementation%20Guide%202013.pdf

Hirschel. J.D., & Dean, C.W. (1995). The relative cost effectiveness of citation and arrest. *Journal of Criminal Justice, 23*(1), 1–12. doi:10.1016/0047-2352(94) 00041-7

Hoffman, P.B. (1983). Screening for risk: A revised salient factor score (SFS 81). *Journal of Criminal Justice, 11*(6), 539–547. doi:10.1016/0047-2352(83)90006-5

Hoffman, P.B. (1994). Twenty years of operational use of a risk prediction instrument: The United States Parole Commission's Salient Factor Score. *Journal of Criminal Justice, 22*(6), 477–494. doi:10.1016/0047-2352(94)90090-6

Hoffman, P.B., & Beck, J.L. (1974). Parole decision-making: A salient factor score. *Journal of Criminal Justice, 2*(3), 195–206. doi:10.1016/0047-2352(74)90031-2

Hoffman, P.B., & Beck, J.L. (1976). Salient factor score validation: A 1972 release cohort. *Journal of Criminal Justice, 4*(1), 69–76. doi:10.1016/0047-2352(76)90041-6

Hoffman, P.B., & Beck, J.L. (1980). Revalidating the salient factor score: A research note. *Journal of Criminal Justice, 8*(3), 185–188. doi:10.1016/0047-2352(80)90025-2

Holmes-Didwania, S. (2018). *The immediate consequences of pretrial detention: Evidence from federal criminal cases* [Working paper]. Retrieved from: https://papers.ssrn.com/sol3/papers.cfm?abstract_id=2809818

Holt, J.C., Garnett, G., & Hudson, J. (2015). *Magna carta* (3rd ed.). Cambridge, UK: Cambridge University Press.

Holtfreter, K., & Cupp, R. (2007). Gender and risk assessment the empirical status of the LSI-R for women. *Journal of Contemporary Criminal Justice, 23*(4), 363–382. doi:10.1177/1043986207309436

Horney, J. (1980). Citation arrest: Extending the reach of the criminal justice system? *Criminology, 17*(4), 419–434. doi:10.1111/j.1745-9125.1980.tb01306.x

Howe, S.W. (2015). The implications of incorporating the Eighth Amendment prohibition on excessive bail. *Hofstra Law Review, 43*, 1039–1085.

Hudson v. Parker, 156 U.S. 277 (1895).

Hughes, J.M., & Henkel, K.S. (2015). The federal probation and pretrial services system since 1975: An era of growth and change. *Federal Probation, 79*(3), 48–54. (Original work published 1997)

Human Rights Watch. (2017). *Not in it for justice: How California's pretrial detention and bail system unfairly punishes poor people.* Retrieved from www.hrw.org/sites/default/files/report_pdf/usbail0417_web_0.pdf

Human Rights Watch. (2018, August 24). *Human Rights Watch urges Governor Brown of California to veto Senate Bill 10, The California Bail Reform Act: The new SB 10 is simply not bail reform.* Retrieved from www.hrw.org/news/2018/08/24/human-rights-watch-urges-governor-brown-california-veto-senate-bill-10-california

Hunt v. Roth, 648 F.2d 1148 (8th Cir. 1981), *vacated as moot sub nom, Murphy v. Hunt,* 455 U.S. 478 (1982).

Huq, A.Z. (2019). Racial equity in algorithmic criminal justice. *Duke Law Journal, 68*, 1043–1134.

Hurrell-Harring v. State, 930 N.E.2d 217 (N.Y. 2010).

*In re* Humphrey, 228 Cal. Rptr. 513 (Cal. Ct. App.), *review granted, sua sponte,* 417 P.3d 769 (Cal. 2018).

Institute for Research on Poverty. (2016). *Who is poor?* Retrieved from www.irp .wisc.edu/faqs/faq3.htm

International Association of Chiefs of Police (IACP). (2016). *Citation in lieu of arrest: Examining law enforcement's use of citation across the United States.* Alexandria, VA: Author. Retrieved from www.theiacp.org/Portals/0/documents /pdfs/IACP%20Citation%20Final%20Report%202016.pdf

Irwin, J. (1985). *The jail: Managing the underclass in American society.* Berkeley, CA: University of California Press.

Jacobs, J. B. (2015). *The eternal criminal record.* Cambridge, MA: Harvard University Press.

Jacobson, L. (2018, October 9). Are U.S., Philippines the only two countries with money bail? *PolitiFact.* Retrieved from www.politifact.com/california /statements/2018/oct/09/gavin-newsom/are-us-philippines-only-two-count ries-money-bail/

Jarecki, A. (Producer & Director), Blum, J. (Producer), & Smerling, M. (Producer). (2015). *The jinx: The life and deaths of Robert Durst* [Television series]. Santa Monica, CA: HBO Documentary Films.

Jeffrey, C. Ray. (1957). The development of crime in early English society. *Journal of Criminal Law, Criminology, and Police Science, 47*(6), 647–666. doi:10.2307/1140057

Johnson, J. L., & Baber, L. M. (2015). State of the system: Federal probation and pretrial services. *Federal Probation, 79*(2), 34–40.

Johnson, L. D. (2015). The politics of the bail system: What's the price for freedom? *Scholar, 17,* 171–217.

Johnson v. Zerbst, 304 U.S. 458 (1938).

Johnston, J. E. (2003). *The complete idiot's guide to psychology* (2nd ed.). New York, NY: Alpha Books/Penguin.

Jonakait, R. N. (1995). The origins of the confrontation clause: An alternative history. *Rutgers Law Journal, 27,* 77–168.

Jones v. City of Clanton, 2015 WL 5387219 (M.D. Ala. 2015).

Kalhous, C., & Meringolo, J. (2012). Bail pending trial: Changing interpretations of the Bail Reform Act and the importance of bail from defense attorneys' perspectives. *Pace Law Review, 32*(3), 800–855.

Kalmthout M. M., Knapen C., & Morgenstern, C. (Eds.). (2009). *Pretrial detention in the European Union.* Oisterwijk, Netherlands: Wolf Legal Publishers.

Kane, D., & Raynor, D. (2017, August 15). 51 NC jail inmates have died in past five years after poor supervision from jailors. *News & Observer.* Retrieved from www.newsobserver.com/news/local/crime/article164829912.html

Kapsch, S., & Sweeny, L. (1990). *Multnomah County DMDA Project: Evaluation final report.* Washington, DC: US Department of Justice, Bureau of Justice Assistance.

Karnow, C.E.A. (2008). Setting bail for public safety. *Berkeley Journal of Criminal Law 16,* 1–30.

Kastenmeier, R.W. (1984). *Bail Reform Act of 1984* (H.R. Rep. No. 98–1121). Washington, DC: Government Printing Office.

Katz, C.M., & Spohn, C.C. (1995). The effect of race and gender on bail outcomes: A test of an interactive model. *American Journal of Criminal Justice, 19*(2), 161–184. doi:10.1007/BF02885913

Katz, L.R. (2013). "Lonesome road": Driving without the Fourth Amendment. *Seattle University Law Review, 36,* 1413–1471.

Keith, C.P. (1917). *Chronicles of Pennsylvania, 1688–1748* (Vol. 2). Philadelphia, PA: Patterson & White.

Kellough, G., & Wortley, S. (2002). Remand for plea: Bail decisions and plea bargaining as commensurate decisions. *British Journal of Criminology, 42*(1), 186–210. doi:10.1093/bjc/42.1.186

Kemshall, H. (1996). A *review of research on the assessment and management of risk and dangerousness: Implications for policy and practice in the probation service.* Birmingham, UK: Home Office Research and Statistics Directorate.

Kennedy, S., House, L., & Williams, M. (2013). Using research to improve pretrial justice and public safety: Results from PSA's risk assessment validation project. *Federal Probation, 77*(1), 28–32.

King, J.D. (2013). Beyond "life and liberty": The evolving right to counsel. *Harvard Civil Rights-Civil Liberties Law Review, 48,* 1–49.

Kirby v. Illinois, 406 U.S. 682 (1972).

Klein, D.J. (1997). The pretrial detention "crisis": The causes and the cure. *Washington University Journal of Urban & Contemporary Law, 52,* 281–306.

Kleinberg, J., Lakkaraju, H., Leskovec, J., Ludwig, J., & Mullainathan, S. (2018). Human decisions and machine predictions. *The Quarterly Journal of Economics, 133*(1), 237–293. doi:10.1093/qje/qjx032

Kleppinger, B. (2018, November 20). How reducing cash bail for the poor can help solve the rural jail crisis. *The Crime Report.* Retrieved from https://thecrimereport.org/2018/11/20/reducing-cash-bail-for-the-poor-first-step-in-solving-the-rural-justice-crisis/

Klockars, C.B., Ivkovich, S.K., Harver, W.E., & Haberfeld, M.R. (2000). *The measurement of police integrity.* Washington, DC: US Department of Justice, National Institute of Justice. Retrieved from www.ncjrs.gov/pdffiles1/nij/181465.pdf

Knowles v. Iowa, 525 U.S. 113 (1998).

Kochel, T. R., Wilson, D. B., & Mastrofski, S. D. (2011). Effect of suspect race on officers' arrest decisions. *Criminology*, *49*(2), 473–512. doi:10.1111/j.1745-9125. 2011.00230.x

Kovaleski, S. F. (2017, September 22). Alabama man who waited 10 years for trial is found guilty. *New York Post*. Retrieved from https://nypost.com/2015/09/10 /inmate-takes-plea-deal-after-nearly-7-years-in-rikers-without-trial/

Kubiak, S. P., Kim, W. J., Bybee, D., & Eshelman, L. (2014). Assessing the validity of the Self-Appraisal Questionnaire in differentiating high-risk and violent female offenders. *Prison Journal*, *94*(3), 305–327. doi:10.1177/0032885514537597

Kubrin, C., Squires, G., & Stewart, E. (2007). Neighborhoods, race, and recidivism: The community-re-offending nexus and its implications for African Americans. *Race Relations Abstracts*, *32*(1), 7–37. doi:10.1177/0307920107073250

Lafler v. Cooper, 566 U.S. 156 (2012).

Laisne, M., Wool, J., & Henrichson, C. (2017). *Past due: Examining the costs and consequences of charging for justice in New Orleans.* New York, NY, Vera Institute of Justice. Retrieved from www.vera.org/publications/past-due-costs -consequences-charging-for-justice-new-orleans

Langbein, J. (2003). *The origins of adversarial criminal trial.* Oxford, UK: Oxford University Press.

Lansing, S. (2012). *New York State COMPAS-probation risk and need assessment study: Examining the recidivism scale's effectiveness and predictive accuracy.* Albany, NY: Division of Criminal Justice Services, Office of Justice Research and Performance. Retrieved from www.criminaljustice.ny.gov/crimnet/ojsa/opca /compas_probation_report_2012.pdf

Larson, J., Mattu, S., Kirchner, L., & Angwin, J. (2016, May 23). *How we analyzed the COMPAS recidivism algorithm.* Retrieved from www.propublica.org/arti cle/how-we-analyzed-the-compas-recidivism-algorithm

Latessa, E. J., Lemke, R., Makarios, M., Smith, P., & Lowenkamp, C. T. (2010). Creation and validation of the Ohio Risk Assessment System (ORAS). *Federal Probation*, *74*(1), 16–22.

Latessa, E. J., Smith, P., Lemke, R., Makarios, M., & Lowenkamp, C. T. (2009). *Creation and validation of the Ohio Risk Assessment System: Final report.* Cincinnati, OH: University of Cincinnati, Center for Criminal Justice Research. Retrieved from www.pretrial.org/download/risk-assessment/Ohio%20 Pretrial%20Risk%20Assessment%202009.pdf

Leistico, A. R., Salekin, R. T., DeCoster, J., & Rogers, R. (2008). A large-scale meta-analysis relating the Hare measures of psychopathy to antisocial conduct. *Law and Human Behavior*, *32*(1), 28–45. doi:10.1007/s10979-007-9096-6

Lemke, A.J. (2009). *Evaluation of the pretrial release pilot program in the Mesa municipal court.* Mesa, AZ: Institute for Court Management Court Executive Development Program. Retrieved from www.ncsc.org/~/media/Files /PDF/Education%20and%20Careers/CEDP%20Papers/2009/Lemke_Eval PretrialReleaseProg.ashx

Leone, M.C. (2002). Net widening. In D. Levinson (Ed.)., *Encyclopedia of crime and punishment* (pp. 1087–1088). Thousand Oaks, CA: Sage. doi:10.4135/97814 12950664.n286

LJAF (The Laura and John Arnold Foundation). (2016a). *Public Safety Assessment: Risk factors and formula.* Retrieved from www.arnoldfoundation.org/wp -content/uploads/PSA-Risk-Factors-and-Formula.pdf

LJAF (The Laura and John Arnold Foundation). (2016b, August 10). N*ew data from Ohio validates PSA impact* [Web log post]. Retrieved from www.arnold foundation.org/new-data-ohio-validates-psa-impact/

Locke, J.W., Penn, R., Rock, J., Bunten, E., & Hare, G. (1970). *Compilation and use of criminal court data in relation to pre-trial release of defendants: Pilot study 1.* Washington, DC: National Bureau of Standards. Retrieved from https:// nvlpubs.nist.gov/nistpubs/Legacy/TN/nbstechnicalnote535.pdf

Logan, W.A. (2002). Street legal: The court affords police constitutional carte blanche. *Indiana Law Journal, 77,* 419–467.

Lowenkamp, C.T., Lemke, R., & Latessa, E.J. (2008). The development and validation of a pretrial screening tool. *Federal Probation, 72*(3), 2–9.

Lowenkamp, C.T., Lovins, B., & Latessa, E.J. (2009). Validating the Level of Service Inventory-Revised and the Level of Service Inventory: Screening version with a sample of probationers. *The Prison Journal, 89*(2), 192–204. doi:10.1177/0032885509334755

Lowenkamp, C.T., VanNostrand, M., & Holsinger, A. (2013). *Investigating the impact of pretrial detention on sentencing outcomes.* Houston, TX: Laura and John Arnold Foundation. Retrieved from www.arnoldfoundation.org/wp-con tent/uploads/2014/02/LJAF_Report_state-sentencing_FNL.pdf

Lowenkamp, C.T., & Whetzel, J. (2009). Federal pretrial risk assessment. *Federal Probation, 76*(2), 33–36.

Loza, W., Neo, L.H., Shahinfar, A., & Loza-Fanous, A. (2005). Cross-validation of the Self-Appraisal Questionnaire: A tool for assessing violent and non-violent recidivism with female offenders. *International Journal of Offender Therapy and Comparative Criminology, 49*(5), 547–560. doi:10.1177/0306624X04 273433

Macartney, S., Bishaw, A., & Fontenot, K. (2013). *Poverty rates for selected detailed race and Hispanic groups by state and place: 2007–2011.* (American Community

Survey Briefs No. 11-17). Washington, DC: US Department of Commerce, Economics and Statistics Administration, U.S. Census Bureau. Retrieved from www.census.gov/prod/2013pubs/acsbr11-17.pdf

Macpherson, G.J. (1997). Psychology and risk assessment. *British Journal of Clinical Psychology, 36*(4), 643–645. doi:10.1111/j.2044-8260.1997.tb01272.x

Mahoney, B., Beaudin, B.D., Carver, J.A., III, Ryan, D.B., & Hoffman, R.B. (2001). *Pretrial service programs: Responsibilities and potential* (NJC 181939). Washington, DC: US Department of Justice, National Institute of Justice. Retrieved from www.ncjrs.gov/pdffiles1/nij/181939.pdf

Main, F. (2016, July 3). Cook county judges not following bail recommendations: Study. *Chicago Sun Times.* Retrieved from https://chicago.suntimes.com/news/cook-county-judges-notfollowing-bail-recommendations-study-find/

Malterer, M.B., Lilienfeld, S.O., Neumann, C.S., & Newman, J.P. (2010). Concurrent validity of the psychopathic personality inventory with offender and community samples. *Assessment, 17*(1), 3–15. doi:10.1177/1073191109349743

Mamalian, C.A. (2011, March). *State of the science of pretrial risk assessment.* Washington, DC: US Department of Justice, Bureau of Justice Assistance. Retrieved fromwww.bja.gov/publications/pji_pretrialriskassessment.pdf

Marceau, J.F. (2012). Embracing a new era of ineffective assistance of counsel. *University of Pennsylvania Journal of Constitutional Law, 14*, 1161–1217.

Marceau, J.F., & Rudolf, N. (2012). The Colorado counsel conundrum: Plea bargaining, misdemeanors, and the right to counsel. *Denver University Law Review, 89*, 327–367.

Maruna, S., Dabney, D., & Topali, V. (2012). Putting a price on prisoner release: The history of bail and a possible future of parole. *Punishment & Society, 14*(3), 315–337. doi:10.1177/1462474512442311

Maryland Office of the Public Defender, Gupta, A., Swanson, D., & Frenchman, E. (2016). *The high cost of bail: How Maryland's reliance on money bail jails the poor and costs the community millions.* Retrieved from www.opd.state.md.us/Portals/0/Downloads/High%20Cost%20of%20Bail.pdf

Massachusetts Bail Fund. (n.d.). *About the Massachusetts Bail Fund.* Retrieved from www.massbailfund.org/about.html

Massiah v. United States, 377 U.S. 201 (1964).

Maxfield, M.G., & Baumer, T.L. (1991). *Final report: Evaluation of pretrial home detention with electronic monitoring.* Bloomington, IN: Indiana University, School of Public and Environmental Affairs.

May, D.C., Applegate, B.K., Ruddell, R., & Wood, P.B. (2014). Going to jail sucks (and it really doesn't matter who you ask). *American Journal of Criminal Justice, 39*(2), 250–266. doi:10.1007/s12103-013-9215-5

Mays, J.C. (2018, November 20). 105 New York City inmates freed in bail reform experiment. *The New York Times*. Retrieved from www.nytimes.com /2018/11/20/nyregion/bail-reform-rikers-rfk-nyc.html

Mays, M. (2014). *Presumption of guilt: The global overuse of pretrial detention*. New York, NY: The Open Society.

Mayson, S.G. (2018). Dangerous defendants. *Yale Law Journal, 127*(3), 490–568.

Mayson, S.G. (In press). " Bias in, bias out. *Yale Law Journal, 128*. Retrieved from https://ssrn.com/abstract=3257004

McDonald v. City of Chicago, Ill., 561 U.S. 742 (2010).

McKehnie, W.S. (1917). The Magna Carta. In H.E. Malden (Ed.), *Magna Carta commemorative essays* (pp. 1–25). London, UK: Royal Historical Society. Retrieved from http://oll.libertyfund.org/titles/339

McKenzie, W., Stemen, D., Coursen, D., & Farid, E. (2009). *Prosecution and racial justice: Using data to advance fairness in criminal prosecution*. New York, NY: Vera Institute of Justice. Retrieved from https://storage.googleapis .com/vera-web-assets/downloads/Publications/prosecution-and-racial-jus tice-using-data-to-advance-fairness-in-criminal-prosecution/legacy_down loads/Using-data-to-advance-fairness-in-criminal-prosecution.pdf

McMahon, M. (1990). Net-widening. *British Journal of Criminology, 30*(2), 121–149. doi:10.1093/oxfordjournals.bjc.a047986

Medwed, D.S. (2010). Emotionally charged: The prosecutorial charging decision and the innocence revolution. *Cardozo Law Review, 31*, 2187–2213.

Meechaicum v. Fountain, 696 F.2d 790 (10th Cir. 1983).

Mellon, L.R., Jacoby, J.E., & Brewer, M.A. (1981). The prosecutor constrained by his environment: A new look at discretionary justice in the United States. *Journal of Criminal Law and Criminology, 72*(1), 52–81. doi:10.2307/1142905

Mempa v. Rhay, 389 U.S. 128 (1967).

Menefee, M.R. (2018). The role of bail and pretrial detention in the reproduction of racial inequalities. *Sociology Compass, 12*(5), e12576. doi:10.1111/soc4.12576

Milgram, A., Holsinger, A., M., VanNostrand, M., & Alsdorf, M.W. (2015). Pretrial risk assessment: Improving public safety and fairness in pretrial decision making. *Federal Sentencing Reporter, 27*(4), 216–221. doi:10.1525/ fsr.2015.27.4.216

Miller, J., & Maloney, C. (2013). Practitioner compliance with risk/needs assessment tools: A theoretical and empirical assessment. *Criminal Justice and Behavior, 40*(7), 716–736. doi:10.1177/0093854812468883

Miller, M.L., & Wright, R.F. (2008). The black box. *Iowa Law Review, 94*, 125–196.

Miller, W. L. (1969). The Bail Reform Act of 1966: The need for reform in 1969. *Catholic University Law Review, 19,* 24–49.

Millon, T., & Davis, R. D. (1998). Ten subtypes of psychopathy. In T. Millon, E. Simonsen, M. Birket-Smith, & R. D. Davis (Eds.), *Psychopathy: Antisocial, criminal, and violent behavior* (pp. 161–170). New York, NY: The Guilford Press.

Mills, J. F., Kroner, D. G., & Hemmati, T. (2007). The validity of violence risk estimates: An issue in item performance. *Psychology Services, 4*(1), 1–12. doi:10.1037/1541-1559.4.1.1

Milsom, S. F. C. (1976). *The legal framework of English feudalism.* Cambridge, UK: Cambridge University Press.

Minton, T. D., & Zeng, Z. (2015). *Jail inmates at midyear—2014.* Washington, DC: US Department of Justice, Bureau of Justice Statistics. Retrieved from www.bjs.gov/content/pub/pdf/jim14.pdf

Mischel, W. (1968). *Personality and assessment.* Hoboken, NJ: John Wiley & Sons Inc.

Missouri v. Frye, 566 U.S. 134 (2012).

Mitchell, O., Caudy, M. S., & MacKenzie, D. L. (2013). A reanalysis of the self-appraisal questionnaire: psychometric properties and predictive validity. *International Journal of Offender Therapy and Comparative Criminology, 57*(4), 445–459. doi:10.1177/0306624X12436504

Monaghan, G., & Bewley-Taylor, D. (2013). *Practical implications of policing alternatives to arrest and prosecution for minor cannabis offences.* London, UK: International Drug Policy Consortium. Retrieved from http://fileserver.idpc .net/library/MDLE-report-4_Practical-implications-of-policing-alternati ves-to-arrest.pdf

Monahan, J. (1981). *The clinical prediction of violent behavior.* Washington, DC: National Institute of Mental Health/Government Printing House.

Monahan, J., & Steadman, H. J. (Eds.). (1994). *Violence and mental disorder: Developments in risk assessment.* Chicago, IL: University of Chicago Press.

Monahan, J., Steadman, H. J., Silver, E., Appelbaum, P. S., Robbins, P. C., Mulvey, E. P., Roth, L. H., Grisso, T., & Banks, S. (2001). *Rethinking risk assessment: The MacArthur study of mental disorder and violence.* New York, NY: Oxford University Press.

Mumola, C. J. (2005). *Suicide and homicide in state prisons and local jails.* Washington, DC: US Department of Justice, Bureau of Justice Statistics. Retrieved from www.bjs.gov/content/pub/pdf/shsplj.pdf

Myers, N. M. (2017). Eroding the presumption of innocence: Pre-trial detention and the use of conditional release on bail. *British Journal of Criminology, 57*(3), 664–683. doi:10.1093/bjc/azw002

Nadel, M.R., Pesta, G., Blomberg, T., Bales, W.D., & Greenwald, M. (2018). Civil citation: Diversion or net widening? *Journal of Research in Crime and Delinquency, 55*(2), 278–315. doi:10.1177/0022427817751571

Nafekh, M., & Motiuk, L.L. (2002). *The statistical information on recidivism– revised 1 (SIR-R1) scale: A psychometric examination.* Correctional Service of Canada, Research Branch. Retrieved from www.csc-scc.gc.ca/research/092 /r126_e.pdf

Nagel, I. (1983). The legal/extra-legal controversy: Judicial decisions in pre-trial release. *Law & Society Review 17*(3), 481–515. doi:10.2307/3053590

National Association of Criminal Defense Lawyers. (2012). *Policy on pretrial release and limited use of financial bond.* Retrieved from www.pretrial .org/download/policy-statements/NACDL%20Pretrial%20Resolution%20 (7-2012).pdf

National Association of Pretrial Services Agencies. (2004). *National Association of Pretrial Service Agencies: Standards on pretrial release* (3rd ed.). Washington, DC: Author.

National Bail Out. (n.d.). *Black mamas bail out.* Retrieved from https://nomore moneybail.org/

National Conference of State Legislatures. (2013a). *Pretrial release eligibility.* Retrieved from www.ncsl.org/research/civil-and-criminal-justice/pretrial -release-eligibility.aspx

National Conference of State Legislatures. (2013b). *Bail bond agent licensure.* Retrieved from www.ncsl.org/research/civil-and-criminal-justice/bail-bond -agent-licensure.aspx

National Conference of State Legislatures. (2016a). *Pretrial release conditions.* Retrieved from www.ncsl.org/research/civil-and-criminal-justice/pretrial -release-conditions.aspx

National Conference of State Legislatures. (2016b). *Pretrial right to counsel.* Retrieved from /www.ncsl.org/research/civil-and-criminal-justice/pretrial -right-to-counsel.aspx

National Conference of State Legislatures. (2017, October 23). *Citation in lieu of arrest.* Retrieved from www.ncsl.org/research/civil-and-criminal-justice /citation-in-lieu-of-arrest.aspx

National Conference of State Legislatures. (2018, June 28). *Pretrial release viola-tions and bail forfeiture.* Retrieved from www.ncsl.org/research/civil-and -criminal-justice/bail-forfeiture-procedures.aspx

National Council on Crime and Delinquency. (2010). *CAIS Correctional Assess-ment and Intervention System: System manual.* Madison, WI: Author.

National Institute of Corrections. (2011). *Measuring what matters: Outcome and performance measures for the pretrial services field.* Washington, DC: US Department of Justice, The National Institute of Corrections Pretrial Executives Network. Retrieved from www.pretrial.org/download/performance-meas ures/Measuring%20What%20Matters.pdf

Neal, M. (2012). *Bail fail: Why the U.S. should end the practice of using money for bail.* Washington, DC: Justice Policy Institute. Retrieved from www.justicepol icy.org/uploads/justicepolicy/documents/bailfail.pdf

Neller, D.J., & Frederick, R.I. (2013). Classification accuracy of actuarial risk assessment instruments. *Behavioral Sciences & the Law, 31*(1), 141–153. doi:10. 1002/bsl.2047

Nellis, A. (2016). *The color of justice: Racial and ethnic disparity in state prisons.* Washington, DC: The Sentencing Project. Retrieved from www.sentenc ingproject.org/wp-content/uploads/2016/06/The-Color-of-Justice-Racial -and-Ethnic-Disparity-in-State-Prisons.pdf

Nellis, M. (1991). Electronic tagging: Grounds for resistance? In J.R. Lilly & J. Himan (Eds.), *The electronic monitoring of offenders: Symposium papers* (2nd series). Leicester, UK: Leicester Polytechnic.

Neubauer, D.W., & Fradella, H.F. (2019). *America's courts and the criminal justice system* (13th ed.). Boston, MA: Cengage.

Nikambule, S. (2018, April 25). Man locked 9 years in jail without trial. *Swazi Observer.* Retrieved from www.pressreader.com/swaziland/swazi-observer /20180425/281479277021236

Northpointe Institute for Public Management. (2012). *Practitioner's guide to COMPAS.* Traverse City, MI: Author. Retrieved from www.northpointeinc .com/files/technical_documents/FieldGuide2_081412.pdf

Nuffield, J. (1989). The "SIR Scale": Some reflections on its applications. *Forum on Corrections Research, 1,* 19–22.

ODonnell v. Harris County, Texas, 251 F. Supp. 3d 1052 (S.D. Tex. 2017), *aff'd in part, rev'd in part,* ODonnell v. Harris County, Texas, 882 F. 3d 528 (5th Cir. 2018).

Ofer, U. (2017). *We can't end mass incarceration without ending money bail* [Web log post]. Retrieved from www.aclu.org/blog/smart-justice/we-cant-end-mass -incarceration-without-ending-money-bail

Office of Probation and Pretrial Services. (2003, January). Pretrial services officers. *Court & Community.* Washington, DC: Administrative Office of the U.S. Courts. Retrieved from https://permanent.access.gpo.gov/lps40966 /2003-pretrial.pdf

Oleson, J.C., Lowenkamp, C.T., Wooldredge, J., VanNostrand, M., & Cadigan, T.P. (2017). The sentencing consequences of federal pretrial supervision. *Crime & Delinquency, 63*(3), 313–333. doi:10.1177/0011128714551406

Oleson, J.C., VanBenschoten, S.W., Robinson, C.R., & Lowenkamp, C.T. (2011). Training to see risk: Measuring the accuracy of clinical and actuarial risk assessments among federal probation officers. *Federal Probation, 75*(2), 52–56.

Oleson, J.C., VanNostrand, M., Lowenkamp, C.T., & Cadigan, T.P., (2014). Federal detention choices and federal sentencing. *Federal Probation, 78*(1), 12–18.

Olusanya, O., & Gau, J.M. (2012). Race, neighborhood context, and risk prediction. *Criminal Justice Studies, 25*(2), 159–175. doi:10.1080/1478601X.2012.699734

Olver, M.E., Stockdale, K.C., & Wormith, J.S. (2009). Risk assessment with young offenders: A meta-analysis of three assessment measures. *Criminal Justice and Behavior, 36*(4), 329–353. doi:10.1177/0093854809331457

Olver, M.E., Stockdale, K.C., & Wormith, J.S. (2014). Thirty years of research on the Level of Service scales: A meta-analytic examination of predictive accuracy and sources of variability. *Psychological Assessment, 26*(1), 156–176. doi:10.1037/a0035080

Olver, M.E., Wong, S.C.P., Nicholaichuk, T., & Gordon, A. (2007). The validity and reliability of the Violence Risk Scale—Sexual Offender Version: Assessing sex offender risk and evaluating therapeutic change. *Psychological Assessment, 19*(3), 318–329. doi:10.1037/1040-3590.19.3.318

Open Society Foundations. (2011). *The socioeconomic impact of pretrial detention.* New York, NY: Author. Retrieved from www.opensocietyfoundations.org /sites/default/files/socioeconomic-impact-pretrial-detention-02012011.pdf

Ostermann, M., & Herrschaft, B.A. (2013). Validating the Level of Service Inventory-Revised: A gendered perspective. *The Prison Journal, 93*(3), 291–312. doi:10.1177/0032885513490278

Ostermann, M., & Salerno, L.M. (2016). The validity of the level of service inventory-revised at the intersection of race and gender. *The Prison Journal, 96*(4), 554–575. doi:10.1177/0032885516650878

Otto, R.K., & Douglas, K.S. (2014). *Handbook of violence risk assessment.* New York, NY: Routledge.

Ottone, S., & Scott-Hayward, C.S. (2018). Pretrial detention and the decision to impose bail in Southern California. *Criminology, Criminal Justice, Law and Society, 19*(2), 24–43.

Padilla v. Kentucky, 559 U.S. 356 (2010).

Page, J. (2017, Spring). Desperation and service in the bail industry. *Contexts.* Retrieved from https://contexts.org/articles/bail/

Page, J., Piehowski, V., & Soss, J. (2019). A debt of care: Commercial bail and the gendered logic of criminal justice predation. *RSF: The Russell Sage Foundation Journal of the Social Sciences, 5*(1), 150–172.

Pasquale, F. (2015). *The black box society: The secret algorithms that control money and information.* Cambridge, MA: Harvard University Press.

Paul, A. M. (1997, November 1). Judging by appearance. *Psychology Today.* Retrieved from www.psychologytoday.com/us/articles/199711/judging-appearance

Pelekai v. White, 861 P.2d 1205 (Haw. 1993).

Pennington, K. (1993). *The prince and the law, 1200–1600: Sovereignty and rights in the western legal tradition.* Oakland, CA: University of California Press.

People *ex rel* Shapiro v. Keeper of City Prisons, 49 N.E.2d 498 (N.Y. 1943).

Pepin, A. W. (2013). *2012–2013 Policy paper: Evidence-based pretrial release.* Williamsburg, VA: National Center for State Courts, Conference of State Court Administrators. Retrieved from www.pretrial.org/download/policy-statements/Evidence%20Based%20Pre-Trial%20Release%20-%20COSCA%202012.pdf

Perbix, M. (2013). *Unintended consequences of cite and release policies.* Sacramento, CA: SEARCH: The National Consortium for Justice Information and Statistics. Retrieved from www.wdmtoolkit.org/~/media/Microsites/Files/Warrants%20and%20Dispositions/Policy/Unintended-Consequences-of-Cite-and-Release-Policies.ashx

Petersdorff, C. (1824). *A practical treatise on the law of bail in civil and criminal proceedings.* London, UK: Joseph Butterworth & Son. Retrieved from https://ia802605.us.archive.org/31/items/apracticaltreatoopetegoog/apracticaltreatoopetegoog.pdf

The Pew Charitable Trusts. (2016). *Alaska's criminal justice reforms.* Washington, DC: Author. Retrieved from www.pewtrusts.org/~/media/assets/2016/12/alaskas_criminal_justice_reforms.pdf

Phillips, M. T. (2012). *A decade of bail research in New York City.* New York, NY: New York City Criminal Justice Agency. Retrieved from www.prisonpolicy.org/scans/DecadeBailResearch12.pdf

Phillips, N. (2013). A case study of the impact of wealth on the criminal justice system in early nineteenth-century England. *Crime, History & Societies, 17*(1), 29–52. doi:10.4000/chs.1409

Pierce, R. (2016, September 26). More corruption in the bail bond industry. *North Carolina Advocate.* Retrieved from http://ncadvocate.net/index.php/2016/09/26/more-corruption-in-the-bail-bond-industry-thanks-wayne-goodwin/

Pilkinton v. Circuit Court, 324 F.2d 45 (8th Cir. 1963).

Pinkerton, J., & Caruba, L. (2015, December 28). Tough bail policies punish the poor and the sick, critics say: 55 died awaiting trial in Harris County jail since 2009. Houston Chronicle. Retrieved from www.houstonchronicle.com/news/houston-texas/houston/article/Tough-bail-policies-punish-the-poor-and-the-sick-6721984.php

Pinto, N. (2012, October 10). Making bail better. The Village Voice. Retrieved from www.villagevoice.com/2012/10/10/making-bail-better/

Pinto, N. (2015, August 13). The bail trap. The New York Times Magazine. Retrieved from www.nytimes.com/2015/08/16/magazine/the-bail-trap.html

Policing and profit. (2015). Harvard Law Review, 128, 1723–1746.

Pollock, F., & Maitland, F. W. (1898). The history of English common law before the time of Edward I. (2nd ed.). Cambridge, UK: Cambridge University Press.

Powell v. Alabama, 287 U.S. 45 (1932).

President's Task Force on 21st Century Policing. (2015). Final report of the President's Task Force on 21st Century Policing. Washington, DC: Office of Community Oriented Policing Services. Retrieved from http://www.theiacp.org/Portals/o/taskforce_finalreport.pdf

Pretrial Detention Reform Workgroup. (2017). Pretrial detention reform: Recommendations to the chief justice. Retrieved from www.courts.ca.gov/documents/PDRReport-20171023.pdf

Pretrial Justice Center for Courts. (n.d.). Pretrial services and supervision. Retrieved from www.ncsc.org/Microsites/PJCC/Home/Topics/Pretrial-Services.aspx

Pretrial Justice Institute. (2009). 2009 survey of pretrial services programs. Washington, DC: Author. Retrieved from www.pretrial.org/download/pji-reports/new-PJI%202009%20Survey%20of%20Pretrial%20Services%20Programs.pdf

Pretrial Justice Institute. (2010). Pretrial justice in America: A survey of county pretrial release policies, practices, and outcomes. Washington, DC: Author. Retrieved from www.pretrial.org/download/research/PJI%20Pretrial%20Justice%20in%20America%20-%20Scan%20of%20Practices%202009.pdf

Pretrial Justice Institute. (2012). Using technology to enhance pretrial services: Current applications and future possibilities. Washington, DC: Author. Retrieved from www.pretrial.org/download/pji-reports/PJI%20USING%20TECHNOLOGY%20TO%20ENHANCE%20PRETRIAL%20SERVICES.pdf

Pretrial Justice Institute. (2015, May). Pretrial risk assessment: Science provides guidance on assessing defendants. Issue Brief. Rockville, MD: Author.

Retrieved from www.pretrial.org/download/advocacy/Issue%20Brief-Pre trial%20Risk%20Assessment%20(May%202015).pdf

Pretrial Justice Institute. (2017). *Pretrial justice: How much does it cost?* Rockville, MD: Author. Retrieved from https://university.pretrial.org/HigherLogic /System/DownloadDocumentFile.ashx?DocumentFileKey=4c666992-0b1b -632a-13cb-b4ddc66fadcd

Pretrial Justice Institute. (2018). *The solution.* Retrieved from https://owl .english.purdue.edu/owl/resource/560/10/

Pretrial Services Agency for the District of Columbia. (n.d.). *Research and data: Performance measures.* Retrieved from www.psa.gov/?q=data/performance _measures

Pretrial Services Resource Center. (1999). *The supervised pretrial release primer.* Washington, DC: American University Criminal Courts Technical Assistance Project. Retrieved from https://jpo.wrlc.org/bitstream/handle/11204/31 47/The%20Supervised%20Release%20Pretrial%20Primer.pdf?sequence=3

Prison Policy Initiative. (2016). *Detaining the poor.* Northampton, MA: Author. Retrieved from www.prisonpolicy.org/reports/DetainingThePoor.pdf

Pryor, D. E., & Smith, W. F. (1982). *Pretrial issues: Significant research findings concerning pretrial release.* Washington, DC: Pretrial Services Resource Center.

Pugh v. Rainwater, 572 F.2d. 1053 (5th Cir. 1978).

Rabuy, B., & Kopf, D. (2016). *Detaining the poor.* Northampton MA: Prison Policy Initiative. Retrieved from www.prisonpolicy.org/reports/Detaining ThePoor.pdf

Raine, A. (1993). *The psychopathology of crime and criminal behaviour as a clinical disorder.* San Diego, CA: Elsevier Science/Academic Press.

Reagan, R. (1982, May 26). Statement on proposed anticrime legislation. Retrieved from www.reagan.utexas.edu/archives/speeches/1982/52682b.htm

Reaves, B. A. (2013). *Felony defendants in large urban counties, 2009—Statistical tables.* Washington, DC: US Department of Justice, Bureau of Justice Statistics. Retrieved from www.bjs.gov/content/pub/pdf/fdluc09.pdf

Reilly, R. J., & Liebelson, D. (2016, December 16). We wanted to find troubled jails, so we counted the bodies. *Huffington Post.* Retrieved from www.huff ingtonpost.com/entry/jail-deaths-statistics_us_58518e13e4b0ee009eb4f1a9

Reitz, K. R. (Ed.). (2017). *American exceptionalism in crime and punishment.* New York, NY: Oxford University Press.

Review of selected 1973 California legislation: Criminal procedure: Adoption of bail schedules. (1974). *Pacific Law Journal, 5,* 334–335.

Reynolds v. United States, 80 S. Ct. 30 (1959).

Rice, M. E., & Harris, G. T. (1997). Cross-validation and extension of the Violence Risk Appraisal Guide for child molesters and rapists. *Law and Human Behavior, 21*(2), 231–241. doi:10.1023/A:1024882430242

Rice, M. E., & Harris, G. T. (2005). Comparing effect sizes in follow-up studies: ROC Area, Cohen's d, and r. *Law and Human Behavior, 29*(5), 615–620. doi:0.1007/s10979-005-6832-7

Richey-Mann, C. (1993) *Unequal justice: A question of color.* Bloomington, IN: Indiana University Press.

Rios, V. M. (2011). *Punished: Policing the lives of black and Latino boys.* New York, NY: New York University Press.

Roberts, J. (2011). Why misdemeanors matter: Defining effective advocacy in the lower criminal courts. *U.C. Davis Law Review, 45,* 277–372.

Robinson v. California, 370 U.S. 660 (1962).

Roman, J. (2013). *Cost-benefit analysis of criminal justice reforms.* Washington DC: US Department of Justice, National Institute of Justice. Retrieved from www.ncjrs.gov/pdffiles1/nij/241929.pdf

Rose, K. J. (2016). *Pretrial services agencies: Risk-informed pretrial decision making in the Commonwealth of Virginia.* [PowerPoint slides]. Retrieved from http:// vscc.virginia.gov/Virginia%20Pretrial%20Services%20Presentation%2012 -5-2016.pdf

Rosenberg, R. (2015, September 15). Inmate takes plea deal after nearly 7 years in Rikers without trial. *New York Post.* Retrieved from https://nypost.com/2015 /09/10/inmate-takes-plea-deal-after-nearly-7-years-in-rikers-without-trial/

Rosenblatt, A. M. (2003). The law's evolution: Long night's journey into day. *Cardozo Law Review, 24*(5), 2119–2148.

Roth, M. T., Hoffner, Jr., H. A., & Michalowski, P. (1997). *Law collections from Mesopotamia and Asia Minor* (2nd ed.). Atlanta, GA: Society of Biblical Literature.

Rothgery v. Gillespie County, 554 U.S. 191 (2008).

Ruggero, T., Dougherty, J., & Klofas, J. (2015). *Measuring recidivism: Definitions, errors, and data sources.* [Working paper]. Rochester, NY: Rochester Institute of Technology Center for Public Safety Initiatives.

Sacks, M., & Ackerman, A. R. (2014). Bail and sentencing: Does pretrial detention lead to harsher punishment. *Criminal Justice Policy Review, 25*(1), 59–77. doi:10.1177/0887403412461501

Sacks, M., Sainato, V. A., & Ackerman, A. R. (2015). Sentenced to pretrial detention: A study of bail decisions and outcomes. *American Journal of Criminal Justice, 40*(3), 661–681. doi:10.1007/s12103-014-9268-0

Salekin, R. T., Rogers, R., & Sewell, K. W. (1996). A review and meta-analysis of the Psychopathy Checklist and Psychopathy Checklist–Revised: Predictive validity of dangerousness. *Clinical Psychology: Science and Practice, 3*(3), 203–215. doi:10.1111/j.1468-2850.1996.tb00071.x

Sawyer v. Barbour, 300 P. 2d 187 (Cal. 1956).

Scherr, A. (2003). *Daubert* & danger: The "fit" of expert predictions in civil commitments. *Hastings Law Journal, 55,* 1–90.

Schilb v. Kuebel, 404 U.S. 357 (1971).

Schlesinger, T. (2005). Racial and ethnic disparity in pretrial criminal processing. *Justice Quarterly, 22*(2), 170–192. doi:10.1080/07418820500088929

Schnacke, T. R. (2014). *Fundamentals of bail: A resource guide for pretrial practitioners and a framework for American pretrial reform.* Retrieved from www.pretrial .org/download/research/Fundamentals%20of%20Bail%20-%20NIC%20 2014.pdf

Schnacke, T. R., Jones, M. R., & Brooker, C. M. (2010). *The history of bail and pretrial release.* Rockville, MD: The Pretrial Justice Institute. Retrieved from https://cdpsdocs.state.co.us/ccjj/Committees/BailSub/Handouts/History ofBail-Pre-TrialRelease-PJI_2010.pdf

Schnacke, T. R., Jones, M. R., & Wilderman, D. M. (2012). Increasing court-appearance rates and other benefits of live-caller telephone court-date reminders: The Jefferson County, Colorado, FTA pilot project and resulting court date notification program. *Court Review, 48,* 86–138.

Schönteich, M. (2014). *Presumption of guilt: The global use of pretrial detention.* New York, NY: Open Society Justice Initiative.

Schug, R. A., & Fradella, H. F. (2014). *Mental illness and crime.* Thousand Oaks, CA: Sage.

Schuppe, J. (2017, August 22). Post bail. *NBC News.* Retrieved from www .nbcnews.com/specials/bailreform

Schwalbe, C. S. (2007). Risk assessment for juvenile justice: A meta-analysis. *Law and Human Behavior, 31*(5), 449–462. doi:10.1007/s10979-006-9071-7

Schwirtz, M., & Winerip, M. (2015, June 8). Kalief Browder, held at Rikers Island for 3 years without trial, commits suicide. *The New York Times.* Retrieved from www.nytimes.com/2015/06/09/nyregion/kalief-browder -held-at-rikers-island-for-3-years-without-trial-commits-suicide.html

Scott v. Illinois, 440 U.S. 367 (1979).

Scott-Hayward, C. S. (2009). *The fiscal crisis in corrections: Rethinking policies and practices.* New York, NY: Vera Institute of Justice. Retrieved from https://storage .googleapis.com/vera-web-assets/downloads/Publications/the-fiscal-crisis

-in-corrections-rethinking-policies-and-practices/legacy_downloads/fiscal
-crisis-corrections-rethinking-policies-and-practices-2.pdf

Scott-Hayward, C. S. (2011). The failure of parole: Rethinking the role of the state in reentry. *New Mexico Law Review, 41*(2), 421–465.

Scott-Hayward, C. S. (2017). Rethinking federal diversion: The rise of specialized criminal courts. *Berkeley Journal of Criminal Law 22*(2), 47–109.

Scott-Hayward, C. S., & Ottone, S. (2018). Punishing poverty: California's unconstitutional bail system. *Stanford Law Review Online, 70*, 167–178.

Sernoffsky, E. (2018, May 3). SF inmate in landmark battle over bail wins release. *San Francisco Chronicle.* Retrieved from www.sfchronicle.com/news/article/Judge-orders-defendant-in-legal-bail-battle-to-be-12885426.php

Shapiro, D. L., & Noe, A. M. (2015). *Risk assessment: Origins, evolution, and implications for practice.* New York, NY: Springer.

Siddiqi, Q. (2009). *Predicting the likelihood of pretrial failure to appear and/or rearrest for a violent offense among New York City defendants: An analysis of the 2001 dataset: Final report.* New York, NY: New York City Criminal Justice Agency, Inc.

Silver, E., & Miller, L. L. (2002). A cautionary note on the use of actuarial risk assessment tools for social control. *Crime and Delinquency, 48*(1), 138–161. doi:10.1177/0011128702048001006

Simmons, R. (2002). Re-examining the grand jury: Is there room for democracy in the criminal justice system? *Boston University Law Review, 82*, 1–76.

Simon, J. (1988). The ideological effects of actuarial practices. *Law & Society Review, 22*(4), 771–800. doi:10.2307/3053709

Simonson, J. (2017). Bail nullification. *Michigan Law Review, 115*(5), 585–638.

Singh, J. P., & Fazel, S. (2010). Forensic risk assessment: A metareview. *Criminal Justice and Behavior, 37*(9), 965–988. doi:10.1177/0093854810374274

Singh, J. P., Grann, M., & Fazel, S. (2011). A comparative study of violence risk assessment tools: A systematic review and metaregression analysis of 68 studies involving 25,980 participants. *Clinical Psychology Review, 31*(3), 499–513. doi:10.1016/j.cpr.2010.11.009

Sistrunk v. Lyons, 646 F.2d 64 (3d Cir. 1981).

Skeem, J. L., Edens, J. F., Camp, J., & Colwell, L. H. (2004). Are there ethnic differences in levels of psychopathy? A meta-analysis. *Law and Human Behavior, 28*(5), 505–527. doi:10.1023/B:LAHU.0000046431.93095.d8

Skeem, J. L., & Lowenkamp, C. T. (2016). Risk, race, and recidivism: Predictive bias and disparate impact. *Criminology, 54*(4), 680–712. doi:10.1111/1745-9125.12123

Skeem, J. L., Polaschek, D. L. L., Patrick, C. J., & Lilienfeld, S. O. (2011). Psychopathic personality: Bridging the gap between scientific evidence and public policy. *Psychological Science in the Public Interest*, 12(3), 95–162. doi:10.1177/1529100611426706

Skolnick, J. H., & Fyfe, J. J. (1993). *Above the law: Police and the excessive use of force.* New York, NY: The Free Press.

Smith, A., & Madden, S. (2011). *Three-minute justice: Haste and waste in Florida's misdemeanor courts.* Washington, DC: National Association of Criminal Defense. Retrieved from www.nacdl.org/WorkArea/DownloadAsset.aspx?id=20794&libID=20764

Smith v. Kelly, 2012 U.S. Dist. LEXIS 64584, 2012 WL 1605123, No. C11-623 (W.D. Wash. 2012).

Solomon, F. F. (2013). CJA's Queens County supervised release program: Impact on court processing and outcomes. New York, NY: New York City Criminal Justice Agency, Inc. Retrieved from www.pretrial.org/download/research/Queens%20County%20Supervised%20Release%20Program-%20Impact%20on%20Court%20Processing%20ad%20Outcomes%20-%20CJA%202013.pdf

Spielkamp, M. (2017, June 12). Inspecting algorithms for bias. *MIT Technology Review.* Retrieved from www.technologyreview.com/s/607955/inspecting-algorithms-for-bias/

Stack v. Boyle, 342 U.S. 1 (1951).

Starr, S. B. (2014). Evidence-based sentencing and the scientific rationalization of discrimination. *Stanford Law Review*, 66, 803–872.

Starr, S. B. (2015). The new profiling: Why punishing based on poverty and identity is unconstitutional and wrong. *Federal Sentencing Reporter*, 27(4), 229–236. doi:10.1525/fsr.2015.27.4.229

State of New Jersey Commission of Investigation. (2014). *Inside out: Questionable and abusive practices in New Jersey's bail-bond industry.* Retrieved from http://dspace.njstatelib.org:8080/xmlui/bitstream/handle/10929/33879/i622014k.pdf

State of Utah Legislative Auditor General. (2017). *A performance audit of Utah's monetary bail system: A report to the Utah legislature.* Retrieved from https://le.utah.gov/audit/17_01rpt.pdf

State v. Askerooth, 681 N.W.2d 353 (Minn. 2004).

State v. Bauer, 36 P.3d 892 (Mont. 2001).

State v. Bayard, 71 P.3d 498 (Nev. 2003).

State v. Bricker, 134 P.3d 800 (N.M. Ct. App. 2006).

State v. Brown, 792 N.E.2d 175 (Ohio 2003).

State v. Detter, 260 S.E.2d 567 (N.C. 1979).

State v. Fann, 571 A.2d 1023 (N.J. Super. Ct. Law Div. 1990).

State v. Hinojosa, 271 S. W. 2d 522 (Mo. 1954).

State v. Jakschitz, 136 Pac. 132 (Wash. 1913).

State v. Rodarte, 125 P.3d 647 (N.M. Ct. App. 2005).

State v. Seibert, 15 P. 2d 281 (Wash. 1932).

Steffensmeier, D., Ulmer, J., & Kramer, J. (1998). The interaction of race, gender, and age in criminal sentencing: The punishment cost of being young, Black, and male. *Criminology*, *36*(4), 763–797. doi:10.1111/j.1745-9125.1998.tb01265.x

Stemen, D., & Frederick, B. (2013). Rules, resources, and relationships: Contextual constraints on prosecutorial decision making. *Quinnipiac Law Review*, *31*, 1–83.

Stevenson, M. T. (2017). *Distortion of justice: How the inability to pay bail affects case outcomes* [Working paper]. Retrieved from https://papers.ssrn.com/sol3/Papers.cfm?abstract_id=2777615

Stevenson, M. T. (2019). Assessing risk assessment in action. *Minnesota Law Review*, *103*, 303–384.

Stevenson, M. T., & Mayson, S. G. (2017). *Bail reform: New directions for pretrial detention and release.* University of Pennsylvania Law School Faculty Scholarship Series (Paper No. 1745). Retrieved from https://scholarship.law.upenn.edu/cgi/viewcontent.cgi?referer=https://www.google.com/&httpsredir=1&article=2747&context=faculty_scholarship

Stewart, J. E. (1980). Defendant's attractiveness as a factor in the outcome of criminal trials: An observational study. *Journal of Applied Social Psychology*, *10*(4), 348–361. doi:10.1111/j.1559-1816.1980.tb00715.x

Stoltze, F. (2012). Sheriff Baca blamed for deputy-on-inmate jail violence; report calls it "persistent." *KPCC*. Retrieved from www.scpr.org/news/2012/09/28/34467/report-deputy-inmate-violence-persistent-l-jails-b/

Subramian, R., Delaney, R., Roberts, S., Fishman, N., & McGarry, P. (2015). *Incarceration's front door: The misuse of jails in America.* New York, NY: Vera Institute of Justice. Retrieved from www.vera.org/publications/incarcerations-front-door-the-misuse-of-jails-in-america

Sullivan, L. (Writer & Cohost). (2010, January 10). Three-part series: Bonding for profit: Behind the bail bond system [Radio program]. In National Public Radio (Producer), *All things considered* and *Morning edition*. Washington, DC: NPR. Retrieved from www.npr.org/2010/01/21/122725771/Bail-Burden-Keeps-U-S-Jails-Stuffed-With-Inmates

Summer, C., & Willis, T. (2010). *Pretrial risk assessment: Research summary.* Arlington, VA: US Department of Justice, Bureau of Justice Assistance. Retrieved from www.bja.gov/Publications/PretrialRiskAssessmentResearchSummary.pdf

Sunstein, C. R. (2002). Probability neglect: Emotions, worst cases, and law. *Yale Law Journal, 112,* 61–107.

Superior Court of California, County of Los Angeles. (2018). *2018 bail schedule.* Retrieved from www.lacourt.org/division/criminal/pdf/felony.pdf

Superior Court of California, County of San Mateo. (2014). *Procedures for posting equity in real property as bond.* Retrieved from www.sanmateocourt.org /documents/criminal/PostingRealPropertyBond.pdf

Sykes, G. (2007). *The society of captives: A study of a maximum-security prison.* Princeton, NJ: Princeton University Press. (Original work published 1958)

Tafoya, S. (2015). *Pretrial detention and jail capacity in California.* San Francisco, CA: Public Policy Institute of California. Retrieved from www.ppic.org /publication/pretrial-detention-and-jail-capacity-in-california/

Tartaro, C., & Sedelmaier, C. M. (2009). A tale of two counties: The impact of pretrial release, race, and ethnicity upon sentencing decisions. *Criminal Justice Studies, 22*(2), 203–221. doi:10.1080/14786010902975507

Theodorakis, N. (2013). Psychopathy and its relationship to criminal behavior. *IALS Student Law Review, 1*(1), 47–56.

Thomas, W. H., Jr. (1976). *Bail reform in America.* Berkeley, CA: University of California Press.

Thompson, C. (2017). *Myths & facts: Using risk and needs assessments to enhance outcomes and reduce disparities in the criminal justice system.* Washington, DC: US Department of Justice, National Institute of Corrections & Community Corrections Collaborative Network. Retrieved from https://s3.amazonaws .com/static.nicic.gov/Library/032859a.pdf

Thompson, S. G. (2016). Do prosecutors really matter? A proposal to ban one-sided bail hearings. *Hofstra Law Review, 44*(4), 1161–1177.

Thorpe, B. (Ed.) (1840). *Ancient laws and institutions of England.* London, UK: Eyre & Spottiswoode. Retrieved from https://archive.org/details/ancient lawsandi00commgoog

Toborg, M. A., Bellasai, J. P., Yezer, A. M. J., & Trost, R. P. (1989). *Assessment of pretrial urine testing in the District of Columbia.* Washington, DC: US Department of Justice. Retrieved from www.ncjrs.gov/pdffiles1/Digitization/1199 68NCJRS.pdf

Tomkovicz, J. J. (2002). *The right to the assistance of counsel.* Westport, CT: Greenwood.

Toobin, J. (2015, May 11). The Milwaukee experiment: What can one prosecutor do about the mass incarceration of African-Americans? *The New Yorker*. Retrieved from www.newyorker.com/magazine/2015/05/11/the-milwaukee-experiment

Ulloa, J. (2019, January 16). California's historic overhaul of cash bail is now on hold, pending a 2020 referendum. *Los Angeles Times*. Retrieved from www.latimes.com/politics/la-pol-ca-bail-overhaul-referendum-20190116-story.html

United States v. Arzberger, 592 F.Supp.2d 590 (S.D.N.Y.2008).

United States v. Barber, 140 U.S. 164 (1891).

United States v. Feely, 25 F. Cas. 1055 (C.C.D. Va. 1813) (No. 15,082).

United States v. Foster, 79 F. Supp. 422 (S.D.N.Y. 1948).

United States v. Lawrence, 26 F. Cas. 887 (C.C.D.C. 1835) (No. 15,557).

United States v. McConnell, 842 F.2d 105 (5th Cir. 1988).

United States v. Motlow, 10 F.2d 657 (7th Cir. 1926).

United States v. Salerno, 481 U.S. 739 (1987).

United States v. Steward, 2 U.S. (2 Dali.) 343 (1795).

United States v. Wade, 388 U.S. 218 (1967).

US Department of Justice. (2014). *CRIPA investigation of the New York City department of correction jails on Rikers Island*. New York, NY: US Department of Justice, US Attorney Southern District of New York. Retrieved from www.justice.gov/sites/default/files/usao-sdny/legacy/2015/03/25/SDNY%20Rikers%20Report.pdf

US Department of Justice. (2015). Investigation of the Ferguson police department. Retrieved from www.justice.gov/sites/default/files/opa/press-releases/attachments/2015/03/04/ferguson_police_department_report.pdf

US Department of Justice & The Vera Foundation, Inc. (1965). *Proceedings and interim report of the national conference on bail and criminal justice*. Retrieved from www.ncjrs.gov/pdffiles1/Photocopy/355NCJRS.pdf

Van Cleve, N.G., & Mayes, L. (2015). Criminal justice through "colorblind" lenses: A call to examine the mutual constitution of race and criminal justice. *Law & Social Inquiry*, 40(2), 406–432. doi:10.1111/lsi.12113

Van Eijk, G. (2017). Socioeconomic marginality in sentencing: The built-in bias in risk assessment tools and the reproduction of social inequality. *Punishment & Society*, 19(4), 463–481. doi:10.1177/1462474516666282

VanBenschoten, S. (2008). Risk/needs assessment: Is this the best we can do? *Federal Probation*, 72(2), 38–42.

VanNostrand, M. (2003). *Assessing risk among pretrial defendants in Virginia: The Virginia Pretrial Risk Assessment Instrument.* Richmond, VA: Virginia Department of Criminal Justice Services. Retrieved from www.dcjs.virginia.gov/sites/dcjs.virginia.gov/files/publications/corrections/assessing-risk-among-pretrial-defendants-virginia-virginia-pretrial-risk-assessment-instrument.pdf

VanNostrand, M. (2011, September 21). *Using evidence to advance effective justice realignment pretrial* [PowerPoint slides]. Presentation at the California Realignment Conference, Sacramento, CA. Retrieved from https://slideblast.com/using-evidence-to-advance-effective-justice-realignment-pretrial_59 7a93641723dd27378db4d6.html

VanNostrand, M., & Crime and Justice Institute. (2007). *Legal and evidence-based practices: Application of legal principles, laws and research to the field of pretrial services.* Washington, DC: US Department of Justice, National Institute of Corrections. Retrieved from https://s3.amazonaws.com/static.nicic.gov/Library/023359.pdf

VanNostrand, M., & Keebler, G. (2009). Pretrial risk assessment in federal court. *Federal Probation, 73*(2), 3–29.

VanNostrand, M., & Rose, K.J. (2009). *Pretrial risk assessment in Virginia: The Virginia Pretrial Risk Assessment Instrument.* St. Petersburg, FL: Luminosity, Inc. Retrieved from www.dcjs.virginia.gov/sites/dcjs.virginia.gov/files/publications/corrections/virginia-pretrial-risk-assessment-report.pdf

VanNostrand, M., Rose, K.J., & Weibrecht, K. (2011). *State of the science of pretrial release recommendations and supervisor.* Washington, DC: Pretrial Justice Institute and US Department of Justice, Bureau of Justice Assistance. Retrieved fromuniversity.pretrial.org/HigherLogic/System/Download DocumentFile.ashx?DocumentFileKey=47063a15-8e11-461e-6ee5-cc109b053 b08&forceDialog=0

Vera Institute of Justice. (1972). *Programs in criminal justice reform: Ten-year report, 1961–1971.* Retrieved from https://storage.googleapis.com/vera-web-assets/downloads/Publications/programs-in-criminal-justice-reform-vera-institute-of-justice-ten-year-report-1961-1971/legacy_downloads/1002.pdf

Vera Institute of Justice. (2011). *Los Angeles County jail overcrowding reduction project: Final report: Revised.* New York, NY: Author. Retrieved from www.vera.org/publications/los-angeles-county-jail-overcrowding-reduction-project-final-report

Vera Institute of Justice. (2014). *A prosecutor's guide for advancing racial equality.* New York, NY: Author. Retrieved from https://cdpsdocs.state.co.us/ccjj/Resources/Ref/prosecutors-advancing-racial-equity_Nov2014.pdf

Virginia v. Moore, 553 U.S. 164 (2008).

Visher, C. A. (1992). Pretrial drug testing: Panacea or Pandora's box? *Annals of the American Academy of Political Science, 521*(1), 112–131. doi:10.1177/0002716 292521001007

Vojt, G., Thomson, L. D. G., & Marshall, L. A. (2013). The predictive validity of the HCR-20 following clinical implementation: Does it work in practice? *Journal of Forensic Psychiatry & Psychology, 24*(3), 371–385. doi:10.1080/14789949 .2013.800894

Vose, B., Smith, P., & Cullen, F. T. (2013). Predictive validity and the impact of change in total LSI-R score on recidivism. *Criminal Justice and Behavior, 40*(12), 1383–1396. doi:10.1177/0093854813508916

Wagenmann v. Adams, 829 F.2d 196 (1st Cir. 1987).

Walker v. City of Calhoun, 2017 U.S. Dist. LEXIS 219543, 2017 WL 2794064 (N.D. Ga. June 16, 2017).

Wallace v. State, 245 S. W. 2d 192 (Tenn. 1952).

Walmsley, R. (2017). *World pre-trial/remand imprisonment list* (3rd ed.). International Centre for Prison Studies. Retrieved from www.prisonstudies.org /sites/default/files/resources/downloads/wptril_3rd_edition.pdf

Walsh, L. (2017, Mar. 2). Email to Robert Brauneis. Retrieved from http:// perma.cc/7CU3-4JQP

Walters, G. D. (2003). Predicting criminal justice outcomes with the Psychopathy Checklist and Lifestyle Criminality Screening Form: A meta-analytic comparison. *Behavioral Sciences and the Law, 21*(1), 89–102. doi:10.1002/bsl.519

Webster, C. D., Douglas, K. S., Eaves, D., & Hart, S. D. (1997). Assessing risk of violence to others. In C. D. Webster & M. A. Jackson (Eds.), *Impulsivity: Theory, assessment, and treatment* (pp. 251–277). New York, NY: Guildford Press.

Weisburd, D., Greenspan, R., Hamilton, E. E., Williams, H., & Bryant, K. A. (2000). *Police attitudes toward abuse of authority: Findings from a national study.* Washington, DC: US Department of Justice, National Institute of Justice. Retrieved from www.ncjrs.gov/pdffiles1/nij/181312.pdf

Western Surety Co. v. People, 208 P. 2d 1164 (Colo. 1949).

Wheeler, G. R., & Wheeler, C. L. (1981). Two faces of bail reform: An analysis of the impact of pretrial status on disposition, pretrial flight, and crime in Houston. *Review of Policy Research, 1*(1), 168–182. doi:10.1111/j.1541-1338.1981. tb00384.x

White, M. D., & Fradella, H. F. (2016). *Stop and frisk: The use and abuse of a controversial policing tactic.* New York, NY: New York University Press.

White, M.D., & Fradella, H.F. (2018). The intersection of law, policy, and police body-worn cameras: An exploration of critical issues. *University of North Carolina Law Review, 96(5),* 1579–1638.

Whiteacre, K.W. (2006). Testing the Level of Service Inventory-Revised (LSI-R) for racial/ethnic bias. *Criminal Justice Policy Review, 17(3),* 330–342. doi:10.1177/0887403405284766

Whitmore, W.H. (Ed.). (1889). *The colonial laws of Massachusetts.* Boston, MA: Rockwell & Churchill. Retrieved from https://archive.org/details/colonial lawsofmaoomass

Williams, M.R. (2017). The effect of attorney type on bail decisions. *Criminal Justice Policy Review, 28(1),* 3–17. doi:10.1177/0887403414562603

Williams, Marian R. (2003). The effect of pretrial detention on imprisonment decisions. *Criminal Justice Review, 28(2),* 299–316. doi:10.1177/0734016803028000206

Williams, Marian R. (2016). From bail to jail: The impact of jail capacity on bail decisions. *American Journal of Criminal Justice, 41(3),* 484–497. doi:10.1007/s12103-015-9305-7

Winterfield, L., Coggeshall, M., & Harrell, A.V. (2003, April). *Development of an empirically-based risk assessment instrument: Final report.* Washington, DC: Urban Institute. Retrieved from www.urban.org/research/publication/develop ment-empirically-based-risk-assessment-instrument/view/full_report

Wiseman, S.R. (2011). *McDonald*'s other right. *Virginia Law Review in Brief, 97,* 23–29.

Wiseman, S.R. (2014). Pretrial detention and the right to be monitored. *Yale Law Journal, 123(5),* 1344–1404.

Wiseman, S.R. (2016). Fixing bail. *George Washington Law Review, 84(2),* 417–479.

Wistrich, A.J., Rachlinski, J.J., & Guthrie, C. (2015). Heart versus head: Do judges follow the law or follow their feelings? *Texas Law Review, 93,* 855–923.

Wolf, T.J. (1997). What United States pretrial services officers do. *Federal Probation, 61,* 19–24.

Wong, S.C.P., & Gordon, A. (2006). The validity and reliability of the Violence Risk Scale: A treatment-friendly violence risk assessment tool. *Psychology, Public Policy, and Law, 12(3),* 279–309. doi:10.1037/1076-8971.12.3.279

Wong, S.C.P., Olver, M.E., & Stockdale, K.C. (2009). The utility of dynamic and static factors in risk assessment, prediction, and treatment. In J.T. Andrade (Ed.), *Handbook of violence risk assessment and treatment* (pp. 83–120). New York, NY: Springer Publishing Company.

Woodruff, M.S. (2013). The excessive bail clause: Achieving pretrial justice reform through incorporation. *Rutgers Law Review, 66*, 241–297.

Wooldredge, J. (2012). Distinguishing race effects on pre-trial release and sentencing decisions. *Justice Quarterly, 29*(1), 41–75. doi:10.1080/07418825.2011.55 9480

Workman v. Cardwell, 338 F. Supp. 893, 898 (N.D. Ohio), *aff'd in part, vacated in part*, 471 F. 2d 909 (6th Cir.), *cert. denied*, 412 U.S. 932 (1972).

World Prison Brief. (2018). *United Kingdom: England & Wales: Pretrial/remand prison population: Trend*. Retrieved from www.prisonstudies.org/country /united-kingdom-england-wales

Wright, R.F., & Miller, M.L. (2002). The screening/bargaining tradeoff. *Stanford Law Review, 55*, 29–118.

Zeng, Z. (2018). *Jail inmates in 2016*. Washington, DC: US Department of Justice, Bureau of Justice Statistics. Retrieved from www.bjs.gov/content /pub/pdf/ji16.pdf

Zimring, F.E., & Hawkins, G. (1986). Dangerousness and criminal justice. *Michigan Law Review, 85*, 481–509.

STATUTES

18 U.S.C. § 3585(b) (2018).

An Act for Regulateing of Tryals in Cases of Treason and Misprision of Treason, 1696, 7 & 8 Will. 3, c. 3, § 1 (Eng.).

ALA. R. CRIM. PROC. RULE 7.2(b).

ALASKA STAT. § 12.25.180(a) (2017).

The Alien Registration Act, Pub. L. 76–670, ch. 460, 54 Stat. 670 (June 28, 1940) (codified as amended at 8 U.S.C. § 451), *repealed by* ch. 477, title IV, § 403(a) (39), 66 Stat. 280 (June 27, 1952).

ARIZ. CONST. art. II, § 22.

ARIZ. REV. STAT. §§ 13-3961 & 13-3967 (2017).

Bail Reform Act of 1966, Pub. L. No. 89-465, § 3146(b), 80 Stat. 214 (codified as amended at 18 U.S.C. § 3142–3151).

CAL. CONST. art. 1, §§ 12, 28 (2018).

CAL. PENAL CODE §§ 853.5, 853.6, 818, 978.5, 1269, 1270, 1275, 1320, & 1320.5 (2018).

CAL. R. CT. § 4.101-102 (2018).

CO. REV. STAT. § 16-7-301(1) (2011) (repealed).

D.C. CODE §§ 23-1321–1322 (2018).

GA. CODE ANN. § 17-6-1 (2017).

Habeas Corpus Act of 1679, 31 Car. 2, ch. 2 (1679).

HAW. REV. STAT. § 8-306 (2017).

LA. CODE CRIM. PROC. art. 211(a)(1).

MAINE REV. STAT. ANN. tit. 15, § 1026 (West, 2013).

MASS. GEN. LAWS ch. 276, § 58A (2017).

MD. CODE ANN., CRIM. PROC. § 4-101 (2018).

MD. R. CT., R. 4-216.

MICH. COMP. LAWS ANN. § 765.5 (2017).

MINN. CRIM. PROC. R. 6.01, subd. 2.

N.C. GEN. STAT. § 15A-401 (1999).

N.H. REV. STAT. § 597:1-d (2017).

N.J. CONST. art. 1. §. 11.

N.J. STAT. ANN. §§ 2A: 162-15, 162-17 (2017).

OHIO CONST. art. I, § 9.

OHIO REV. CODE § 2935.26 (2017).

OR. CONST. art I. § 14.

OR. REV. STAT. § 133.055 (2017).

PA. CONST. art 1. § 14 (1969).

The Prisoners' Counsel Act of 1836, 6 & 7 Will. 4, ch.14 (1836).

R.I. GEN. LAWS § 12-7-3 (2000).

S.C. CODE § 22-5-510 (2017).

S.D. CODIFIED LAWS §23A-3-2 (1998).

Statute of Westminster, 3 Edw., ch. 15 (1275), 3 Hen. 7, ch. 3 (1486).

TEX. CODE CRIM. PROC. Art. 14.06(b) (2017).

TENN. CODE ANN. §§ 40-7-118, 55-10-203 & 55-10-207 (2018).

UTAH CONST., art I, § 8.

VA. CODE ANN. §§ 19.2-74, & 19.2–81 (2018).

VT. STAT. tit. 13, § 7553 (2018).

W. VA. CODE §§ 62-1C-7 & 62-1-5a (2018).

WYO. CONST. art 1, § 14 (1889).

WYO. STAT. § 7-2-103 (2017).

# INDEX

Founded in 1893,
UNIVERSITY OF CALIFORNIA PRESS
publishes bold, progressive books and journals
on topics in the arts, humanities, social sciences,
and natural sciences—with a focus on social
justice issues—that inspire thought and action
among readers worldwide.

The UC PRESS FOUNDATION
raises funds to uphold the press's vital role
as an independent, nonprofit publisher, and
receives philanthropic support from a wide
range of individuals and institutions—and from
committed readers like you. To learn more, visit
ucpress.edu/supportus.